The Christian Healing Ministry

1985.

The Christian Healing Ministry

MORRIS MADDOCKS

First published 1981
Sixth impression 1984
SPCK
Holy Trinity Church
Marylebone Road
London NW1 4DU

Typeset by Malvern Typesetting Services
Printed in Great Britain by Redwood Burn Limited, Trowbridge
and bound by Pegasus Bookbinding, Melksham

ISBN 0 281 03760 4

Contents

PART ONE
Health and the Kingdom of God

PART TWO
Healing in the Church

PART THREE
Health and Society

APPENDIX

Acknowledgements

Biblical quotations, except where it is indicated otherwise, are from the Revised Standard Version of the Bible, copyrighted 1946, 1952 © 1971, 1973 by the Division of Christian Education of the National Council of the Churches of Christ in the U.S.A., and are used by permission.

Thanks are also due to Darton, Longman & Todd for permission to quote from *But Deliver Us From Evil* by J. Richards.

Foreword by the Archbishop of York

The Lambeth Bishops' Meeting in 1978 delivered themselves of the opinion that 'the healing of the sick in his name is as much part of the proclamation of the Kingdom as the preaching of the Good News of Jesus Christ'. The Bishop of Selby's book, therefore, could hardly be more timely and I commend it enthusiastically to those who are concerned with the healing ministry—and even more so to those who, for whatever reasons, are not concerned. The reader will find here an orderly and well-documented study which allows due place to modern critical scholarship of the Bible, makes allowance for the radical differences in cultural and mental climate between the twentieth century and the first and, I am glad to say, honours the part which the so-called 'secular agencies' play in the whole process of healing. This book is no exercise in indoctrination or special pleading. It is written by one who has had a long experience in the ministry and is thoroughly familiar not only with the history but with the practice of healing. It contains material which will exercise the minds of the professionals—the doctors and the clergy; but at the same time it is written in such a way as to be well within the grasp of those for whom the subject is at present unfamiliar. I wish the writer and his readers 'shalom' in the name of the Lord.

Bishopthorpe   STUART EBOR:
29th January 1980

Preface

The words of the Preacher: 'Of making many books there is no end, and much study is a weariness of the flesh' (Eccles. 12.12) might well apply to the rapidly increasing number of books on the subject of healing. Granted it is 'an idea whose time has come', why yet another book on this subject?

My *apologia* would centre round certain convictions, the first being a strong belief in the power of the Lord present to heal, which deepens as time goes by. I feel compelled to bear witness to this conviction. I also believe the Lord of the Church has spoken a word to his Church in our time recalling it to proclaim the Good News by preaching *and* healing. His renewed commission sends us out especially among the sick and the poor, the underprivileged and the hungry, the anxiety-ridden and the downtrodden, to proclaim the fact that Christ heals and saves. It is a commission to exalt in our time the healing Christ universally. Hopefully a fruitful dialogue and joint action across national, cultural, ecclesiastical and disciplinary divides will lead to a healing of unhealthy polarization in this quest, so that the Church catholic may make its contribution to the health of man which it alone can make, by enabling the vital, spiritual element to be brought into all thinking and action concerning health and healing throughout the world.

The subject is vast, and my preparatory reading as well as the writing of the book has had to be fitted into a fairly full life. I trust the reader will forgive the resulting faults and omissions.

Among the many people who have helped me with this book, too numerous to mention by name, I would include all my colleagues with whom I work both clerical and lay, all to whom I have ministered and who have ministered to me. Also, all with whom I have shared seminars, teaching days, dialogue and prayer in this work, including the members of our Prayer Fellowship and many others who have prayed about this book. I am especially grateful to the three Archbishops of York under whom I have served during the past twenty-one years and from whom I have learned much; and particularly to the present incumbent of the See for his encouragement in this ministry and concerning this book, as well as for writing the foreword.

I should like to thank my colleagues of the Churches' Council for Health and Healing for their assistance and inspiration, especially my Co-chairman Dr Kenneth Leese, the Reverends Peter Smith and John Richards, and Mr Brian Frost who has stimulated my thinking and reading and has kindly offered many constructive criticisms about Part III. Professor G. Hudson, Dean of the Faculty of Medicine in Sheffield University has more than earned my gratitude for reading the manuscript and offering many valuable comments. I am also grateful to the Reverends David Watson and Geoffrey Hunter for their helpful suggestions about Parts I and II respectively, to Dr Joan Llewellyn-Jones for her researches and to Mrs June Hall who has tirelessly and cheerfully typed and retyped the manuscript. Principally, I thank my beloved wife Anne for all her love, encouragement and joyful partnership in this work and ministry, to whom, as an act of thanksgiving to God for the many blessings we have received together, I dedicate this book.

Upper Poppleton, York   ✠ MORRIS SELBY
Feast of the Conversion of St Paul, 1980

PART ONE

Health and the Kingdom of God

1

Healing and Wholeness

1 *What things belong to man's health?*

The complexities of modern life seem to be proliferating at a rate similar to that of our fast-expanding universe. The inventions of modern man have so intensified the pace and pressures that it is small wonder many find the running too hard. Jet travel has made the world a small place: television has made it even smaller. Epoch-making events and violent turbulence (of nature or man) are brought directly into the living room of most Western families. The development in the use of fossil fuels with the resulting wealth and higher earning ability of Western man to make use of them has led to great advances in technology and a mercurial rate of living, seemingly an effort to catch up with the machines man has made. Much of his time is spent in travel, to and from work and leisure. Man is on the go, a study in perpetual motion. Inactivity leads to a feeling of guilt, for the world is running wild with the brilliant discoveries he has made, and he feels he should run too.

But so fast is the rate of development—we used to call it progress—that man has begun to suffer from a backlash of his own ingenuity. The speed of the expansion in the electronics and computer industries, which have helped man walk on the moon and survey himself in detail from outer space, is but one example. Micro-electronics was born in 1948 with the invention of the transistor. Whereas there were 10 components per silicon chip in 1960, increasing to several hundred by 1970, by 1976 there were 10,000 and a year later over 30,000. Very large-scale integration (VLSI) will bring the production of microcircuits to an equivalent of 100,000 on a chip, which is less than the size of your finger nail, by 1981, and one million components on a quarter-inch square chip are forecast for the mid 1980s. The advent of the microprocessor in this field of development now means that a wide range of intellectual or intuitive skills can be extended or even displaced.

This serves as but one example of the fast rate of change in technology which inevitably will have its repercussion on society and man himself. A university professor forecasts that the next

3

generation may need no more than 10 per cent of its labour force. 'The primary activity then will become education, health and social care. The new productivity would provide society with the wealth needed to sustain these other sectors of society.'[1] How is man to adapt to such a situation? What things belong to man's health?

With these developments and so many others which tend to make life more full and complex and yet paradoxically less fulfilled, it is not surprising to find signs that man is thinking again about his health. Western man's increase in wealth may well have led to a decrease in general health, despite medicine's magnificent advances in combating disease. In fact, we are beginning to see that health is not a mere absence of disease. Western man is learning that health involves positive care of the body, and so he dons his shorts and jogs off his outsize meals, freed for a few moments from the pressure of powerful advertisements to eat and drink himself silly. The very rich still take the easier and vastly more expensive way of attending the health farms. An increasing number of food operators sell their products more subtly, by encouraging the buyers to watch their calorie intake. Tour operators increase the pace of life by advertising a jet-propelled journey to the sun in answer to northern man's quest for warmth for his body. Others believe that health rests in the quietude of the mind, and so they join a meditation school. As a result, the teaching of meditation in its varied forms is now big business. The East has come into its own: the Beatles were only the first in a long line of Western pilgrims to India. One group in Bombay can now leave the source of their anxiety and stress behind, in a 'more meaningful' *mindless* existence! As Bishop Hensley Henson might have remarked: They will find life to be somewhat less difficult with no minds to go out of! The cross-fertilization of culture may have opened our eyes to the riches of the world in which we live, but it has also contributed to the complexity of life. It has by no means led to the spiritual health of man. What things belong to his health?

So far, because I am white and live in a comparatively rich country of the Western (first) world, we have only begun to consider a tiny part of man's total milieu. If I am having to slim for my health, the majority of my brothers and sisters in the southern (third) part of the world are having to fight starvation for their survival. Health has a very different meaning for each of us, but one thing is certain: neither of us can talk about total health in isolation from the other. I am unhealthy however brilliant my mind and fit my body, if from the comfortable chair in my living room I can watch my brother and sister in the third world starve or destroy themselves in violent efforts to obtain the necessities of life. Health and healing are universal symbols that embrace the whole creation. As John Donne said more than three centuries ago: 'No man is an island to himself.' There are, as the researchers for the Treaty of Rome Powers reminded us, 'Limits to growth'. The speed and complexity of global development in science and technology have led to the many strands of man's existence being woven together in a web of life. 'If one member suffers, all suffer together' (1 Cor. 12.26) is becoming equally true of the world today as it was true of the Church in the time of St Paul. What then belongs to man's health?

It was Carl Jung, perhaps *the* greatest mind in this century, whose researches led him to find that there is a purposeful centre of reality with which man needs to be in conscious contact for his full health. Man is seldom in sound physical and mental health unless he can find some way to relate to this centre of being whom he calls God. Man's very life requires for its full health acknowledgement of God and his direct influence on the world. Sooner or later by the route of religious experience or scientific research or by some other way, man has to come to this realization if he is to survive. In this he will be aided by what Jung saw as an instinctual drive toward wholeness in his psyche. Such wholeness may be experienced in real religion which enables man to be touched by the reality of God. It is this experience which can weld man into a whole, can integrate him, and give his life meaning. As Morton Kelsey remarks 'In the last analysis, real health of body and mind depends upon one's religious life',[2] though I would add that such a life must, like the universe, the creation of our Creator, be a constantly expanding and enlarging experience. A stunting of growth in the spiritual experience can be as counter-productive as omitting to plant the seed or till the soil.

It was during one of my ministries in the normal course of pastoral routine that I came to realize the powerful healing which contact with the Creator and the centre of his creation can bring. 'C.' was a busy Member of Parliament whose mother was dying of cancer in the north of England. I told him I should like her to receive the healing sacraments of the Church, but I would wait until he could leave the House to come to her bedside. I well remember how we battled our way to the hospital through a snow storm. His mother looked pathetically frail as the disease had taken its toll. So recently she had been a robust, fine looking woman, actively campaigning for him, supportive of so much in public life and always surrounded by many friends and adoring grand-children. Now we viewed her in the extremity of human weakness. He knelt down at her bedside while I anointed her. I never cease to wonder at the majestic brevity and beauty of the rite of anointing nor at the peace which invariably accompanies the 'celebration' of this sacrament of healing. 'E.' was to die a week later, but a very remarkable thing happened during her last week. She seemed to be separated from her disease and became her old 'self'. It was as if a healing force of explosive energy had effected this transformation internally for she sat up, demanded menus and wine lists and had many farewell parties for her friends, presiding over them as she used to do in her home. She seemed to be enjoying the anticipation of the banquet in the Kingdom. Her work done and her farewells over, she died in peace.

Her son later wrote to say that never before had he experienced such a nearness to his Creator and to all that was good in creation as when he had been kneeling at his mother's bedside during her anointing. He had been given a glimpse of the things that belong unto his true health, that communication with the divine centre of all being, the Creator of the universe whom we call God. It was a 'religious experience' that has maintained its mark on him ever since in a new integrity of being. I believe it was also for me a disclosure moment of health-giving significance whose redolence has been maintained by a deep friendship with 'C.'. Let us reiterate the question, therefore more personally:

What belongs to our health?

Michael Wilson ends his most helpful book *Health is for People* in a reflective mood:

> Health is a concept like truth which cannot be defined. To define it is to kill it. Nor can it be possessed. It can only be shared. There is no health for me without my brother. There is no health for Britain without Bangladesh. . . . Man's vision of his wholeness constantly 'breaks the shell of his understanding', disturbs his complacency and tempts him to new adventures

beyond the next ridge. . . . Health comes as a surprise . . . a gift, a grace. . . . Health is a foretaste of wholeness to come. . . . Health is now being reborn as an explosive vision with disturbing consequences for the Western style of life. Health is an idea whose time has come.

At the end of these reflections he asks, 'Healthy for what?' and his answer comes:

For God. For that which is at the heart of all that is, in which we live and move and have our being. For the ultimate Context. The experience of health, because it is a foretaste of wholeness to come, contains, like beauty, love and joy, the answer in itself. For what are we healthy? Just for the fun of it![3]

I have quoted at length because I find his reflections lead one to be reflective and dream dreams and see wider visions. Health can never be equated with human wellness and an absence of disease. Health is to do with the totality of creation, with the Creator himself. It is the divine gift and grace to creation by the Creator who 'saw everything that it was good', i.e. like the human psyche as Jung saw it, it was motivated towards wholeness. What is needed is a vision of the fullness of human life which alone will inspire us to build again a healthy society. Christians believe Jesus came not only to give us this vision, but also the means to implement it. 'I came that they may have life, and have it abundantly' (John 10.10).

Health then, though it defies definition, can and must be reflected on by man if he is to survive. He can never possess it for himself: it is something that he can only share in community as he learns to adjust to his environment and live at peace with his neighbour. Man is therefore always in the process of health: he can never cease his effort to obtain that wholeness, even if that attempt is a cessation from activity and a learning from silence and solitude. For man must be still for his health from time to time, as the Psalmist saw. He must be still to know his God and the things that belong to his peace. Otherwise he will never see his health for what it is—a foretaste of that wholeness to come, when the Kingdom is established and creation healed. Mercifully there are signs of this search now going on, as man enters a more reflective era. It will be for his health if he can put behind him the reckless activity of the last decades and, without becoming idle, become more contemplative. Many of our young people are giving a lead in this.

I well remember an occasion when the senior dancer of the Black and White Minstrels gave a telling witness. I had prepared several members of the show for Confirmation in the mid-sixties and the media naturally took an interest. Being a blonde bombshell 'S.' was selected from the group by the male interviewer to be grilled. He ended his questions by asking whether she didn't think it odd that a young, healthy (his word for dashingly beautiful) girl like her should be going in for out of date beliefs such as were held by the Church. At that moment, as the camera zoomed in for a close-up, she slew him (and the television viewers) with one of her most potent smiles and said: 'That's just where you're wrong: all my generation are searching for a more healthy way of living and many of us are finding the end of our search in Jesus Christ.' Cut! As one friend wrote to me, 'That was worth a thousand of your sermons!', to which I could only say 'Amen'. Many of our young people, I should like to think the majority, are indeed engaging fully in life, always looking forward, filled with the spirit of exploration and adventure, acutely conscious of their colleagues in the poorer nations, critical of the unhealthy style of much of Western life. Health is truly a vision being reborn amongst them, an idea whose time has come. And more young people than we are led to think are seeing that God lies at the centre of their search for a new life-style, that God is their health. And it is fun.

One of the most healthy gatherings Anne and I recently attended—I am fortunate to have a wife who is a partner both in marriage and ministry—was at a church hall in the London West End, where once a month two hundred and fifty to three hundred young people, many of whom are married, meet together for three hours' solid 'work'. On the other Tuesdays in the month they meet in thirty-two study groups in each others' houses. On the Tuesday of the plenary sessions they enjoy a buffet supper together—and how they enjoy it—having come straight from work. Then there is a time of praise and singing, a scripture reading, silence, an instructive talk and questions, prayer in groups where burdens are shared and prayed through and any ministry needed is given, and finally an act of closing worship. Then they just talk! I have seldom experienced such a healthy atmosphere and attitude to life among such a gathering of young people. Their priorities are right and health and life an adventure for God which is fun. 'What is the chief end of man?' asked the Westminster Catechism of the

Puritans (1647) and the answer came 'Man's chief end is to glorify God and to *enjoy* him for ever.' The things that belong unto our health in this life are reflections of the life of the world to come where as Martin Luther saw: 'All creatures shall have their fun, love and joy, and shall laugh with thee and thou with them, even according to the body.' There are few better pictures of ultimate health.

2 *What is healing?*

Dr R. A. Lambourne once offered this definition of healing, 'Healing is a satisfactory response to a crisis, made by a group of people, both individually and corporately.' This was quoted by Michael Wilson who then supplemented it by explaining the 'satisfactory response' as 'restoration to purposeful living in society'.[4] It is in fact the process which brings about the restoration to health. However we must dig a little more deeply. Dr Coggan, who has done much to underline the healing dimension in the Church's witness, prefers to begin with the name Jesus. 'Here was an idea whose roots went deep down into Jewish soil. Jesus—Joshua—deliverance *from* and *to* . . . . The Name which is above every name is derived from a Hebrew root that denotes "to be spacious."'[5] A Christian can never discuss healing without having Jesus in mind. His very name, the equivalent of Saviour from the root save/heal, speaks of growth and enlargement, a process whereby a power is unleashed that brings the life of man (or society) back into a new spaciousness in which all the cells (or members) are released and delivered to perform their full and purposeful function. Little wonder, as we shall see later on, that Jesus spent so much of his time in healing; it was part of his very nature to do so. As we proceed with this study in healing we must not forget this idea of spaciousness and growth. It goes back to the unleashing of the explosive force inherent in the act of creation, a power in nature that can even use suffering for an eventual good and takes setbacks into its evolutionary process.

Healing is as wide as creation and is the motive force within it. It must never be narrowed to a part of the whole. Too often we tend to think of physical healing only but the purpose of our Creator for us is infinitely greater. He has unleashed a power that must heal totally and bring us into that spaciousness of health. Tyndale so

9

rightly translated *soteria* in this way at Luke 19.9 when Jesus declared on being received by Zacchaeus, 'Today *health* has come to this house.' Had we kept Tyndale's translation *health* and *heal* through the Bible instead of *salvation* and *save*, our ideas on the subject might have been more spacious!

So often in our ministry we are confronted by this explosive force that needs space to move. One of my priests had a motor accident in which the whole of the front of his car was sliced off. He was within inches of death. The shock began to affect his sight. As it deteriorated he 'called for the elders of the Church'. When the service of anointing was over instead of taking the advice to lie down and rest, he jumped up and began to dance—all the way down the stairs for the chapel was at the top of the house. 'I don't want to lie down, I want to dance', was a demand for spaciousness for the healing force to grow. 'I was going blind and now I can see' was an affirmation of faith in him whose nature is to heal. It was all a little bit of heaven, a projection of the end time of history which Jürgen Moltmann engagingly (and appropriately) describes as 'an ever-varying round dance of the redeemed in the trinitarian fullness of God, the complete harmony of soul and body.'[6] The Lord of the dance needs space in which to move! The healed also become healers (a matter of growth once more) and this priest's ministry has been enlarged in many wonderful ways: he constantly finds himself used as a channel of healing, while this event in his life, together with the healing of one of his daughters prior to his own, led to the formation of my Healing Prayer Fellowship of which he was the secretary for five years, circulating its five hundred members around the British Isles with a monthly prayer leaflet.

Let us now turn to some of the other biblical words which will enlarge our concept of healing.

3 *Peace–Shalom*

Peace was a word frequently found on Jesus' lips; it was his first gift to his followers after his resurrection. Its general sense is determined by the positive conception of the Hebrew word *shalom*, which in the Old Testament covers the idea of well-being in the widest sense of the word—prosperity, bodily health, contentedness, good relations between nations and men, salvation. It has political connotations and a public significance far beyond the purely personal. J. I. Durham contends that it is often indicative 'of a comprehensive kind of fulfilment or completion, indeed of a perfection in life and spirit which quite transcends any success which man alone, even under the best of circumstances, is able to attain'. And again, '(Shalom) is the gift of God, and can be received only in his Presence.'[7] Jesus' act on the first Easter Day was therefore of supreme significance.

The state of *shalom* comes about when the will of God is being done, when there is a harmony of being at one with the purposes of the Creator, the popular symbol for which was the ideal time when every man could sit under his vine and fig tree. It is left to Jeremiah to discern that true peace can come only through a radical change of heart and the writing of a new covenant deep within (31.33). One of the messianic titles was Prince of Peace (Isaiah 9.6) and so Jesus 'came and preached peace to you who were far off and peace to those who were near' (Eph. 2.17). It was peace that would involve suffering and not yield to any easy solution: 'Do not think that I have come to bring peace on earth; I have not come to bring peace, but a sword' (Matt. 10.34/Luke 12.51). He pronounces 'Woes' on the Pharisees and drives out from the Temple those whose lives are set on selfish gain. But always one is left with the feeling that here is the Prince of Peace fighting for the ultimate good, the health and *shalom* of his people and his Father's creation. This is the supreme cause for which the Prince of Peace dies—the fullness and perfection of God's creation, the perfect time when God's Kingdom becomes creation healed. The peacemakers, those who follow the Prince in this work, are therefore accorded a special title and position: 'Blessed are the peacemakers, for they shall be called the Sons of God' (Matt. 5.9). To be a fellow son and heir with Christ is healing indeed, but we have to experience peace *with* God before we can know the peace *of* God (cf. Rom. 5 and Eph. 2).

4 *Forgiveness and Reconciliation*

All life is a question of relationships and we have already seen how these must be kept in good working order if man is to be healthy. Bishop Stephen Neill once wrote: 'The life of man can develop fully'—we are still close to our concept of spaciousness—'only through the harmonious evolution of a fourfold relationship—to the good earth beneath his feet, his physical environment; to other men, to his living and human environment; to himself, through a right ordering of his own inner and complex existence; to God, the source of all his being.'[8] He went on to point out that once the last has been impaired, all the others go wrong. Healing is needed for a return to the full health of right relationship. For sin is a failure to recognize our dependence on God and our need to be in a state of reconciliation with our Creator and all that is good in his creation; it is setting up ourselves on our own, claiming to be the masters of our own destiny (pride) and to be our own gods (idolatry). When a person is in the centre of his own picture there is not much room for God or anyone else. This is what the Bible calls sin, the state of alienation from God which is the cause of all other alienations. There is only one answer if man is to survive and become healthy.

Basically there are three words for forgiveness in the Old Testament, all metaphors for the removal of sin. The first renders the idea of sin being covered so that it no longer obtrudes between man and God (*kipper*): the second conveys the idea of sin being carried away, the barrier between God and man thereby being removed (*nasa*): the third the actual concept of forgiveness so that no resentment or anger is left in the injured party (*salach*). The New Testament also has three words: *apoluo*, loose away, is used only twice: *charizomai*, be gracious, is used eleven times; and *aphiemi*, send away, fifty-six times. This last word belongs almost entirely to the Gospels and Acts. The second is Pauline, connected with his great word for grace, *charis*, though of course the whole idea of forgiveness is involved in his great concept of justification, which has as its basic idea that of restoration to fellowship. It is a healing through judgement since the word comes from the vocabulary of the law courts.

Forgiveness is always conditional on repentance. Jesus deepened the requirement of repentance and made it a condition of entry into the Kingdom of God. 'Repent and believe' was the keynote of his early preaching (Mark 1.15). The New Testament word is *metanoia*, which means far more than our traditional notion of dust and ashes. Literally it means a change of mind and so a complete turning round, a reorientation of the whole personality. It is called for as the response to the proclamation of the Good News.

For Jesus and his followers, there is therefore no limit to forgiveness. It must be unto 'seventy times seven' in response to repentance—the one condition attached to being forgiven, as Jesus made plain in the Lord's Prayer. In short it is God's own free and health-giving act to his creation which as his creatures we must make our own if we would be healed.

Reconciliation is also a word that is supremely concerned with the healing of relationships. It is the New Testament word (*katallage*) used to describe the changed relationship between God and man consequent upon the death and resurrection of Jesus. Reconciliation is the activity of God: man is the recipient (cf. Rom. 5.10f). The mighty act of the New Covenant has effected the reconciliation of the two ethnic groups, Jew and Gentile, hitherto diametrically opposed (Eph. 2.16). Even more than for the healing of nations, God's supreme act in Jesus has cosmic effectiveness, reconciling to himself 'all things, whether on earth or in heaven' (Col. 1.20). The classic passage is in 2 Corinthians 5. 17–19: 'If anyone is in Christ, he is a new creation; the old has passed away, behold the new has come. All this is from God, who through Christ reconciled us to himself and gave us the ministry of reconciliation; that is, God was in Christ reconciling the world to himself, not counting their trespasses against them, and entrusting to us the message of reconciliation.' Freely we have received such healing: freely must we be channels of this healing power to others. The initiative for the world's health lies with Christians. It is high time to wake out of sleep: our health is nearer now than when we first believed! Are we sufficiently concerned for the health of others? As Cardinal Basil Hume told his monks:

> The Gospel is not only a programme for action, it is also a proclamation of the power at our disposal. Forgiving and healing should characterize our treatment of each other. Christ's manner of action has to be the model for ours. As pastors, we need to learn how to use his healing power, or how to be instruments enabling him to exercise that power on one another.[9]

The ball is in our court.

5 *Wholeness and Holiness*

The root meaning of the Old Testament word for holy is that of separation. Isaiah in his vision in the Temple heard the Trisanctus, the song of the angels adoring Jahweh, the holy God. His response was to realize Jahweh's separation from him and his from Jahweh.

13

'And I said "Woe is me! For I am lost; for I am a man of unclean lips, and I dwell in the midst of a people of unclean lips"' (Isa. 6.5). Confronted by the holiness of his God, he knew immediately his need of healing. His vision continued with the appearance of cleansing fire which took away his guilt and he knew he was forgiven. Restored to health he was able to be used as Jahweh's messenger: 'Then I said, "Here am I! Send me"'. Isaiah's great contribution to religious consciousness was that he stumbled upon the truth that a holy God demands a like holiness from his people. Only with this new-found wholeness was he enabled to be one of 'his servants the prophets'. Holiness is a reflection of the holy God. It is other-wordly equipment if you like which enables a human being to be more whole in this world. Bishop Michael Ramsey puts it like this: 'The men and women whom we call saints have been marked by a growing reflection of the divine character mingled with awe, penitence, humility.'[10] It was after Peter had received the ministry of the risen Christ for the healing of his memories, that he could 'turn again' and strengthen his brethren. The three times repeated question was no mere reminder of his threefold denial of Christ early on Good Friday morning. It was a deliberate searching and cleansing by Christ of the inner recesses of Peter's consciousness, evoking a new confession of loving obedience. It was a catharsis, potent with healing, that led to a new wholeness. Appropriately it is the gospel, proper to the consecration of Anglican bishops, who are then commissioned to heal the sick. Only the healed can become healers.

Or again, it was only after Saul of Tarsus had come face to face with the risen Christ before the gates of Damascus that he was able to be 'turned round' and brought to new health by the healing Christ. His 'threatenings and slaughter' were not only motivated towards the destruction of Christians: they were the instrument of his own destruction. A devout Pharisee, basically he was an unhealthy person. In such a house, 'divided against itself', wholeness was an impossibility. Saul received a true vision of the God he served, a vision so wonderful and so contrary to his own model, that he was blinded by it. He 'came to himself' with the realization that he had been going in exactly the opposite direction to what he thought; not only that, but he had never listened to the God whom he thought he heard and obeyed. A new vision, a new obedience, a new humility were the fruits of this momentary encounter, sealed by the ministry of the early Church, expressed in the obedience of a very unwilling Ananias to the basic commission to his profession: Love (God and man), preach and heal, baptize and do this. Such obedience was a contributary factor in the making of Saul into the wholeness of Paul.

It is in the lives of the saints that we see the process of this coming to wholeness most clearly, that alone prepares man for the gift and goal of holiness which God wills for him. Holiness is Christlikeness which the Spirit alone can effect in man. The Holy Spirit's work is to bring us the things of Christ. The essential mark of holiness is Christlike love, of which Jesus was the incarnate expression. Love like his, selflessiy devoted to his heavenly Father's will and poured out in self-sacrificing service towards man—this is the essence of Christian holiness. In Christian terms it is also the mark of a whole personality. It is a gift given in due measure to our response to him in this life, but the fruit can ripen and blossom fully only in the life of the world to come. It is therefore important for Christians to be other-worldly in the positive sense of being consciously at one with their brothers and sisters in Christ who are in this fuller state of wholeness. All have received the call of God and that call is to a holiness consonant with the attribute of him who calls. Both Israel and the Christian Church are called the 'holy nation' (Exod. 19.6 and 1 Pet. 2.9) and all their members are 'holy ones', the holiness dependent on the holy God who calls. As Dr R. A. Lambourne has said: 'the definition for Christians of a "whole man" is epitomised in the "whole" life of Christ, his disciples, and the early Church, a life of fellowship with man (and God), of loving the weak, of power and praise and prayer, of full living and full suffering, of preaching and healing.'[11]

The chief emphasis of this holiness/wholeness in the Old Testament is naturally placed on the corporate aspect. To be made whole is to be 'at-oned' with all those who are enjoying salvation and healing. The Hebrew mind thought of the day of judgement as a corporate raising of the righteous and the bringing of the universe as a whole directly under the divine rule. This corporate aspect of salvation is also to be found in the New Testament. For Paul, baptism was a dying and rising again with Christ to a state of wholeness in order to be grafted into the new Israel of God. 'To be made whole is (therefore) to be joined to a group chosen to accomplish a particular task for God'.[12] The healed become by the very act of healing, part of the healing community. It is this experience of coming into wholeness that enables them to identify with the sick, the suffering, and the abandoned and so to be used as an instrument of the divine will.

This sharing in the wholeness and holiness of Christ is not only the essence of life in this world; it reflects the wholeness of the communion of saints. It is this dimension which is too frequently forgotten or ignored when the satisfactory community relations required of man for his wholeness are under discussion. The Bible is concerned with the wholeness of a community for whom the grave is no barrier or confinement. The grave is no interruption to the life of the redeemed community. We ignore the life of the world to come and its fellowship of wholeness/holiness at our peril and to our eternal loss. Much of the sickness and dis-ease of men and women today is due to a severed or wrong relationship with their ancestors, a relationship with someone 'gone before' which has not been healed. Neither are individuals the only unhealthy ones. Nations with a record of violence need reconciliation and healing too. Nor are Churches immune in this regard. Is it so remarkable that the Churches who have neglected this other dimension of wholeness in their liturgical life and theology have been most prone to the dis-ease of schism? Just as there can be no health for the world without an identification with the starving brother or abandoned sister, so can there be no healing for the Church without its realization of being part of a holy and innumerable multitude in whose call to wholeness by a holy God lies the key to the Kingdom of God which is creation healed.

At the centre of the Kingdom stands the King. He alone is whole, the perfect pattern for our health. Luke, a doctor, records that at the beginning of his earthly life, his growth to full manhood had been in four major areas: 'Jesus increased in wisdom and in stature, and in favour with God and man' (Luke 2.52). In effect he is saying that Jesus grew mentally (in wisdom) and physically (in stature), and also spiritually (in favour with God) and socially (in favour with man). These are the four areas of growth that need to be cultivated for perfect health. When wholeness comes in these four areas, there is holiness indeed. Holiness is the goal and Jesus has revealed that holiness in all its perfection. He is the Way, the Truth, and the Life, of whose gift alone comes that wholeness and perfect health.

2

Health and the Kingdom of God in the teaching of Jesus

God's kingdom is creation healed.
Hans Kung, *On being a Christian*, p. 231

1 *Why did Jesus come?*

Why did Jesus come? What did he stand for? What was his cause? We shall hope to take a close look at his life and work and that of his early followers. We shall attempt to gain some guidelines for the work of his followers today. But first we must ascertain what was central to his proclamation and what motivated his life and work.

A reading of the Gospels will reveal that Jesus did not come for his own cause. He did not come to proclaim himself. He always kept himself subordinated to his cause. 'I seek not my own will but the will of him who sent me' (John 5.30) is a theme to be found more than once in the Fourth Gospel. His attitude bespoke a continual passivity, an obedience to a cause outside himself and yet one in which he was totally identified and to which he was entirely committed. 'I have a baptism to be baptized with; and how I am constrained until it is accomplished!' (Luke 12.50)

In a word, his cause is the cause of God, the cause of establishing God's will and rule in the world. He came to further God's purpose of putting things to rights. In the thinking and mission of Jesus God's cause is paramount. It may appear that Jesus is entirely concerned with man's cause, and so he is; but he is only concerned with man's cause because first and foremost he is wholly concerned with God's. And Jesus proclaims God's cause in terms of the Kingdom of God. The Kingdom of his Father was always the core of his proclamation. 'In the thought of the kingdom of his Father Jesus lived and worked and died.'[1] Mark sums up the message of Jesus: 'The time is fulfilled, and the Kingdom of God is at hand; repent, and believe in the gospel' (1.15). Matthew (4.23 and 9.35) and Luke (4.43 and 8.1) have similar summary verses, but neither can match the genius of Mark in encapsulating in the minimum of

17

words the essential message he wishes to convey, in this case the reason why Jesus came.

Our word kingdom is a misleading translation of *basileia/malkut*. It is not a territorial or static but a dynamic symbol.[2] The Kingdom of God therefore refers to God reigning, God actively ruling in his royal power, God visiting and redeeming his people. It means that God is setting the world to rights, saving men from sin, sickness, and evil and establishing a new order of things. This is how Jesus furthered God's cause: he made this dynamic symbol of the Kingdom of God the central theme of his public proclamation. Statistics alone serve to underline this. In Mark we find it 14 times and in Luke 32. Matthew, who was writing for Jewish readers with a preference for using a 'one-off' description of God rather than the divine name itself used Kingdom of heaven 33 times and Kingdom of God 4.

2 *How did Jesus view the Kingdom?*

In Judaistic thought, there were two reigns of God corresponding to the two aeons, present and future. His lasting reign was his kingly rule over Israel during the present age: in the age to come his (future) reign would be over all nations. When Jesus came, he brought a new urgency to the situation by claiming that what would happen in the future Kingdom was being determined now by the way in which people reacted to him and his message. 'Everyone who acknowledges me before men, I also will acknowledge before my Father who is in heaven' (Matt. 10.32). Jesus' view of the Kingdom therefore differs from the Judaistic model in that he believes it to be bound up with himself. In short, the future rule of God has already begun to break through into the present in the words and works of Jesus. This is what some contemporary scholars call 'inaugurated eschatology' as opposed to the extreme eschatological views which are completely 'futuristic', or 'realized'. Jesus proclaimed the Kingdom of God neither solely as a future event nor only as a present reality. Central to his message is the urgent proximity of God's reign, that God is about to set the world to rights. Its inauguration will be by God's free act of grace: men can only await its coming watchfully, patiently, expectantly.

This seems to be the most balanced view of Jesus' attitude to the Kingdom, 'an eschatology in process of realization'.[3] It holds the

urgency of Jesus' message and mission in the here and now in a
healthy tension with the expectancy of a new creation to be perfected in the absolute future.

Jesus therefore showed by his words and actions that he believed
he had come to inaugurate the Kingdom of God. The unconditional grace and goodness of God was now particularly
available to the abandoned and destitute, the sick who need the
physician, the outcast and rejected, the little ones and the simple
ones, the abandoned and the poor. 'Blessed are the eyes which see
what you see! For I tell you that many prophets and kings desired
to see what you see, and did not see it, and to hear what you hear,
and did not hear it' (Luke 10.23f). It is this unconditionality of
God's grace and goodness, characteristic of the Kingdom, which is
the essentially new element in Jesus' view of his Father's reign. It is
brought out clearly in a well-authenticated saying, Jesus' reply to
John's disciples. It is a statement of fact, of what is happening
now, in phrases culled from the prophets.[4] Jesus makes it all the
more striking by expressing it in a form he made his own, a sixfold
parallelism in two-beat rhythm. To gain the effect in English,
emphasis should be placed on the two salient words in each line:

> The blind see (receive their sight, RSV)
> The lame walk
> Lepers are cleansed
> And the deaf hear,
> The dead are raised up,
> The poor have the good news preached to them.

> And blessed is he who takes no offence at me
> (Luke 7.22f/Matt. 11.5f).

These images were familiar phrases of some antiquity in the East
used to signify the time of salvation. This new aeon would be
marked by an absence of all sorrow, crying, and grief. The case of
the lepers and dead is not mentioned in Isaiah but Jesus included
them to show that the fulfilment exceeds by far all prophecy and
expectation. The most distinctive feature however in those important *ipsissima verba* of Jesus which describe the conditions of
the Kingdom, is that the people who hear this good news are the
poor. In the six-fold parallelism, it is the sixth clause that receives
the emphasis and upon which the final clause is dependent. To a

Jew, poverty was a mark of God's disfavour. Jesus reverses this value-judgement and adds a benediction for those who don't take offence at this new teaching. The beatitudes further emphasize the fact that this lay at the heart of Jesus' teaching. The Lucan quartet begins: 'Blessed are you poor, for yours is the Kingdom of God' (Luke 6.20). The destitute and humiliated are now being called to inherit the Kingdom. Here was new and radical thinking, articulated for the first time by this Galilean rabbi. It was to be backed by equally radical action as Jesus went about amongst the poor and despised, even sharing meals with them. The boundlessness of God's grace, so much to the fore in the consciousness of the early Church, was lived and taught by Jesus as he proclaimed the Kingdom. 'This man eats with publicans and sinners' was the invariable complaint of his enemies. 'Fear not, little flock, for it is your Father's good pleasure to give you the Kingdom' (Luke 12.32) was the assurance he gave to his despised friends. It was his table fellowship with the abandoned in the form of 'publicans and sinners' more than any other factor that sent Jesus to the cross.

Jesus viewed the Kingdom as a new era of blessing for the 'poor'. He invited 'those who labour and are heavy laden' to come to him. He used these terms in the prophetic sense of those who are oppressed and thrown completely on God's mercy. For him they are the hungry, those who weep, the sick, those who labour and bear burdens, the least and the simple, the lost and sinners. It is these who need health and salvation from the physician of life, not those who are well (cf. Mark 2.17). The old attitudes enshrined in a severe orthodoxy must change to a realization of the blessedness of those who know their need of God. There could be no view of the Kingdom for Jesus which did not include the poor.

Thus viewed, the Kingdom will be the source of health for all people. The God who reigns is the infinitely gracious and loving God whose will and purpose for his creation is health and wholeness. Like the father of the prodigal, he goes out to meet his erring children and accepts them back into their rightful home unconditionally. He hears the cry of the distressed and answers the prayer of the despairing publican. This is what the Kingdom will be because this is what God is like. Health will be a free gift for these poor ones, these little ones. Jesus knew the Kingdom from the inside because he knew his heavenly Father. For him the Kingdom of God meant the compassionate love of his Father present and active in his creation. The coming of the Kingdom would mean its final healing.

How did he go about proclaiming his Father's Kingdom?

3 *Jesus proclaims the Kingdom through—*

a His sayings

Three of Jesus' sayings about the Kingdom call for special mention. The most important is one in which he is interpreting his exorcisms:

'But if it is by the finger of God I cast out demons, then the Kingdom of God has come upon you' (Luke 11.20).[5]

The saying demonstrates Jesus' belief that his exorcisms were a manifestation of God's kingly rule. The Kingdom is a symbol of God's activity on behalf of his people. Jesus urges his hearers to see that they take into their own experience that divine activity as they witness his exorcisms. Of course the exorcisms are by no means the only demonstrable activity of God, but they are at least one of those activities and have a lesson to teach those with ears to hear and eyes to see. In adding 'upon you', Jesus is making plain that the kingly power of God has drawn near to his hearers and is there for them to lay hold of. The proof of this is that the power has been manifested in the lives of other people through Jesus' exorcisms. Perhaps we are also meant to see in this saying a reference to the Kaddish prayer, 'May he establish his Kingdom in your lifetime'. Constant use of this very personal petititon would lead to an expectancy of that kingly power not only in the cosmic realm but also in the personal. It was a prayer for health both for the individual and the nation, though the Jews who thought in terms of corporate solidarity would not make too much distinction between the two. The point is that Jesus' exorcisms and healings proclaimed the Kingdom in terms of health and wholeness. God was putting his creation right by healing it. In Jesus' work, the touch (finger) of God was revealed and his kingly rule asserted.

A similar saying is found in Luke 17.20f:

'The Kingdom of God is not coming with signs to be observed; nor will they say, "Lo, here it is!" or "There!" for behold, the Kingdom of God is in the midst of you' (*entos humon estin*). This is a negative saying, concerned to guard against false proclamation and yet it affirms the same truth as the last. God in his kingly activity is confronting the hearers of Jesus, who uses the Kingdom symbol again to mediate a living experience of his Father's work among them. It may be significant that this passage follows the healing of the ten lepers. Nine of them had failed to see the presence of the kingly power in Jesus. The Pharisees, to whom this saying was addressed, showed a similar failure. The saying declares that the saving benefits are now available to all—in Jesus.

One further saying occurs in Matthew 11.12 (par. Luke 16.16):

'From the days of John the Baptist until now the Kingdom of heaven has suffered violence, and the men of violence take it by force.' Again, this saying seems to envisage the Kingdom as a present fact, but what do the references to violence mean? Norman Perrin is of the opinion that Jesus, with his high regard for the Baptist, must have reflected deeply on his passion and its meaning in relation to the Kingdom and that this saying is a result of that reflection. Furthermore, 'it reflects not on the fate of the Baptist only but also on the potential fate of Jesus and his disciples.'[6] The Kingdom is now present in such measure among men that it has become vulnerable and open to attack from its enemies.

Matthew emphasizes the presence of the Kingdom by his thrice repeated 'The Kingdom of heaven has drawn near' (3.2; 4.17; 10.7). He firmly believed it to be a transcendent reality which, while to be consummated in God's absolute future, was confronting men and women in the present with the possibility of new health and wholeness.

As a postscript to this section I quote two sayings from the Gospel of Thomas for their interest alone and without comment, except to say that the last two sentences of the first quotation have deep implications for our health.

Thomas 3. Jesus said: "If those who lead you say to you: 'See, the Kingdom is in heaven', then the birds of the heaven will precede you. If they say to you: 'It is in the sea', then fish will precede you. But the Kingdom is within you **and** without you. If you (will) know yourselves, then you will be **known** and you will know that you are the sons of the living **Father**. But if you do not know yourselves, then you are in poverty and you are poverty."

Thomas 113. His disciples said to him: "When will the Kingdom come?" (Jesus said) "It will not come by expectation; they will not say: 'See here', or 'See there'. But the Kingdom of the Father is spread upon the earth and men do not see it."

b His parables.

One of P. G. Wodehouse's characters defines a parable as 'one of those stories in the bible which sounds at first like a pleasant yarn, but keeps something up its sleeve which suddenly pops up and knocks you flat!' It was not a bad description of the effect the parables have had on people! Parable means a comparison, usually drawn from nature or daily life and designed to teach some spiritual truth. Jesus' parables for the most part brought light to bear on the Kingdom. Here is one of them:

'(Jesus) said, "To what shall I compare the Kingdom of God? It is like leaven which a woman took and hid in three measures of meal, till it was all leavened"' (Luke 13.20f; par. Matt. 13.33). Jesus here points out that just as leaven in flour becomes a heaving mass of explosive energy, so when the rule of God takes effect in a personality, his healing power becomes an explosive force bringing new life and energy and radiant joy. The Kingdom of God is health-giving and Jesus' work is to make men whole. A similar lesson can be drawn from the parable of the mustard seed and both could be interpreted on the cosmic level as well as the personal. The Kingdom has small beginnings, but the rule of God enlarges everyone and everything it touches, imparting life and health. This is the lesson to be drawn from all the parables of growth. As A. M. Hunter puts it: 'Just as in nature (which is God's creation) there is a freely-given power which man does not make or direct, so in history there is a divine power—the Spirit of God—which brings God's Kingdom from seed to harvest.'[7] And seed needs space to grow into its destined fruition and wholeness.

Some parables like the Hidden Treasure and the Pearl of great Price (Matt. 13. 44-6) teach about the commitment necessary for the Kingdom. There must be a readiness to sacrifice all for God's cause and an unyielding obedience once the decision of commitment is taken. These twin parables point to the blessedness of a place in God's Kingdom which is worth any sacrifice. Others like the Unjust Steward (Luke 16. 1-8) and the Ten Virgins (Matt. 25. 1-12) warn of the urgency concerning the coming of the Kingdom. Men must discern the signs of the times and respond with repentance, lest they find they have refused the invitation into the Kingdom by their unreadiness. We should see even more signs of the Kingdom today if Christians showed a similar commitment to God's cause as, for instance, many do to the Marxist cause, and respond to the urgency of the situations confronting them with like resolution. It is the steadfast devotion of the children of the Kingdom, watching in prayerful awareness and obedience, in forgiveness and love, which will lighten the path to the Kingdom and prepare the way for the King. Watchfulness is the necessary Christian attitude, for God's time is always *now*.

The most important set of parables, however, were evoked by the religious people of the day who severely criticized Jesus for 'eating with sinners' and going among those whom 'society' despised. These parables therefore demonstrated the boundlessness of the grace of God and the wideness of his mercy. They showed that the Kingdom was for such as the abandoned and rejected, the despised and the desolate, and so came nearest to the heart of Jesus' teaching. It was these who needed the Physician, for whom health and the Kingdom of God was a vital necessity. Jesus came to fulfil their need. He therefore accepted the ministry of 'the woman' at Simon's feast and proceeded to tell the story of the Two Debtors (Luke 7. 36–50) to open his host's mind to the amazing grace of God, who exercises his kingly rule for healing rather than condemnation. In effect he told him that the rewards of God's Kingdom can never be measured by what people deserve or fail to deserve, but only by the grace and goodness of God. Time and again the teaching of Jesus on the Kingdom and also some of his signs were evoked by the opposition of the critics to his table-fellowship with the outcast and 'sinners'. Much of the didactic material is an apologia to the gainsayers for the good news he came to bring, and incidentally forms a constructive commentary on Jesus' creative use of stress.

There is no better illustration of this positive response to negative criticism than the three parables of 'the lost' in Luke 15. How fortunate that the Pharisees and Scribes murmured about his table-fellowship! We should not have had this glorious vignette of the love of God in action. The reason for Jesus' concern for the abandoned and destitute is because they are God's concern. This is what health and the Kingdom mean—God going out in his fatherly love to the destitute and unloved, for his will is health and wholeness for all his creation. The implementation of that will is the Kingdom. Only when God rules is there true health.

God is therefore like a shepherd, searching for his one lost sheep. Finding it brings him consummate joy. Lifting it on his shoulder he returns to his friends with a spring in his walk: 'Rejoice with me, for I have found the lost one.' Joy is the health-giving characteristic of the Kingdom. The abandoned are reinstated. The lost have the way home found for them and become reintegrated. Or again, God is like a thorough and conscientious housewife. What an encouraging illustration! This humble housewife loses a silver coin and then turns the house upside down to find it. When she does so, she feels the situation calls for a party and, like the shepherd, she calls together her friends and neighbours to make merry. Such is the joy when anyone receives the health-giving life of God's rule, a road that will lead through repentance and forgiveness to reconciliation in the Father's house. And this is the great message of hope held out to the lost and abandoned today: the Kingdom is for you: if you are feeling hopelessly sick and bewildered in an unhealthy society, be assured that behind the sickness you feel, behind this immense and mysterious universe in which we are but a grain of dust, reigns the One who cares infinitely for you and wills your health. Pray that it may not be a message of judgement to the Church whose task is to continue the work of Christ among the abandoned and destitute, bringing them the good news of Jesus, the joy of salvation, the health of God's Kingdom.

The best wine of this great chapter is however saved until last. Rather than the somewhat misleading title 'the prodigal son', A. M. Hunter, following Thielicke, prefers to call it 'the waiting Father', a title, like Jeremias' 'the parable of the Father's love', which places the emphasis more correctly. If ever a parable spoke to a generation, this one speaks to ours. It is a real life situation— until the homecoming. The son is then met by no ordinary father. Jesus' story is seen to be larger than life, for here he depicts the 'amazing grace' of the heavenly Father going out to the undeserving. No single parable epitomizes more completely Jesus' teaching concerning the health of the Kingdom at whose centre is the God of all grace, freely offering it to the abandoned and destitute, going beyond the limits of fatherly duty in his all-healing love. It is a truth that is hard for human beings in a rational, scientific age to grasp, yet to be possessed by it is our only health and salvation; healing comes not by our own effort but by his grace alone.

The depths of this great parable are not easily plumbed and there is more to come. If Jesus is pointing to the unlimited love of God, he is also hinting that he is acting for him in making his grace and goodness available to his hearers. In his ministry the wholeness which God wills even for the sick and suffering, the lost and abandoned, is being actualized. The Kingdom means health and wholeness for those who return and enter it: it means the best robe, the ring, the joy of the feast to celebrate the coming to life out of death, the being found after being lost. This is the parable that was to be acted out on Calvary in the person of Jesus himself. 'In this is love, not that we loved God but that he loved us and sent his Son to be the expiation of our sins' (1 John 4.10). It was God's demonstration of his love, as Paul was to call it in Romans 5.8, that 'while we were yet sinners Christ died for us'. The cross showed and effected that love which has now made the health of the Kingdom available to all. The door to the Kingdom stands open: do we know the things that belong to our health? That was the question posed by many of Jesus' parables which pointed to a joyful life of exploding health under God's rule of Fatherly love.

c The Lord's Prayer

Most scholars are now prepared to accept a version substantially similar to that in Luke 11. 2–4 as authentic:[8]

> Father,
> Hallowed be thy name,
> Thy Kingdom come.
> Give us each day our daily bread;
> And forgive us our sins, for we ourselves forgive
> every one who is indebted to us;
> And lead us not into temptation.

The prayer undoubtedly goes back to Jesus himself. Who else could have given the prayer the opening address of *Abba*? However, it bears similarity to the Kaddish prayer which Jesus would have regularly used in the synagogue worship:

Magnified and sanctified be his
great name in the world that he
has created according to his will.
May he establish his Kingdom in your
lifetime and in your days and in
the lifetime of all the house of Israel,
ever speedily and at a near time.
Praised be his great name from eternity to eternity.
And to this, say: Amen.

It is a prayer for the health and healing of creation and the
establishment of the Kingdom, an urgent prayer for it asks for
fulfilment, both corporate (all the house of Israel) and personal (in
your lifetime and in your days), in the present generation. It is both
immediate and eschatological. Jesus, who obediently observed the
Jewish hours of prayer and assumed throughout his life the whole
atmosphere of Jewish orthodoxy, was deeply influenced by the
eschatology and urgency of the Kaddish prayer and took it one
stage further when he taught his disciples to pray. As Jeremias puts
it: 'In the Kaddish, a community is praying which is still completely
in the courts of waiting. The Lord's Prayer is prayed by men who
know that God's gracious work, the great turning-point, has
already begun.'[9] The very first word 'Father' in all its brevity
sounds the urgent note. It would have been for Jesus' contemporaries a strikingly new privilege even to name God in prayer,
certainly to call him 'Father' following Jesus' own custom. But this
was to be the new relationship in the Kingdom. God is our Father;
we are his children, and children talk with their Father. In this very
new relationship the power and health of the Kingdom are already
to hand. Being a child of God is a gift of health-giving power that
will put its seal on Jesus' disciples to the end of time. It assures
them of a share in future salvation, for 'it is not the will of your
Father who is in heaven that one of these little ones should perish'
(Matt. 18.14). It also assures them of security now for 'your Father
knows what you need before you ask him (Matt. 6.8). From a
position of such security, all relationships can be made healthy:
enemies can be loved and persecutors prayed for (Matt. 5.44). God
extends his special protection to the smallest: in the heavenlies it is
the guardian angels of the little ones who stand in the innermost
circle (Matt. 18.10). Again, being a child of God brings assurance

in the face of suffering. Indeed, suffering is transformed into an instrument of God's glory and an occasion of joy (Matt. 5.11f: par. Luke 6.22f). Never has such a truth been verified as it was by Jesus on Calvary where the tree of defeat became the tree of glory. Yes, for the children of God even death appears in a new light for God 'is not God of the dead, but of the living' (Mark 12.27). As Jeremias concludes: 'Stronger than all questions, riddles and anxieties is the one word *Abba*. The Father knows.'[10] The new relationship in the Kingdom is the recipe for health.

The two petitions couched in the second person singular that follow the address are obviously taken from the Kaddish prayer and follow its eschatology. They look to God's appearance as Lord, when his glory will become visible and he enters upon his kingly rule. It is a prayer for the overthrow of the rule of Satan and the revelation of the Kingdom of God, the only way to health and wholeness for the children of God. Is Jesus intending this prayer for the use of his little ones to be the prayer of the Kingdom?

The two first person plural petitions that follow tend towards this view. If the first two petitions closely followed the Kaddish, in this second couplet, two half-lines asking for bread and forgiveness, Jesus strikes new ground. The word *epiousios* in the first petition has occasioned the use of many tons of paper and gallons of ink. Scholars seem to be returning to Jerome's view that it refers to the *future* bread and this agrees with the eschatological trend of the prayer. The phrase might strikingly be rendered: 'Tomorrow's bread give us today.' As for the meaning of 'bread', it must be remembered that there was no contradiction in Jesus' mind between earthly bread and the bread of life for in the realm of the Kingdom all things are holy. The bread he broke, not only at the Last Supper but whenever he ate with his disciples, had an eschatological significance. The prayer for tomorrow's bread to be given today was a petition for the bread of life, i.e. the health-giving power of the life of the world to come, to be made available to today's children in their present situation as the food of pilgrims, the 'life-imparting heavenly manna', on their journey to the land of promise.

The most striking feature of the second part of this doublet is its own second clause, 'for we ourselves forgive everyone who is indebted to us'. It is the only reference to human action in the prayer. It is an important reminder of God's forgiveness of us and a declaration of our readiness to pass it on to others. It is a prayer, well illustrated by the warning contained in the parable of the Wicked Servant, requesting that the health-giving circumstances of the Kingdom seen in forgiveness should be a living experience for us, the children of the Father's Kingdom, today. At the same time it asserts our readiness to be instruments in God's work of passing on that experience to others. His saving health is for 'all nations and people and tongues' and is the endemic characteristic of the Kingdom.[11]

The final petition falls outside the structured framework of the prayer and appears harsh and out of place. It is also the only petition in the negative. All this only serves to underline its originality and importance. It is doubtful if Jeremias' view of the *peirasmos* referring to the last great trial can be correct. Surely Jesus is here bringing the disciples 'down to earth' in a petition that they may not succumb to the temptations that surround them in this life both from without and also from within. In the midst of temptation and tribulation, God is still *our* Father, who wills health for his children under his rule of love.

Though the doxology is not part of the original, a fixed form must have been in general use by the end of the first century A.D. The first form only included an ascription containing the power and the glory. Perhaps the Church's further experience of the prayer led to a realization of its true character—an articulation before the heavenly Father of the life-style and health of the coming Kingdom. For the Kingdom will be characterized by the universal acknowledgement of God's fatherhood and the hallowing of his name. It will be an experience of the bread of life enjoyed in the eternal today, of *shalom* lived out in a perfection of all relationships; it will be the end of Satan's tormenting rule; God's power and glory will be fully revealed and all creation fully healed. The Kingdom experience is one of total health.

The fourth way in which Jesus proclaimed the Kingdom, in his miracles and healing work, requires another chapter.

3

Jesus proclaims the Kingdom through his healing ministry

The Bible constantly demonstrates that word and deed are linked indissolubly together. God can demand a loving response from his children because he acts as a loving Father. This is also true of the ministry of Jesus. He was, as the two disciples remarked on the Emmaus road, 'a prophet mighty in *deed* and *word* before God and all the people' (Luke 24.19). For Jesus the two were all of a piece. His deeds therefore, seen in his healing work and his exorcisms, were as much part of the proclamation of the Kingdom as his words. They are signs that point to God's great work of constantly renewing the health of his creation. Indeed, the concern of the biblical writers is more for the significance of the mighty works than for the works themselves. This also reflects the attitude of Jesus. 'If it is by the finger of God that I cast out demons, then the Kingdom of God has come upon you' (Luke 11.20/Matt. 12.28). His works interpret his words and both are essential to the proclamation. The climax is seen when the final word is uttered in the mighty work of the New Testament, the cross/resurrection, the word and work of God combining to open the Kingdom to all believers and inaugurate the new creation. This is to anticipate, however, the theme of the next chapter and first we must begin our study of Jesus' healing work with an examination of the biblical vocabulary.

1 *The biblical words used to describe the healing miracles*

The most important word in the synoptic Gospels for miracle is *dunamis* = mighty work or power, from which is derived our word 'dynamite', meaning an explosive force. *Dunamis* suggests an act of God who is the source of all power and connects the miracles with the mighty work of history, the Christ event, in whose context they alone have meaning. R. H. Fuller calls them preliminary or accompanying miracles, just as the plagues and the dividing of the Red Sea were the preliminaries and the accompaniments of the Exodus, the mighty work of the Old Testament.[1]

Another word is *semeion* = sign, which has a somewhat infelicitous connotation in the synoptic Gospels where Jesus consistently refuses to give a sign. The Old Testament equivalent, *ôth*, used of the plagues in Exodus 7.3, suggests an event which points beyond itself to some further meaning, in this case the Exodus. The writer of the Fourth Gospel uses *semeion* in this sense as a God-given sign pointing beyond itself to the cross/resurrection event. The beginning of the signs at Cana was preliminary to the supreme glorification of Jesus in his death and resurrection. The word is similarly used in Acts 4.22. of the miraculous healing of the lame man which the Apostles claimed was indicative of the power of the holy name of Jesus.

Another word in the Fourth Gospel is *ergon* = work. Like *semeion*, this was also a pagan word for miracle to which the Evangelist gave a Christian meaning by associating it with his profound doctrine of Christ's person, for he sees Jesus' works as the works of the Father (John 9.3f; 14.10).

Teras = wonder usually has a depreciatory sense. It is not used in the synoptic Gospels and only once by John (4.48). Wonders are not to be looked for. It is used in a positive sense at Acts 2.22 in combination with *semeia*. There are three other nouns: *thaumasia* = wonderful things, Matt. 21.15; *paradoxa* = strange things, Luke 5.26; and *aretai* = wonderful deeds, 1 Peter 2.9, which only occur once.

The Bible has no one distinctive word for miracle; what is noteworthy is that each of the main nouns, once rescued from pagan usage, is given a theological meaning, deriving its distinctive character from association with the biblical view of God and his creation. Now we must turn to the verbs.

Iaomai = heal, or cure, is a medical term in classical Greek and it is not therefore surprising to find it is chiefly used by Luke, in both his writings. Although it also had a moral connotation, and could refer to the healing of moral sickness, Luke invariably used it of the healing of physical disease. He even used it in the commissioning of the Twelve (Luke 9.2) where Matthew used *therapeuo* (Matt. 10.8).

Therapeuo = heal, restore, or cure, is (obviously) the word from which our words therapy and its adjective therapeutic are derived. Again it was a common medical word, used for the treatment and healing of disease. Originally it had meant the giving of service of various kinds, including having a care for the gods. Moses was described as the *therapon* (= retainer or servant) of Jahweh in the LXX version of Numbers 12.7, cf. Joshua 1.2 etc. and Heb. 3. 1–6 which makes the contrast with Christ who is the Son. Whether Jesus had a consciousness of the therapeutic content of his role as servant is an interesting question which does not seem as yet to have been asked. A servant was certainly one with a message, 'my servants the prophets': if a therapeutic role was also endemic in his character, it was natural for Christ to combine both the preaching and healing roles in his person as the Man who serves and trains his followers to do and be the same. They were to be heralds and healers. This was to be the kind of *service* the Church would offer the world. This is Matthew's favourite word for 'heal', but it is also frequently used by Luke.

Sozo = preserve or keep from harm, save (from death), or rescue. It is employed in a variety of senses including being used in classical Greek as a medical term for healing in the sense of saving a person from illness or death. This is the word which is used when Christ declares that the faith of someone he has healed has saved them, e.g. in the case of the woman with a haemorrhage (Luke 8.48), or the Samaritan leper (Luke 17.19). It is from this that has sprung the erroneous conception of 'faith healing'. When the original word is understood then it will readily be seen that Jesus was saying that faith had brought the person to him and he had healed them. In this sense it had *rescued* them from prolonged sickness or even death which is the basic meaning of *sozo*. It was Jesus however who had healed the person, not their faith.

This verb is to be found more than a hundred times in the New Testament and is used some fourteen times in the Gospels in the sense of 'make whole' in connection with Jesus' miracles of healing. On these occasions the *double entendre* of save/heal is never far from the surface, for the Isaianic prophecies are fulfilled: the promised salvation has come through Jesus, a prophet mighty in deed and word, who brings the longed-for *shalom*. *He* is the good news of God's saving power (Rom. 1.16).

The verb *sozo* must of course be considered against the whole background of soteriology. The Old Testament word stemmed from the root meaning of being wide and spacious, of developing without hindrance and so of having victory in battle. The Israelite leaders and kings thus brought salvation to the people, but it was Jahweh who raised them up and so he was the author of salvation: 'salvation belongeth unto the Lord' (Ps. 3.8). The last of the Servant Songs (Isa. 53) saw that this saving work would be carried out only through suffering. The New Testament is the record of God's mighty work of salvation through Christ, who came to seek and *save* those who were lost (Luke 19.10) and so inaugurate God's kingly reign. This he accomplished when he had overcome the sharpness of death.

Hugiaino = to be in good health. Taken from the name Hygeia who was the Greek goddess of health, the word could refer to having a sound and healthy state of the body or even of religious and political affairs. A basic word in Greek medical usage, it is of course the origin of our word hygiene. The word is used mostly by Luke whose medical training possibly gave him a preference for it, e.g. at Luke 5.31, where Matthew and Mark had used another word; it is also used by the author of the Fourth Gospel.

2 *Miracles and Signs in the Synoptic Gospels*

One of the many positive blessings of modern critical methods with regard to the Gospels is that they have demonstrated beyond all doubt that Jesus healed and exorcized. It will therefore no longer do to dismiss the whole of Jesus' healing work on the single piece of evidence that he was reluctant to give 'an evil and adulterous generation' a sign. His rejection was not of miracles as such but of miracles as spectacles. He would also have rejected them as proofs of his divinity, as he seems to have done in the temptation on the pinnacle of the Temple. The evangelists for their part accepted miracles as a fact of their time. It must be remembered that the historical and natural sciences had not been developed in those days and so the idea that the miracle might be investigated and a scientific explanation might be sought never entered their heads. Their one concern was to show what great things God had done and thereby elicit from their readers a faith in God of whose activity in Jesus the 'mighty works' were 'signs'.

All the main gospel strata contain references to Jesus' healings.

The most valuable evidence is Jesus' own words concerning his exorcisms and healings (as we have seen above), from which it can readily be seen how Jesus regarded his ministry of healing as a priority. Furthermore, it is highly unlikely that Jesus would have commissioned his disciples to exorcize and heal had this not been an integral part of his own ministry. And would the Sanhedrin have insisted on Jesus' crucifixion had he only been a teacher from Galilee? Surely it was his 'signs' that alarmed them: they were clever enough to realize the implications as the writer of the Fourth Gospel perceived: 'This man performs many signs. If we let him go on thus, everyone will believe in him, and the Romans will come and destroy both our holy place and our nation' (John 11.47f). The question that troubled them was not whether Jesus healed and exorcized: it was by what authority he did so (cf. Mark 11.28).

We must not be afraid therefore to employ the tools of modern scientific criticism. The Holy Spirit surely uses them as one of the many avenues by which he leads us into all the truth. Historical and especially literary criticism are useful in our search for the living Jesus. Before we list his healing miracles and say a word about each, some brief examples of how the findings of modern scholarship can assist our quest may be helpful.

The miracle stories rest upon a single primary source, i.e. there are no miracles that are found both in Mark and Q. The source critics' work is therefore too simple. If we turn to literary and linguistic criticism, inevitably the material diminishes. A tendency to heighten the element of miracle (a perfectly natural tendency in those days when men and women had time to see and listen to wonder-workers), to multiply and elaborate, is discerned. For example, the summaries of Jesus' healings are accurate in that they summarize the fact that he healed, if not entirely accurate in their description of the events. In some cases a linguistic misunderstanding is found, possibly for instance in the case of the Gerasene demoniac: the Aramaic word *ligyona* may mean legion or *legionary*. The sufferer may have said: 'My name is soldier, and there are many like me' (soldiers resemble each other). There would be but a short step from such a linguistic error to the incident of the 'legion' spirits entering the herd of swine.

Comparison with Rabbinic and Hellenistic miracle stories shows many similarities between them and the miracles of Jesus: exorcisms, healings, raisings from the dead, stilling of storms, miracles with wine are all there. But why should there not be similarities? The needs of men and women for healing are present in every milieu. It is more likely that the early Christians drew upon their store of generalized memory about Jesus, relating the kind of healings he used to perform, while sometimes actual incidents are preserved, e.g. the Syrophoenician woman and the centurion's servant, remarkable in that Jesus went beyond 'the house of Israel' in these cases. Out of this comes one further step—an insight of the form-critics: they help us to distinguish an early Palestinian from a later Hellenistic stratum of tradition. It is naturally the simple narratives of the former (e.g. the healing of blind Bartimaeus, Mark 10. 46–52) which bring the authority of Jesus into the centre by omitting the details of the case and other elaborations. Another distinction made by the form-critics is between two types of miracle stories, those which provide a setting for a saying of Jesus, and those in which the miracle itself provides the climax. Inevitably these constantly overlap the previous Palestinian/Hellenistic distinction. A more helpful distinction when we look at the gospel healings and exorcisms may be to place them in three categories: the Isaianic signs, the exorcisms, and the more elaborately theological parable-miracle,[2] though again there may naturally be some overlapping. It is of course the Isaianic signs and the exorcisms that come from the firmest strata in the gospel tradition of Jesus' healings.

We may therefore summarize the situation thus far: even when critical methods have been applied to the gospel material with the utmost strictness—and the result is an inevitable reduction in that material—an historical nucleus remains to demonstrate beyond all doubt that 'Jesus performed healings which astonished his contemporaries. These were primarily healings of psychogenous suffering. . . . There were also however, healings of lepers (in the broad sense of the word as understood at that time), of the paralysed and the blind. These are happenings along the lines of what doctors call "overpowering therapy."'[3] As for these findings, we might well bear in mind a comment by R. H. Fuller: 'If we find the results of historical and literary criticism conflict with the modern scientific world view, we ought in principle to be ready to widen our world view to make room for these results.'[4] No science can in fact set its limits any longer. Let us now turn to the actual material.

a The Marcan Material

Mark's Gospel has been called a passion story with an extended introduction, the inference being that the author has connected originally isolated units, including the miracle stories, and given them a new interpretation in relation to the passion and resurrection of Jesus. We may discern five groupings of the miracles in his Gospel.

Group 1 1. 21–34 (Matt. 8. 14–17; Luke 4. 33–41).

The demoniac in the Capernaum synagogue 1.21–28 (Luke 4. 33–37). This first exorcism which follows the baptism of Jesus and Mark's summary of Jesus' basic gospel message (1.15), immediately demonstrates the conflict to come, both with the supernatural powers—and therefore the initial work for God's Kingdom must be the storming of Satan's citadel; and also with earthly authority—for Mark emphasizes that the people recognized in Jesus a new authority and a new teaching. It is perhaps significant that Jesus' first mighty work is an exorcism in view of his temptation conflict in the wilderness; of greater significance is the remarkable impression made by this first miracle on the spectators and the whole neighbourhood. The unconventional feature is the recognition of Jesus by the supernatural power. Mark does not miss any opportunity of interpreting Jesus' exorcisms. They are necessary conflicts in the cause of God and open the way for the coming of the Kingdom.

Peter's mother-in-law 1.29–31 (Matt. 8.14f; Luke 4.38f). Presumably Mark recorded this healing, like the previous exorcism, as a reminiscence from Peter's own lips and in his simple style of speaking. For Luke, the fact that the person healed was a woman had some significance. Jesus' concern for both men and women, for demoniacs and the sick, is brought out in this pair of narratives. The woman's healing prepared her for service in the Kingdom, something of which we should be mindful today. What are people healed for? Why does God give them new health? The answer must be to serve him through service of others and one way of responding to the blessing received by the healing Christ is to become a member of a praying fellowship.

This group ends with one of Mark's summaries, 1.32–34 (Matt. 8.16f; Luke 4.40f), closing the first phase of the ministry. It contains a reference to the messianic secret, perceived immediately by the supernatural powers, but only disclosed to the disciples half way through Jesus' ministry at Caesarea Philippi. This particular summary inspired H. Twells' hymn, 'At even ere the sun was set', a favourite at services of healing.

Group 2   1.40—3.6 (Matt. 8.1–4; 9.1–8; 12.9–14; Luke 5.12–26; 6.6–11)

The second group is set in the context of a series of conflicts with human enemies. If the first group followed his 'retreat' in the wilderness and the call of the disciples, this group follows his 'retreat' for prayer and the disciples' interruption and calling of him. Fellowship is only given meaning by knowing how to be alone: to fulfil the call to the fellowship of the Holy Spirit means being able to be alone in the Spirit, as Jesus was in his baptism and during his times 'in the desert'.

The leper[5]   1.40–45 (Matt. 8.1–4; Luke 5.12–16).   The miracles in this section would probably be classified as theological parable-miracles by some scholars. The healing of the leper, in itself a fulfilment of Isaianic prophecy, also introduces the theme of the Mosaic law showing Jesus to be the one who fulfils both the law and the prophets. He is the one to whom both bear witness, as they are seen to do at the Transfiguration, which is the most important link between the 'preliminary' miracles and the mighty work of the cross/resurrection. Jesus' act in touching the leper is both a demonstration of the higher and new law of love and of the fact that the good news of the Kingdom is proclaimed not only in words but in action and is able to break through the barriers of anxiety, fear, and scrupulosity. The strong word *embrimaomai* in v.43 originally means to snort and is used to express indignation.[6] Jesus was angry at the disfiguration of his Father's perfect creation. It is also used to denote the sound made by an exorcist when expelling a demon and since this verse also includes *ekballo* it may be an exorcistic formula. Another summary verse shows the difficulties under which Jesus was ministering. Should we in our ministry expect an easier way?

The paralysed man carried by four friends   2.1–12 (Matt. 9.1–8; Luke 5.17–26).   Here is a profoundly biblical and Christian story, first because it is so personal. Jesus notices the faith of the four friends and accepts their energy and ingenuity in seeking God's help for the sick man. They have in fact made the perfect act of intercession, bringing their friend into the presence of Jesus, who responds by treating the man's plight not merely as physical illness, but as the symptom of a deeper sickness. He offers him freedom from the bondage of sin. Remission is here a stronger translation than forgiveness. 'The remission of sins is the total gift of salvation of which physical healing is a part.'[7] It is this deep healing which Jesus came to bring a fallen race and, as the insertion in the story explains, the Son of man *has* authority (*exousia*) on earth to remit (*aphienai*) sins. This is part of the Good News and prepares men and women for the Kingdom, by making available in advance the blessings of 'the life of the world to come', that perfect *shalom*.

Finally the crowd glorifies God, by which Mark means us to notice that Jesus is the person in whom God acts. This would provide additional encouragement for the early Christian community in which the Gospel was written: God still does through word and sacrament what Jesus did in the days of his flesh. Let the Church today also take this lesson to heart.

The man with the withered hand 3.1–6 (Matt. 12.9–14; Luke 6.6–11). The details of the sickness, which may have been some form of muscular atrophy, possibly a psychosomatic complaint, are kept to a minimum, and all centres round Jesus' question which he puts to his onlookers with the man in the midst: 'Is it lawful on the Sabbath to do good or to do harm, to save life or to kill?' This is a profound question for all time. The word 'good' has a long Old Testament history from the creation narrative, through the blessings brought about by the Exodus even to the blessings of the age to come. It is taken up in the New Testament to define the blessings of the Christ event.[8] The sabbath was regarded as a prefigurement of the Kingdom of God and to save a life was to establish the characteristics of the Kingdom, to do God's work, to do good.

Group 3 3.7–12 (Matt. 12.15–21; Luke 6.17–19).

These may be described as the Galilean healings. They are a series of healings and exorcisms introducing the Beelzebul controversy, which highlights the conflict between the power of the Holy Spirit and the kingdom of Satan. Failure to distinguish between the two in this conflict is the unpardonable sin.[9] Mark shows again that in Jesus' exorcisms the strong man is being bound prior to the plundering of his house in the cross/resurrection. Luke significantly places this group as the introduction to the Sermon on the Plain, once again showing how the preaching and healing ministry of Jesus was all of a piece.

Group 4   4. 35—5.43 (Matt. 8. 23—9.26; Luke 8.22-56).

The scene for this group is the neighbourhood of the Sea of Galilee. Probably the collection was already in existence as an oral tradition. Mark has placed it significantly after Jesus has revealed the secret of the Kingdom of God to the privileged group of disciples in the parables that open the fourth chapter. The disciples are for the most part involved in this group of miracles as though Jesus is now demonstrating that secret to them. Once again, the word and the deed go together.

The stilling of the storm   4.35-41 (Matt. 8.23-27; Luke 8.22-25). This is not of course a healing miracle and yet it serves to demonstrate something entirely relevant to our purpose. The words 'Peace, be still' addressed to the creation, are to say the least a moment of power and truth and evoke the significant question from the disciples which is left unanswered: 'Who then is this, that even the wind and sea obey him?'[10] The Psalmist however had answered this when praising his God:

> Then they cried to the Lord in their trouble
> and he delivered them from their distress;
> he made the storm be still
> and the waves of the sea were hushed
> (Psalm 107. 28f).

Mark is inferring that the power of Jahweh active in his creation is now present in Jesus, who can similarly speak a word to creation. God is setting his world to rights in Jesus, who will bring in the Kingdom, creation healed.

The Gerasene demoniac   5.1-20 (Matt. 8.28-34; Luke 8.26-39). Jesus' exorcisms are a sign of God's imminent rule and that the devil's rule is at an end. That is why, according to Luke, Satan is seen falling like lightning from heaven as Jesus rejoices with his disciples after their first successful mission. But as Hans Kung remarks, this work is no mythological act. Rather it constitutes 'the beginning of a de-demonizing and demythologizing of man and the world and a liberation of true creatureliness and humanity'.[11] Jesus

39

in that same spirit of joy orders the man to go home to his friends to celebrate the beginning of this new creatureliness, this new start in creation. 'If any one is in Christ, he is a new creation; the old has passed away, behold, the new has come' (2 Cor. 5.17). The close of the story indicates what true healing involves: the responsibility to evangelize.

The raising of Jairus' daughter and the woman with the haemorrhage 5.21–43 (Matt. 9.18–26; Luke 8.40–56). The raising of the dead is not one of the predictions of the Isaianic passages, though it is contained in the answer to John and therefore is clearly meant to be a sign of the approach of God's reign, preliminary to the cross/resurrection of Jesus. The narrator—it was probably the oral tradition which joined these two narratives together—is at pains to insist that the raising of the girl is an act of the long-awaited Messiah. 'The girl is sleeping', i.e. she will rise again. The mighty act of the New Testament puts an end to the finality of death. Here is he who is 'the resurrection and the life', who summons into close involvement the three disciples, not long before he sends them out to continue his ministry.

Delay is a common feature in ancient resuscitation stories (cf. John 11.21) and, according to the form-critics, the story of the woman with the haemorrhage was inserted to explain that delay. Despite other features of a 'popular tale', the whole narrative is transformed by the personal encounter between Jesus and the woman, who falls at Jesus' feet in an attitude of humble supplication—and thanksgiving. Jesus addresses her personally, 'daughter', and commends her faith. Here we see the powerful conjunction of divine grace and human faith by which she is made whole. In the formula 'your faith has saved you' there is a deeper healing conveyed than the physical.

The generalized summary, expected at the end of a section, is seen here in a negative form—the rejection at Nazareth, as Jesus comes into conflict with his own countrymen (6.5f). Their unbelief was a lack of awareness of the power of God, of which the healings were signs, and proved them to be totally unready for the coming of the Kingdom. Despite this, Jesus did heal a few sick people, laying his hands upon them, signs that there had been 'a prophet' among them. The sending forth of the Twelve follows (6.7–13), and forms a climax to this fourth group of miracles which has chiefly been concerned with the training of the disciples for ministry.

Group 5 6.30—8.26 (For Matt. and Luke see each separate reference).

There are two strands that run through this group: one is the continued misunderstanding of the disciples. Mark keeps us guessing about the mystery, but the section ends with the opening of the eyes of the blind man and the healing of the disciples' 'blindness' soon afterwards at Caesarea Philippi in Peter's confession. The other strand is the loaves and eating of bread in which is found language that anticipates the messianic banquet and the coming of the Kingdom.

The feedings: The 5,000 6.30-34 (Matt. 14.13-21/Luke 9.10-17) *The 4,000* 8.1-10 (Matt. 15.32-39). Though not strictly part of our purpose, the feedings are extremely relevant and are integral to this fifth group of miracles. They are narrated in popular style and may well be different versions of the same incident.

The connection with the Christian Eucharist may not have been so overt in the primitive oral tradition. The actions of Jesus after all are the actions of a devout Jew presiding at a meal. The significant fact is that the happening was located in the desert and so recalls the eating of manna in the wilderness at the hands of the first Moses (Exod. 16.4ff); in both cases the people 'ate and were satisfied'. When the people of God were rebellious, they became unsatisfied (Isa. 9.20; Mic. 6.14) and so the prophets looked forward to the day when the people would again eat and be satisfied (Jer. 31.14). The feedings both look back to the wilderness and forward to the feast of the messianic age, 'when the meek shall eat and be satisfied'. Could they also have been connected with an attempt by Jesus at political reconciliation and healing? T. W. Manson offers the suggestion that originally this was the story of Jesus' meeting with zealots, 'a maccabean host with no Judas Maccabeus, a leaderless mob, a danger to themselves and everyone else. He speaks to them at some length and later they share a meal, at which Jesus uses symbols which afterwards came to be associated with the suffering and death of Messiah'.[12] However this may be, like the exorcisms and healings, these are signs of the imminent reign of God; Jesus is the agent of the new creation and ushers in the dawn of the Kingdom.

The walking on the water 6.45-52 (Matt. 14.22-33). The theological point of the story is this: the sea in the Old Testament symbolizes the mysterious power of chaos and death which is a constant threat to God's reign. In Jesus therefore, God is asserting his kingly power over Satan's realm. The moral of the story is the same as Jesus' thematic proclamation through his healing work: 'The reign of God is at hand.'

Healings in Gennesaret 6.53–56(Matt. 14.31–36). As R.H.Fuller remarks, these summaries, 'in spite of their late origin, are valuable as supplementary testimony to the general tradition. They show that the separate stories which have been preserved are only a selection from a larger body of memories.'[13] The truth which they encapsulate to an even greater degree than the miracle stories, is that Jesus not only healed, but spent a substantial amount of his time and energy in healing. To ignore this fact is to diminish the gospel deposit and to proclaim less than the good news of God's reign.

The Syro-Phoenician woman 7.24–30 (Matt. 15.21–28). This is the only Gentile healing in Mark: it has many points in common with the Centurion's servant, which is the only Gentile healing in the Q material (Matt. 8.5–13/Luke 7.1–10). As regards the Marcan material, perhaps Austin Farrer was right and the Evangelist is thinking of twelve healings among the Jews and one among the Gentiles, to correspond with the twelve apostles *and* Levi, in turn corresponding to the twelve tribes of Israel *and* Levi in the Old Testament.[14] The theological point made by both the Gentile healings is that it is only through faith in the Christ who heals that the barriers between Jew and Gentile can be broken down and the Gentiles become part of God's people. It is a lesson which the Church must learn and apply today. The healing charisms are given for the healing of the nations as well as for the healing of the Church and individuals, and are indicative of the healing thrust towards the perfection of the new creation.

The deaf mute 7.31–37. *The blind man of Bethsaida* 8.22–26. Mark ends this group with two healings which could easily be placed in the neat pigeon-hole of 'popular miracle stories'. They are twins and share certain 'secular' peculiarities. However, Mark is not quite so naive. Here are two of the signs of the Kingdom as detailed in the answer to John: the deaf hear and the blind see; while the summary of the crowd in v.37 'He has done all things well . . .', reminiscent of lines from a Greek chorus, is also a reminder of 'And God saw that it was good' in the creation narrative. God is even now restoring his sovereign rule. To emphasize this, sacramental acts and dramatic words are used. The touch of the Son of Man restores in a son of God the image of his creator.

There are two more healings in Mark's Gospel, but Peter's confession at Caesarea Philippi and the transfiguration precede them and reveal the secret of the gospel: Peter confesses for all the disciples that Jesus is the Messiah and immediately the chosen three see the vision of Christ in glory.

The two healings follow naturally. The first is:

The epileptic boy 9.14–29 (Matt. 17.14–21; Luke 9.37–43a). The Exodus event forms the background to this healing, as it did to much of the preceding group. Moses also found confusion on his descent from Sinai, Exod. 32. 15–24, and dealt strongly with the faithlessness he found. This present story is transformed by Jesus' discourse with the father into an illustration of faith (vv. 23f), ending with the father's *cri de coeur*, 'I believe; help my unbelief.' Man in his extremity is incapable of that 'energetic grasping' after God and is compelled to fling himself on God's mercy. It is at this point that God can act and that we enter the atmosphere of miracle in the true biblical sense. St Paul found the meaning of 'power in weakness' through his thorn in the flesh. God can enter the situation at the point where the weakness, in this case the unbelief, is confessed. If in Mark the emphasis is laid on the didactic usefulness of the incident for the disciples' own healing ministry, in Luke it is rather on the transfigured person of Christ who comes to heal in an unwelcoming world for which he must in the end suffer in order to effect that healing.

Blind Bartimaeus 10.46–52 (Matt. 20.29–34; Luke 18.35–43). This final healing sets the seal on the secret. It is a messianic miracle, indicated by the twice repeated 'Son of David, have mercy on me.' It also certifies that Jesus is even now opening the Kingdom to all believers. Here is the Son of David, and when the Davidic King is restored to Israel, the blessings of the Kingdom will be an actuality:

> Then the eyes of the blind shall be opened,
>   and the ears of the deaf unstopped;
> Then shall the lame man leap like a hart,
>   and the tongue of the dumb sing for joy
>   (Isa. 35.5f).

The narrative brings out the concern of Jesus for the poor and needy. The healing of Bartimaeus demonstrates that God's reign is here for those whose eyes of faith have been healed.

b The miracles in Matthew

Matthew's Gospel has been described as a new edition of Mark. We must remember he was writing for a Jewish public and his purpose is therefore theological (like Mark?) and Christological, for because of his readers' knowledge, he is able to use the Old Testament extensively to prove that 'this is very Christ', the second Moses. Jesus delivers the new law on the mount (chapters 5–7) as Moses was given the law on Mount Sinai. He then performs the miracles (chapters 8 and 9) as Moses brought about the ten plagues. These ten miracles form Matthew's first group and comprise the Capernaum miracles of Mark 1, the conflict stories of Mark 2.— 3.6 and the divine revelations of Mark 4.35—5.43, together with one from Q (the centurion's servant 8.5-13) and some of his own material.

A second group (chapter 12) is built round the Beelzebul controversy containing the man with the withered hand, a summary, the controversy, the demand for a sign, and the deaf and dumb demoniac; the third group (14.13—15.39) is taken from Mark 6—8, edited to show Jesus as the Lord of the Church, working through his disciples, especially in the feedings which take on a more eucharistic connotation. However it is Matthew's additions that are of chief interest to our present purpose and require a short comment.

Matthew's summaries of the healings are strikingly placed in the gospel record. Apart from those which come in a group of healings, there are two that demand the notice of the reader for they are placed at the very beginning and at the end of Jesus' ministry. Immediately after the temptation and the call of the first disciples comes the first: Matthew 4. 23-24. We have already noted how the summaries give emphasis to the indelible impression left on the people who handed on the oral tradition that Jesus' ministry consisted of preaching *and* healing. Here Matthew is saying that the two always went together from the very first and that they formed the proclamation of the Kingdom. He also stresses the completeness of Jesus' healing ministry—it was '*every* disease and *every* infirmity . . . they brought him *all* the sick', and then proceeds to list them, 'various diseases and pains, demoniacs, epileptics and paralytics, and he healed them'. The writer must have been convicted of the truth that this was an indispensable part of Jesus' work.

The second summary comes at the end of the ministry after the cleansing of the Temple: Matthew 21.14–16. It is the blind and the lame who are specifically mentioned this time, perhaps noting that this is still the Kingdom being proclaimed, and it is these *actions* that lead to the controversy the following day. It is the deeds, as we have noted above, for which Jesus was crucified, more than for the words. Is it surprising that his Church is regarded as innocuous if it only deals in words? Moses could not have become one of the great religious leaders of all time had he confined himself to preaching courses of sermons on the decalogue; if Jesus had not healed he might well not have been crucified. But he did heal, he was crucified and he did rise again and Matthew's purpose is to present Jesus as the Lord of the continuing Church. He expounds the definite tradition he has received in a way that will encourage the contemporary Church to continue Jesus' ministry of preaching *and* healing in the sure knowledge that he promises, 'Lo, I am with you always, to the close of the age' (Matt. 28.20).

c *The message of Luke*

Luke is certainly—and primarily—concerned with the 'works' of Jesus. In the introduction to his second volume (Acts) he writes of his first volume (the Gospel), 'In the first book, O Theophilus, I have dealt with all that Jesus began to *do* and teach' (Acts 1.1). Some scholars see the master plan of Luke's Gospel in Jesus' statement about his ministry, 'Behold, I cast out demons and perform cures today and tomorrow, and the third day I finish my course' (Luke 13.32), in which case the deeds would seem to be basic to Jesus' ministry. The three phases of the ministry would then work out like this:

1. In Galilee (4.14—9.50)—'today'.
2. The journey to Jerusalem (9.51—18.34)—'tomorrow'.
3. The passion and resurrection (18.35—end)—'the third day'.

The first phase opens with Jesus' anointing at his baptism and his sermon at Nazareth containing the statement from Isaiah (61.1f). Here is the theme of the Kingdom, Jesus claiming the anointing of

45

the Spirit in order to bring about the conditions of God's reign—release for the captives, sight for the blind, liberty for the oppressed—and claiming it today, 'Today this scripture has been fulfilled in your hearing' (Luke 4.21). The reign of God, shown in salvation/healing, is now present in the world and Old Testament prophecy has been fulfilled. The Church must now make the Psalmist's injunction her own—'O come, let us sing to the Lord; let us make a joyful noise to the rock of our salvation! . . . O that *today* you would hearken to his voice!' (Ps 95. 1, 7b). There is an immediacy about the good news and Luke's narrative of the works of Jesus is designed to evoke an immediate response. Certainly the response at Nazareth was immediate; it was rejection. Rejected by their own people, the prophets of old turned to outsiders. Jesus, rejected by the people of his own town, was to turn to the outcast: to women, Samaritans, and the Gentiles. The example of the prophets is never far from Luke's mind. The deeds of Jesus are a fulfilment of prophecy. The healings, exorcisms, and raisings are all signs that Jesus is God's anointed, the prophet-Messiah. Jesus makes the salvation of God present 'today'.

The *tomorrow* section of the Gospel again begins with rejection, but this time from the Samaritans. Jesus therefore concentrates once more on the training of the disciples and sends out the Seventy. As in the sending out of the Twelve, 'He called the Twelve together and gave them power and authority over all demons and to cure diseases, and he sent them out to preach the Kingdom of God and to heal' (9.1f), so now Jesus commissions the Seventy to heal, 'When you enter a town and they receive you, eat what is set before you; heal the sick in it and say to them, "The Kingdom of God has come near to you"' (10.8f). Luke obviously intends his readers to understand that the healing ministry was not only part of Jesus' ministry, but is to be part, and an integral and central part, of the ministry of the Church. It is essential to the proclamation of the Kingdom because it brings about the conditions of the Kingdom. In his second volume, Luke sets out to demonstrate how integral is the healing to the outward thrust of the Church's mission, emphasizing the obedience of the first Christians to Jesus' commission to preach and heal.

But even the miracles, despite their indispensable place in Jesus' mission, are not the final and conclusive testimony. The rising again on the *third day* is the mighty act of the new covenant, the supreme miracle of healing and the source of the disciples' joy. 'Do not rejoice in this, that the spirits are subject to you, but rejoice that your names are written in heaven' (10.20). The third day (= the first day of the week) is the celebration of the triumph of God in healing and putting his world to rights; it is the beginning of the new age, the inauguration of the Kingdom. That is why Christians have set it aside as the day of worship, when they meet to proclaim the Lord's death until he comes' (1 Cor. 11.26), in the supreme sacrament of healing.

3 *The Johannine Signs*

The author of the Fourth Gospel (FG) uses the word *semeion* (= sign) for Jesus' miracles throughout his narrative. The synoptic writers do not use this word for the miracles though they clearly regard them in this light (e.g. Matt. 12.28/Luke 11.20). Rather they use the word eschatologically, both of the signs of the false Christs and also of 'the sign of the Son of Man' (Matt. 24.30). In the FG however there is what some commentators call a transvaluation of eschatology, a shift from the eschatological to the ontological, for example in the development of the meaning of *zoe aionios* from the life of the age to come to 'eternal life'.[15] We shall find therefore that the writer attaches a real significance to Jesus' acts of healing and other miracles as signs of the power of God active in the world *now*, and so preserves an original element in the teaching of Jesus, a useful corrective to some of the Church's misunderstandings. It is not within the scope or purpose of this book to discuss the original book of signs the writer found nor his selection of the six (or seven if you include the walking on the water).[16] Let us rather take a brief look at the signs and seek their significance in the proclamation of the Kingdom and its application today.

i *The wedding at Cana* (2.1–11) was an appropriate setting for the first sign, the showing forth of Christ's glory, since a wedding feast is a parabolic model for the messianic Kingdom (cf. Matt. 22.2ff). There is no need to fantasize the occasion with the form-critics and see it as a transplantation from the Dionysus legend; after all it has more affinity with the feeding of the multitude. The miracles from the book of signs are part of the genuine tradition, placed and edited by the Evangelist to suit his theological purpose. They are, as here, actual events which the Evangelist sees as signs with a Christian message, that God's power is active in Jesus. Here, at the beginning of his ministry, Jesus is in fact declaring its purpose, as he did in the sermon at Nazareth in Luke. The wine he gives is a symbol of the messianic salvation/healing, revealed through his ministry especially here in the signs, and supremely accomplished in the cross/resurrection (the seventh sign?), *the* mighty work of the New Testament. Here at the very beginning the writer shows his ontological colours. The glory of Christ is at once revealed; God is active for the salvation/healing of mankind *now*, even before its full revelation in the passion. It is indeed the beginning of signs and its corollary is the cleansing of the Temple, which follows immediately after a link verse. There has to be a constant cleaning out of any ossified traditions, presuppositions, and moribund customs in the Church if the glory of Christ manifested in his constant signs is to be seen and acted upon in its mission.

ii   The setting for *The official's son* (4.46–54) is also Cana and illustrates the Johannine theme of life. It links the signs on each side of it and together the three form the first of the two groups of signs, each containing a nature miracle and its corollary, together with two healings. The similarity of this healing with that of the centurion's servant in Matthew 8 and the centurion's slave in Luke 7 is worthy of note and all three should be compared. The rebuke to the official in verse 48 is presumably a warning from the Evangelist not to seek for merely physical healing, but for the whole salvation of God, a warning that must be heeded in the healing ministry today. This sign, like the others, elicits a total response of faith. The official took Jesus at his word and went home: on ascertaining the truth of the healing 'he himself believed and all his household' (verse 53). The sign had pointed him to 'the glory of God revealed in the face of Jesus Christ'.

iii   *The lame man at Bethesda*[17] (5.1–9) is linked to the previous healing in this first group by a series of contrasts: in the first a child is healed, here an adult; in the first he is healed at a distance, here face to face; in the first it is an acute attack of fever, here a chronic complaint of long standing.

   Out of the crowd of invalids, blind, lame, and paralysed, Jesus was moved to approach one. 'One man was there, who had been ill for thirty-eight years.' He must have been the most 'chronic' of all the cases! And Jesus knew that over the years he had got so used to his illness that it was part of him. Here was not just a man with a sickness but a sick man. 'Do you want to be healed?' The question can be asked of many sick people in any generation. If they are healed they will lose sympathy and be no longer the centre of attention. 'Sir I have no man' might be the words from a proud heart. Healing has to go very deep to make a person whole and only the power of Jesus can bring total life to our mortal personalities by healing the deep recesses of our subconscious.

The theme of judgement is also implicit in this healing. It was done on the sabbath day when God rested from his creative work, but, according to rabbinic teaching, still passed judgement on sin. The healing of the lame man was a work of judgement as well as salvation/healing in its challenge to faith. Jesus was doing God's work on the sabbath and once again a healing demonstrates that in Jesus we are confronted with the work and presence of God himself.

iv *The feeding of the five thousand* (6. 1–13).   As in Mark, this completes the Galilean ministry. The ministry among God's poor, the inheritors of the Kingdom, comes to a climax with an anticipation of the Kingdom banquet. Jesus is hailed by the crowd as the Prophet-Messiah (v.14), imparting a foretaste of things to come. The word for 'gave thanks' is of course the same as that from which our word Eucharist is derived; the Church's Eucharist is also an anticipation of the messianic banquet. The signs point to the reality of the Kingdom, as do the sacraments of the Church, but in Jesus, the reality of the Kingdom is already here: he is indeed *really* present!

iva *The walking on the water* (6. 16–21).   John found this story in his source and retained it as a 'corollary' to the (4th) sign of the loaves. 'The life' manifested there is now shown to be 'the light of men', a fact that is heightened by the mention of the darkness, pointing to the bewilderment of the disciples because Jesus 'had not yet come to them' (v.17). There are many similarities to the Marcan version (Mark 6.47–51), including the fact that Jesus walked *on* the water (*epi* with the genitive) and the words that gave recognition: 'It is I; do not be afraid.' The ultimate healing is when Christ comes to be with the disciple, to abide with him as the guiding light at the centre of his personality, so banishing all fear and anxiety.

49

v *The man born blind* (9.1–41).   The theme of light and darkness
again forms the background to this fifth sign, Jesus being the light,
and the attitude of the Jews representing the darkness. The man
born blind is symbolic of the helplessness of those trapped in
darkness who can only receive illumination from him whom the
darkness is powerless to overcome, the Light of the world. But the
work of God Jesus performs is also a work of judgement:

> For judgement I came into this world
> that those who do not see may see,
> and that those who see may become blind (v.39).

This healing is symbolic of this work; the Jews' messianic presuppositions made them blind to the new revelation in Christ, while the
man born blind was aware of his inability to see and was therefore
open to the revelation of God in the light of Christ.

There are several interesting points in the narrative. The disciples
ask Jesus in verse 2, 'Rabbi, who sinned, this man or his parents,
that he was born blind?', thereby expressing the common belief of
the day that sickness and other misfortunes were a punishment for
sin. The 'comforters' of Job held a similar view. Jesus shows that
he did not share it.[18] The glory of God is the purpose of all healing,
so that God's work of perfection in his creation can be shown forth
in the wholeness of personality.

Again, Jesus proceeds to the cure without even asking the man if
he wishes to be healed. And he uses sacramental acts. Spittle,
symbolic of the healer's life, was frequently used in ancient times,
but Jesus used it here to make mud from the dust of the soil as a
primitive poultice for the man's eyes. The material of creation—
'remember, O man, that dust thou art and unto dust thou shalt
return'—is used by Jesus in the work of the new creation. The cure
is effected by washing in the pool of Siloam, symbolic of the waters
of baptism, the sacrament of the new creation. Siloam is also an
obvious allusion to Christ who was 'sent' for the salvation/healing
of the world. As for Naaman, so with this man it was a test of faith.
The response of obedience led to the cure, which the Evangelist
emphasizes by using a word for seeing (*blepo*) that invariably has a
literal interpretation. Once more we note that the healing took
place on the sabbath, the continuation of the Father's work of
judgement. Also that the healing gave the man a robust confidence!
When asked, somewhat ironically, to give glory to God, he did

indeed glorify God by his eloquent witness: 'one thing I know, that though I was blind, now I see' (v.25). At the further meeting, the faith of the man elicited during cross-examination is transformed by Jesus' questions into worship (v.38). The purpose of all healing is a deeper vision of the glory of God in the face of Jesus Christ and in the power of the Spirit, a vision that can only evoke 'wonder, love, and praise'.

vi *The raising of Lazarus* (11.1–44). The sixth sign forms the climax to the ministry and points to the final sign, the resurrection of Jesus himself. The theme of resurrection also links it with the corresponding sign in the first group, the healing of the man at Bethesda. It is not our purpose to discuss questions of historicity. But since many have doubted the credibility of this story, let it be said that some commentators think it not unreasonable that if historical evidence alone can establish the credibility of any miracle, this has as good a claim as any to reliable testimony. [19]

Once again we find that the key word, summarizing the purpose of all miracle, is glory: it is to be a revelation of the glory of God (v.4). The full glory will be shown in the saving action of God in Jesus on the cross: this sign is the curtain-raiser for the passion. The remark of Thomas (v.16) keeps the goal of the passion in the reader's mind. The references to light and darkness occur once again.

The profound teaching of this sign is found in the dialogues with the sisters, especially in the climax of that with Martha, where Jesus, having led her to a deeper faith, elicits its final expression by declaring: 'I am the resurrection and the life: he who believes in me, though he die, yet shall he live, and whoever lives and believes in me shall never die' (11.25f). It is a pity we usually hear these words only at funerals! Jesus is proclaiming more than resurrection in the last day. Most Jews believed this already. Jesus is saying that for those who accept him resurrection and life are available here and now. The incarnation has made that passing from death to life a present possibility and that 'touch has still its ancient power'. The raising of Lazarus that follows his teaching demonstrates this newness of life in Christ. Passing from death to life is no theological platitude but an actual event consequent upon the words and works of Jesus, who raises men and women and children to life, as many are finding today. Resurrection is an actual happening, for Jesus is *the* resurrection and *the* life. From now on, in R. H. Fuller's words, 'for those who have accepted Jesus' word, death, though still a biological occurrence ("though he die"), becomes theologically irrelevant ("yet shall he live").'[20]

Of all the signs this most profoundly penetrates the heart of the mystery of the incarnation—that in a human being is disclosed 'God's presence and his very self', his saving power in action. John used it as the grand finale of Jesus' ministry and of his 'book of signs'. The epilogue is to be found in chapter 12, verses 37 to 43, a summary which the Evangelist has taken from the book of signs. Isaiah saw the glory (v.41). If all our eyes were open to that glory we also should turn to him for healing. It is a sad but true comment, that the praise of men weighs more heavily (with us) than the praise of God (v.43). Mercifully the glory of God is an eternal fact and is only revealed to us as our mortal senses are able to bear it. He who has ears . . . and eyes too . . . .

4 *The call and the commission*

Jesus' method of training entailed both a calling and a commissioning. He chose those he wanted to be with him that he might send them out 'two by two' to preach and heal. He always said 'Come' in order to say 'Go'. This much we learn from the call of the Twelve in Mark 3.13ff: 'He went up into the hills, and called to him those whom he desired; and they came to him. And he appointed twelve, to be with him, and to be sent out to preach and have authority to cast out demons'. When he *commissioned* them later on (6.7–13), he again *called* them to him 'and began to send them out two by two and gave them authority over the unclean spirits'. He charged them about their equipment and apparel and their conduct in each place and then 'They went out and preached that men should repent. And they cast out many demons, and anointed with oil many that were sick and healed them.' Mark follows this commissioning with the account of the beheading of John Baptist as if to show that the completion of one mission leads to the launching of another, and then records the disciples' return somewhat briefly (6.30f). They 'told him all that they had done and taught' and his reply was a *re-calling*, a constant experience in Christian discipleship as Jesus deepens the commitment: 'Come away by yourselves to a lonely place and rest a while.'[21] And then an interesting comment from the Evangelist; born out of his experience it still rings true for those engaged in ministry today: 'For many were coming and going and they had no leisure even to eat.'

A call, a commissioning, and a re-calling of which there may be very many as most of us know from our experience of discipleship. Too little emphasis has been given to the call by Jesus of his disciples and the reason for that call. For what did he call them? Ralph Morton has written a percipient little book in which he draws attention to the unique place of 'the disciples' in the gospel story.[22] They were those who responded to Jesus' words and deeds. 'His life was his call. His every word and action called men (and women) to his way of life.' His call was an open invitation. There were many disciples. But of these he called twelve, 'to be with him', as a community within a community, just as the three were to become among the Twelve. Jesus being a Jew automatically thought in terms of the community rather than of the individual. For a Jew, corporate solidarity was a way of life and basic to his thought. These Twelve were men whom he 'invited to share in a work that had its purpose in the nation'. They were no individuals seeking personal salvation: they were men under obedience who were given a mission. That is why 'the men whom he called were the adult, the healthy, the responsible . . . who carried the burden of the world's work, who had responsibilities in family and society.' They were those who were to continue with him in his trials and temptations. They were called to live a common life that was utterly different because it was *his* way of life, the life of the Kingdom, and for this they needed that leisure. When he commissioned them, he sent them out in pairs, that is, 'in community'.

Matthew places the call and the commissioning of the Twelve together (chapter 10). In the *call*, authority is also given 'to heal every disease and every infirmity' (v.1). The *commissioning* is more elaborate and contains fuller instruction: 'Preach as you go saying "The Kingdom of heaven is at hand." Heal the sick, raise the dead, cleanse lepers, cast out demons.' The instructions on equipment and method follow and then a passage about persecution which probably is coloured by the experience of the Church at the time of writing. It contains valuable teaching on discipleship while the many 'uncomfortable' words and reversal sayings show that it must be close to the actual words of Jesus. The eschatological tension between life lived now and life in the future Kingdom which characterizes Christian discipleship is also present.

Luke's *calling* and *sending* of the Twelve, and their return, are more briefly related (chapter 9). Jesus *calls* them and gives 'power and authority over all demons and to cure diseases' and then sends them out 'to preach the Kingdom of God and to heal'. A short instruction on equipment and method follows. Their return and report is briefly noted in the first half of verse 10. There is no list of the Twelve in Luke but they are mentioned (8.1) as accompanying Jesus on a preaching tour 'bringing the good news of the Kingdom of God', preliminary training for their own sending out. Typical of Luke, his list at that point is of the women who accompanied them on the tour: Mary Magdalene, who had been healed, Joanna, Susanna 'and many others'. His writing frequently attempts to heal male pride! Luke's major contribution to the commissioning material is his account of a commissioning of Seventy (chapter 10). Much of the material is also found in Matthew, but the significance of their appointment is to be found in the Old Testament. In Numbers 11. 4–25 the Lord directed Moses to appoint seventy elders who received the Spirit of the Lord to assist Moses in governing the 'rabble' (mixed multitude). According to rabbinic learning there were seventy nations, for whom seventy interpreters had already made the Scriptures available. The alternative reading seventy-two derives from the fact that the addition of Eldad and Medad in Numbers 11 may mean that the total should be seventy-two. Luke has included the equipment and method material of the commissioning of the Twelve but has added other material of his own and again from the Old Testament, especially from the Elijah/Elisha saga (e.g. 1 Kings 17 and 2 Kings 4). Luke knew where to go for his 'healing' sources. The Seventy are instructed to 'heal the sick' and to say, 'the Kingdom of God has come near to you', in the towns where they are received. 'The word alone is an empty shell; action alone can be the work of the devil. The reign of God is manifested only in word and action together.'[23]

Luke also is emphatic about the salutation. Matthew barely mentions it, taking it for granted his readers would know the Jewish salutation. But Luke spells it out in full: 'Whatever house you enter, first say, "Peace be to this house!" And if a son of peace is there, your peace shall rest upon him; but if not, it shall return to you' (10.5f). This greeting was immediately taken over by the Christian Church and has again become more meaningful in our time through the giving of the peace during the liturgy, in some places less shyly and more demonstrably than others! From the first this has been the custom in visiting a sick house: the minister goes in Christ's name as a harbinger of Christ's peace. As our formularies enjoin him, 'Coming into the sick person's house (the minister) shall say: Peace be to this house, and to all that dwell in it.'[24] Peace was the first gift the risen Christ gave to his disciples after his resurrection. That same peace is shared within and also given from, the community of the resurrection, the Church of Christ. The greeting itself has become a proclamation of the risen Christ and his Kingdom.

The commissioning of the Seventy inaugurated the Gentile mission. If the first Moses had appointed seventy to help him govern 'the rabble', the second Moses appointed seventy disciples to assist him in the mission beyond Israel to the Gentiles. The good news must be preached to 'other cities' also for the healing of the nations, until the fulness of the Gentiles shall be gathered in and all Israel shall be saved. Healing was an essential element in the method to be used in the proclamation. It was also part of the overall purpose of the God who heals from the beginning, who therefore sent his Son to proclaim the salvation/healing of the world.

Luke immediately records the return of the Seventy who are filled with joy, having tasted the perfect freedom of the Lord's service. 'Lord even the demons are subject to us in your name!' (v.17). Jesus' reply has no parallel in the synoptics: 'I saw Satan fall like lightning from heaven' (v.18). It may be inspired by Isaiah 14.12, which seems most likely since the Capernaum passage in v.15 contained recollections of the same chapter. But Jesus himself saw the fall of Satan's kingdom as a necessary preliminary to the establishment of the eschatological Kingdom of God, and the Seventy's successful mission, marked by an obedience to his instructions to heal and exorcize, did mean that the Kingdom of God had come nearer to them (v.9) and that Satan's kingdom was being stormed. The expectation of the final defeat of Satan had a place in late Judaistic literature, but the actual idea of Satan's falling from heaven is not found until the seventh-century 'Targum Jerushalmi'. The Seventy are not however to rejoice in the subjugation of the spirits, the negative forces in creation, through their ministry of exorcism, but in the fact that their names are in the 'Lamb's book of life', that they have been chosen to enjoy the eternal life of the

Kingdom. The Church today must learn again how 'to abide', to wait still upon God, lest we fail to discern 'the magnificent scale on which he is acting at the present moment', to borrow a phrase from David Edwards.[25] We must learn to rejoice that our names are written in heaven. We must learn again 'to be with him'.

The epilogue to this passage is also of interest. It is Jesus' turn to rejoice. He rejoices in the Holy Spirit as his mother Mary and her cousin Elizabeth had done when they were given a share in the knowledge of God's plan of salvation. Jesus rejoices because he sees this plan being worked out as the preliminary signs of the Kingdom appear. As if by explanation he then turns to the disciples privately (probably therefore the Twelve, not the Seventy) and says: 'Blessed are the eyes which see what you see! For I tell you that many prophets and kings desired to see what you see and did not see it, and to hear what you hear, and did not hear it' (vv.23f). The disciples are witnessing the new creation taking place before their eyes: in Christ's healing miracles they are seeing the fulfilment of the Isaianic signs of the Kingdom. Jesus had said as much to the Baptist's disciples. The significance of these signs is that they are the works of Christ, who is 'he that should come'. They are the fulfilment of Old Testament prophecy: 'Then the eyes of those who see will not be closed, and the ears of those who hear will hearken. The mind of the rash will have good judgement and the tongue of the stammerers will speak readily and distinctly' (Isaiah 32.3f). They are in accord with God's plan of salvation, which indicates Jesus is the Saviour, God's anointed, 'great David's greater son'. Those who have witnessed these works of the Christ, and even more those like the Twelve and the Seventy who have shared in these signs of the Kingdom by healing and exorcizing, have already 'tasted the goodness of the word of God and the powers of the age to come' (Heb. 6.5).

In the Fourth Gospel, where there are accounts of individual disciples being called, no act of commissioning of the Twelve is recorded. However the Upper Room discourses encapsulate what must have been a large tradition of teaching given to the disciples, and it is here we find an expression of the same essential attitude as in the synoptic material: 'Truly, truly, I say to you, he who believes in me will also do the works that I do; and greater works than these will he do, because I go to the Father. Whatever you ask in my name, I will do it, that the Father may be glorified in the Son; if you ask anything in my name, I will do it' (John 14. 12–14). The disciples will be able to do the works of Christ which will be even greater in effect; that is the thrust of the passage. The miracles of Jesus involved only those who were healed and a few others. The 'signs and wonders' to be done by the disciples will reap a rich harvest of souls as the mission moves outwards. And the reason why the obedient disciples will be able to do this is that Jesus is going to the Father, whence the Spirit proceeds. It is Jesus' death that enables the Spirit to be given and the disciples to be empowered to the works of Christ.[26] It is through the new creative power unleashed into the world by the death/resurrection of Jesus that these greater works will take place, but only if the disciples are obedient to Christ's challenge to faith and to ask anything in his name. If we fail to do this, to take Christ at his word, then we are failing to give glory to the Father, for we are failing to give Christ the opportunity to fulfil his promise. How many times each one of us has fallen short of the mark in this regard. We are too frequently a community of 'little faiths'. The age of reason and the resulting intellectualism have tended to introduce an attitude of doubt concerning the simplicity of faith demanded of the disciples. Now is the time for the Church again to turn to its pristine obedience and take Jesus at his word: 'If you ask anything in my name . . . .'

The call of Jesus to be numbered among the disciples must once more be seen as a call into community, for we can only proclaim the Kingdom of our God and of his Christ from within the community of Christ, as part of his body, the sharing of whose life is 'healing to your flesh and refreshment to your bones' (Proverbs 3.8). From this 'health centre' he will commission us to go out— into surprising company. He led his first disciples amongst the outcasts and the underprivileged, the dissolute and the disreputable, the irreligious and the diseased. They were all to be part of the Kingdom community. There was to be no health for the nation (salvation was of the Jews) without them. God wills all to be healed. We must hear his call again. But 'unless our discipleship begins with something of the amazed wonder and fascinated joy with which the first disciples heard Jesus speak and followed him, we are not likely to progress far in our obedience. . . . We too have to learn to be disciples from the beginning. And that means learning to be disciples together.'[27]

5 *The message of Jesus' ministry to the Church of today*

From the brief review of Jesus' miracles and signs one fact cannot have escaped the notice of the persevering reader: Jesus spent a large proportion of his ministry in healing the sick. The healings described in detail were those that had impressed themselves on the consciousness of witnesses, on account of either the dramatic effect or the new dynamic of the teaching. These formed only a small part of Jesus' total healing ministry. In the synoptic Gospels there are nineteen other instances in the form of summary passages which state that people were healed, sometimes a general reference to all kinds of diseases or to 'those who were sick'; sometimes these include cases of demon possession; other diseases mentioned in the summaries include lunacy, paralysis, blindness, dumbness, and lameness. The Fourth Gospel writer is near the truth when he states, 'There are also many other things which Jesus did' (21.25). Constantly Jesus was surrounded by crowds who sought him out and invariably he healed their sick. The fact that Jesus healed, and healed so consistently, ministering to the total personality and to all who were brought to him, has too frequently been disregarded in the history and theology of the Church, and yet the evidence of the New Testament is there for all to see. This contrasts with the evidence which can be produced on behalf of any other religious leader. Jesus' interest in the total health of men and women was far greater than that of any religious leader or religious system, past or present. It is moreover a distortion of the New Testament evidence to say that Jesus pronounced more on moral, than on physical and mental, health. It seems that the latter has been allowed to be ignored owing to a 'spiritualizing' tendency of New Testament interpreters who have substituted a belief in Jesus' moral healing, which, though such took place, e.g. in the case of Zacchaeus (Luke 19) and the woman at the well (John 4), is only fractionally evident when compared with the physical and mental healings. Such a tendency does scant service to a full doctrine of the incarnation. Jesus' healing work was a most significant part of his ministry. A portrait of Jesus that does not contain a substantial element of healing is a false one.

Then again, his healing work was totally consonant with his person and his teaching. His healings found their origin in the essential nature of God and were a direct expression of his in-carnation. He loved people—he was the human expression of the divine love of God for his creation, 'God so loved the world . . . .'—and was utterly caring and compassionate. Compassion is the act of knowing and feeling suffering together. He suffered along with his people because he had to be tested in all points like them apart from sin. His healings flowed naturally from a nature that was essentially compassionate: they were not only the ex-pression but the logical result of the incarnation. The recording of one after another especially in the Marcan groupings demonstrates how dedicated Jesus was to ministering to people with mental and physical diseases, so much so that in order that the work should continue, he commanded his disciples to do the same.

This healing and caring ministry is all of a piece with his teaching on caring and having compassion for one's neighbour. The prime example is of course the parable of the Good Samaritan which has caught the imagination down the centuries and has been the in-spiration to millions as the expression of what lies at the heart of Christianity. Many have seen in the Samaritan the person of Christ himself, who *comes where we are* and ministers to our many wounds. This is the caring in depth that man needs and Christ came to give. It is an expression of God's limitless love, that he is putting the world to rights and cares desperately for his people. They have a right to sit in his Kingdom and Jesus' caring and compassion shown in his healing ministry is direct evidence that the Kingdom is breaking forth.

Moreover Jesus obviously saw himself as engaging in a spiritual warfare on a cosmic level, as a glance at the early part of the Marcan material will demonstrate. Paul also had this experience: 'We are not contending against flesh and blood, but against the principalities, against the powers, against the world rulers of this present darkness, against the spiritual hosts of wickedness in the heavenly places' (Eph. 6.12). Jesus saw that beyond the present illness, beyond even its underlying cause, was frequently a cause that was beyond human control. He therefore was able to respond openly to that person and take direct action to meet the need. He accepted people as they were without a word of recrimination or reproof. People in sickness and moral trouble needed compassion, not judgement. They were up against real forces that, humanly speaking, could not be handled on their own. 'He knew what was in man', and what man encountered within his psyche. To judge him would only increase the despair. Men and women needed the love and compassion, the greater reality of God which not only could release them from, and expel, these alien invaders, but also put something good in their place and recreate them in the divine image. Emptiness of life was—and is!—an open invitation to alien powers to invade the personality and Jesus gave a humorous warning about it (Matt. 12. 43–5/Luke 11. 24–6). Jesus saw himself as fighting a warfare against evil powers on a level where man was powerless to help himself. He saw it as one of his major tasks to set men and women free from the bondage that prevented them from being free agents of God, from following in the way that leads to the glorious liberty of the children of God. In Jesus we realize that there is now a greater power available to mankind.

Again, Jesus' life and teaching were based on a deep conviction about the Kingdom. It was his Father's purpose to reign in his creation and that meant in the hearts of all people, especially in the hearts of the poor and the outcast. This conviction undergirded all Jesus' healing work and his care for the underprivileged. If the Church would be true to its Lord today, it must be rooted theologically in the Kingdom and express its theology in a deep commitment to, and outgoing concern for, the sick, the refugees, the underprivileged, the prisoners, the outcast, the poor. This is the healing ministry committed to the Church, for which it is equipped with the healing power of its risen Lord. That healing power was always available to Jesus in his ministry because of his constant communion with his Father. A Church which is in continual communion with its Lord in the power of the Spirit will find that the reservoir of power to heal never runs dry. The Lord's presence to a Church alert, watchful, and obedient ensures the presence of that power to heal.

Finally it will be noted that Jesus' healing methods were largely sacramental in nature. He usually healed by word and/or touch. The touch has become 'the laying-on-of-hands', the word is still spoken in Jesus' name. In almost half the examples of Jesus' healings we have examined, this method was employed. Mark tells us (6.13) that the disciples used oil when Jesus sent them out on their first tour of duty and although it is never mentioned, it may well be presumed Jesus himself used oil. We might even infer this from the technique used by the Good Samaritan. People also touched Jesus and found healing. The particular instance of this is the woman with the haemorrhage, while in a Marcan summary (6.56) it is noted that people begged Jesus to allow their sick to touch even the fringe of his cloak 'and all those who touched him were cured'. Three times Jesus used saliva, once to make a mud poultice, on the other occasions more to convey his personality than as a direct agent of healing. The faith of the individual, a prayer of thanksgiving, the forgiveness of sins, are further elements that play their part in the healings, but on the whole it is the immediate response of compassion expressed in touch or word that characterizes the ministry of Jesus.

It is in the healing ministry of Jesus that we see the love of God incarnate, the Word made flesh, full of grace and truth. It is the direct outcome of the incarnation. His healing work also included the whole relationship between the sexes (his attitude to women was way ahead of his time, as was his treatment of children), while his relationship with the created Universe brought a healing into man's response to his environment. Again, in his work with the disciples, in his reinterpretation for his own race of historical truth, and finally in the way he responded to and handled the group pressures that surrounded him as he approached his death, Jesus showed how profound was his understanding of the ultimate salvation/healing he came to bring. More work needs to be done on these vital facets of Christology.

All this and more was part of his healing work and was a significant indication that the rule of God had begun and that the divine power would continue to manifest itself in signs following until the Kingdom is revealed in a healed creation. It is for this reason that he called his disciples and commissioned them to continue his work. That call and commission are being heard and answered with renewed conviction in the present century.

4

The unleashing of Healing Power

1 *The Calvary Christ*

On the altar in my private chapel stands an Oberammergau crucifix. It is, as its inscription reads, 'memoria passionis Jesu Christi'. It had been brought back by a priest's wife from her pilgrimage in 1922 to that remarkable place, which, in thanksgiving for its deliverance and healing, has faithfully continued to make this 'memoria' every ten years. Like every 'memoria passionis', whether it be a simple crucifix or the celebration of the Lord's Supper, it recalls him who is the 'Light of the World', who died on the cross, who is both true God and true man. This is the great mystery of our redemption. This is the central fact of our faith. This is the event of cosmic significance, which has changed the order of things: the life of man is no longer hopeless because evil can no longer be triumphant. Central to the Christian's faith and whole philosophy of history stands the cross. From it shines out a redemptive inevitability: within it lies the reservoir of power, whose waters hold the salvific medicine for the healing of creation.

It was the prophet of the Exile, the second Isaiah, possibly influenced by the sufferings of Jeremiah, who was the first to point to the possibility of cosmic redemption through suffering in a remarkable series of prophecies known as the Servant Songs. A special strand within the book, which did not come into being at the same time as its context, it nevertheless owes its origin to Deutero-Isaiah. The comparison of the Servant with Jesus was soon made: early in his Gospel, Matthew (3.17; cf. 12.18–21) sees the significance of the first Servant Song (Isa. 42. 1–4). The song had begun with a designation of the Servant and his work, which was to 'bring forth justice to the nations . . . till he establishes justice in the earth'. Jesus' ministry began with a similar designation at his baptism and temptation. There is also an interesting connection with Moses: he was especially Jahweh's servant in the Old Testament, whose ministry was both by way of action and by word of mouth. These strands later parted company, but were to be reunited in the Servant, and especially in Jesus, the second Moses, whose teaching and healing were both part of his proclamation, as we have seen. In the verses that follow this first Servant Song (Isa. 42. 5-9), the Creator of the universe who gives life and breath to mankind calls Israel to be the instrument of his salvation. The enlightenment and healing he is to bring—the opening of the eyes of the blind and the release of prisoners—speak of the messianic age and the Kingdom.

The second Servant Song (Isa. 49. 1-6) takes up the two main points of the first, his installation as God's Servant and the commission to bring salvation/healing to the Gentiles, a call that approximates closely to that of the prophets. Like Jeremiah, being hid with God ('in the shadow of his hand') is part of the Servant's equipment. But his work is wider and has cosmic dimensions. His special call is for the healing of the nations:

> It is too light a thing that you should be my servant
> to raise up the tribes of Jacob
> and to restore the preserved of Israel;
> I will give you as a light to the nations,
> that my salvation may reach to the end of the earth (v.6).

The third Servant Song (Isa. 50. 4-9) has at first sight close similarities to the Covenants of Jeremiah. The cry of the mediator voiced by Jeremiah is silenced and for the first time suffering for the sake of the task is assented to and accepted. Here is a new factor of revolutionary importance in God's dealings with his people. The healing of the nations, accepted in a positive response by the Servant in the first two Songs, is to be accomplished through the Servant's acceptance of suffering in obedience to a deeper call within the call:

> The Lord God has opened my ear,
> and I was not rebellious,
> I turned not backward.
> I gave my back to the smiters,
> and my cheeks to those who pulled out the beard;
> I hid not my face from shame and spitting (vv. 5 and 6).

If this Servant Song bears similarities to the story of Jesus' passion, the fourth Servant Song (Isa. 52.13—53.12) is almost the description of an eye-witness and is now part of the Good Friday liturgy in the Christian Church. The passage furthermore bears a credal structure: born, suffered, died, and was buried. The astonishment that finds it hard to comprehend what has come about is also significant, viz. that the power of God has been revealed in weakness. We are reminded of the revelation to Paul about his thorn in the flesh (2 Cor. 12.9). And this weakness embraces a whole life span from birth to death, isolating him in the community, 'as one from whom men hide their faces he was despised, and we esteemed him not' (v.3). It is out of this feeble and ordinary person's suffering, the suffering that had brought him nothing but contempt, that the power of healing came. This is one of the great insights of the Old Testament. The discovery made by the speakers in this passage was that:

> Surely he has borne our griefs
>   and carried our sorrows; . . .
> he was wounded for our transgressions,
>   he was bruised for our iniquities;
> upon him was the chastisement that made us whole,
>   and with his stripes we are healed (vv. 4 and 5).

Truly an amazing insight into the realm of suffering and healing, a healing that not only includes the forgiveness of sin but also the removal of suffering, expressed well in Luther's rendering, 'the punishment lies in him, in order that we might have peace (*shalom*). 'With his stripes we are healed;' here is an experience that is revolutionary in its novelty. The final verse of the song:

> He poured out his soul to death,
>   and was numbered with the transgressors;
> yet he bore the sin of many,
>   and made intercession for the transgressors (v.12)

demonstrates that it is also prophetic, for contrary to what some editors may say, this act of intercession is more than the offering of prayer (word); it is the offering of the Servant's life (deed) for suffering and death on behalf of others, by which he took their place and underwent punishment in their stead. It is from this point of 'weakness', marked by a free submission to the Lord's will (cf. v.10), that came the power to heal. Here was an insight scarcely glimpsed even by Job, let alone by his friends. The very act of innocent suffering had within it the power to heal the sufferings of others. The Gospels claim that it is in these Servant Songs, especially in Isaiah 53, that Jesus found the meaning of his sufferings. It is a claim that can be substantiated.[1]

It was in fact Isaiah's Servant of the Lord that pointed the way to the cross and with whom Jesus must have identified himself, certainly from his baptism at which the word from heaven 'with thee I am well pleased' echoes the formula of blessing given to the Servant (Isa. 42.1). He came among us 'as one who serves' (Luke 22.27) and so the baptism had to be undergone, the cup drained, the price paid, and the road trodden. In the light of the resurrection and Pentecost the disciples came to see the significance of the cross. It had to happen. It was part of God's putting the world to rights, his mighty work inaugurating the new Covenant. It was 'according to the definite plan and foreknowledge of God' (Acts 2.23). It was the work upon which the opening of the Kingdom to all was dependent, in which Christ entered with us and for us into God's judgement on sin, making before his Father a perfect confession of our sin, taking it all into his innocence and suffering, and so healing us into a new acceptance, a new peace, with the Father. Such, and so much more, is Christ's *work* for us on the cross. It is also the *word* of God's love, as the writer of the Fourth Gospel makes luminously clear (John 3.16 etc), in which he has destroyed the works of the devil and powers of evil (John 12.31; 1 John 3.8). 'Such is Christ's work *for* us', remarks A. M. Hunter and continues, 'Yet to be effective, it must also become Christ's work *in* us.'[2] The power unleashed in the cross to heal creation has to be received and accepted and used according to God's purpose until the Kingdom is a fact, when 'at the name of Jesus *every* knee shall bow' (Phil. 2.10), for 'on the cross, God stretched out his hands to embrace the ends of the earth' (Cyril of Jerusalem). This act of redemption has included the poor and the abandoned, the destitute and the hopeless. As we read in the aprocryphal Acts of Andrew, the cross is 'set up in the cosmos to establish the unstable'. Jürgen Moltmann, commenting on this says, 'There is a truth here: it is set up in the cosmos in order to give future to that which is passing away, firmness to that which is unsteady, openness to that which is fixed, hope to the hopeless, and in this way to gather all that is and all that is no more into the new creation.'[3] It was on the cross that the Servant accomplished his task and through the weakness of his suffering in some way unleashed a power to heal not only in individuals, but in the structures of the society in which they live and even in the universe. His death, both as word and work, was the ultimate proclamation of the Kingdom and a 'sign' pointing towards its fulfilment.

The first symbol therefore which may help us to understand the inner meaning of the crucifixion of Jesus is 'power-through-weakness'. The very weakness of Christ in his suffering and abandonment, holds the secret of his power. 'Christ helps us, not by virtue of his omnipotence, but by virtue of his weakness and suffering', wrote Dietrich Bonhoeffer shortly before his own death. 'Only the suffering God can help. . . . Man is summoned to share in God's sufferings at the hands of a godless world.' A Japanese theologian, Kazoh Kitamori, writing at about the same time from a similar political situation in his country wrote a book entitled *Theology of the Pain of God*, in which he sought to show how the pain of God heals our pains.[4] From such situations of suffering, like the experience of slavery which inspired the negro spirituals— 'Were you there when they crucified my Lord? We, the black slaves, were there with him in his agony'—comes the knowledge that from weakness and suffering healing is born.

Again, the death of Jesus was not a beautiful death like that of Socrates. Jesus died not only forsaken by man, but by God. He was utterly abandoned to suffering. 'Is there a death', asks Hans Kung, 'which has shaken but perhaps also exalted mankind in its long history more than this death so infinitely human-inhuman in the immensity of its suffering?'[5] We must not gloss over the finality of Jesus' death and his abandonment by man and God: it really did mean the failure of his mission *at that point*, that his proclamation and his action had been repudiated. The disciples had nowhere near reached the point of consciousness held by the second Isaiah. Had it all ended here, they would not have known the saving and healing power that comes out of suffering and weakness. For them Good Friday was 'Good-bye'. It was the end. Jesus was totally identified in his death with the abandoned, the destitute, and the sufferers of all time for a purpose.

It is this very fact that gives the clue to the 'amazing grace', this power that heals, which finds its source in the cross of Jesus. 'The unassumed is the unhealed' is a well-tried principle, tested by such fathers of the Church as Athanasius. The principle infers that it was necessary for the incarnate Son of God to have assumed every element which belongs to human nature in order for his salvific grace to have healed every dimension of the life of man. 'Nothing was healed unless it was assumed.' Gerald O'Collins in a stimulating work,[6] takes this principle which attributes man's redemption to a full incarnation, and applies it to the crucifixion, changing it (he admits 'drastically') to, 'The un*crucified* is the unhealed.' In so doing he stresses the inevitability of the crucifixion: it had to be. Both Mark and Luke introduce this ineluctable theme with regard to the passion of Christ, the former as if by way of emphasis no less than three times (Mark 8.31; 9.31; and 10.33). Paul strikes a similar note of necessity reciting an early Christian creed, 'Christ died for our sins in accordance with the scriptures' (1 Cor. 15.3). The early Christians discerned this necessity in the divine plan. A rationalizing of Jesus' conduct and teaching and attitudes would lead to a feeling of inevitability about his suffering and death.

Fr O'Collins takes up this *dei pathein* theme of Mark and other New Testament writers and uses it to support the principle 'the uncrucified is the unhealed'. He sees it as containing two affirmations:

1. Before Jesus could cause our healing, he had to be crucified. His execution prompted the healing. In that sense, if uncrucified he would not have been our healer. Being made perfect 'through what he suffered', he could become 'the source of eternal salvation to all who obey him' (Heb. 5.8f). 2. It was the whole Jesus who was crucified, not—so to speak—just some part of him. Crucifixion destroyed his entire human existence. What remained uncrucified in him would be unhealed in us.

Here we see the 'power in weakness' principle with which the writings of Paul make us familiar. Its roots however lie back in Jesus' ministry as well as in Paul's own experience related in 2 Corinthians 12. 7-9.

In his teaching Jesus exalted the weak. In the beatitudes he declared that such as the poor, the meek, and the persecuted are in fact the blessed ones. It is such as those who will enter the Kingdom first and their sorrow will be turned to joy. As always, Jesus acted out what he taught. In this case he acted out the beatitudes on the cross. In a very real sense, 'how blest' he was in suffering crucifixion for the cause of right: the Kingdom of heaven was indeed his (Matt. 5.10). And through the principle of solidarity, so much a part of Jewish thought, how blest are we also who are 'found in him': his crucifixion has opened the Kingdom of heaven to us. 'The crucifixion dramatized the beatitudes.' Already his words had proclaimed the principle that divine power is made perfect in human weakness, or 'the uncrucified is the unhealed'.

This same principle was evident in the works of Jesus. He sought out the marginal people of society, the sick, the underprivileged and the sinful. It was among these that 'he exploded with power', healing their broken bodies, forgiving their guilty consciences and restoring them to the wholeness which their Creator had meant for them. He pointed them all to the joy of the Kingdom banquet of which his own eating with them was a foretaste. He came not to call the righteous, but sinners (Mark 2.17). He was at his most powerful in the company of the weak. His 'first eleven' was a team of nobodies. The historical Jesus could have well remarked of himself, 'When I am with the weak, then am I strong'. His works of healing are visible demonstrations of the principle that divine power is made perfect in human weakness. His words and works pointed forward to the cross on which they merged into one. The cross is the mighty work *and* the mighty word of God, where divine power is perfected in human weakness. It is the climax of the Servant's mission for the healing of the nations and the inauguration of the Kingdom, declaring for all time that the 'uncrucified is the unhealed'.

The other symbol that is helpful to our understanding of the power which emanates from the crucified Christ is that of reconciliation. It has been a favourite quarry for theologians, Karl Barth among others, while Pope Paul VI chose it as the theme in 1975 for the Holy Year. It occurs prominently, though not frequently, in the New Testament, because Paul gives it a significant place in two of his major letters, Romans and 2 Corinthians.[7] In these passages he makes the following points:

1 Reconciliation is God's work, not man's. In the Old Testament human beings frequently make atonement for sin. This idea is totally foreign to the New Testament. It is God alone, God in Christ, who makes the reconciliation (2 Cor. 5.18f, Rom. 5.11).

2 The work of reconciliation was on a cosmic scale. 'In Christ, God was reconciling the *cosmos* to himself.' This does not mean only the world of men, but the world which included the hostile,

fallen, elemental powers. Through him God was pleased 'to reconcile to himself all things, whether on earth or in heaven, making peace by the blood of his cross' (Col. 1.20). The reconciliation wrought by Christ's death was total and cosmic.

3   It is the actual death of Christ which effects the reconciliation (Rom. 5.10, cf. Eph. 2.13, etc.) and that death is an act of God on man's behalf. It is part of God's plan for putting the world to rights.

4   This act of God is effective in reconciling not only man with God but man with man. It has 'broken down the middle wall of partition' between Jew and Gentile. Out of the two God has created 'one new man' so that both alike now have access (another great Pauline word) to the Father (See esp. Eph.2).

5   This reconciling work of God is now committed to us (2 Cor. 5.18f). As Bultmann wrote (*Exegetica*, p.228): 'With the cross, God instituted the office of reconciliation, the word of reconciliation; in other words, the preaching itself also belongs to the event of salvation . . . in it Christ is encountered.' Such is the privilege and responsibility of this ministry.

The final verse in the Corinthian passage (5.21), emphasizes the totally representative nature of Christ's work on the cross and the overflow of healing power from the person thus reconciled, who is now 'in Christ'. It is impossible to remain a spectator of the passion drama: no one can recognize in Jesus' death the source of his hope and values without being drawn within the orbit of its saving power. The healed are those who have identified themselves with the crucified Christ and have been brought through that 'baptism' into a new peace, as the Israelites were brought through the Red Sea waters to the promised land, to be part of God's new creation. And all this is the work of God through the cross of Jesus for 'God experiences history in order to effect history. He goes out of himself in order to gather into himself. He is vulnerable, takes suffering and death on himself in order to heal, to liberate and to confer new life.'[8] 'Finish then thy new creation. . . .'

2 *The Risen Christ*

The mighty work of the New Testament is the Christ event. It is impossible to consider *only* the incarnation or the crucifixion or the resurrection. They are all of a piece and all part of God's mighty demonstration of his love, just as Jesus' life was all of a piece and the supreme revelation of that love. It was the resurrection which vindicated the whole Christ event and set God's seal upon the sacrifice of the cross. It also vindicated the purposes of God as 'merciful and mighty'. Because of the resurrection Paul was able to proclaim:

> I am sure that neither death, nor life, nor angels, nor principalities, nor powers, nor things present, nor things to come, nor height, nor depth, nor anything else in all creation, will be able to separate us from the love of God in Christ Jesus our Lord (Rom. 8.38f).

The whole Christian faith stands or falls on the resurrection. Those who claim it to be a falsehood have an enormous, and to my mind impossible, job in front of them, unless of course they stick their head in the sand like an ostrich and so become deaf and blind to the evidence. They have to give an explanation first of the textual evidence. A German historian called Mark's story of the empty tomb (16.1–8) unshakeable. Together with the opening verses of 1 Corinthians 15 it forms the earliest evidence and seems incontrovertible. Certainly no Jew would have made three women the first recipients of the news that the tomb was empty! Their wondering about who would roll the stone away and their flight in sheer terror strike the reader as authentic recollections. But there are other things to explain:

1   The existence of the Christian Church today twenty centuries later, when on the night Christ was crucified the disciples had run for it and were ready to put an end to it all. What transformed them from the cowards of that evening into those who 'spoke the word with boldness' and eventually 'turned the world upside down'?

2   The keeping of Sunday as the day of Christian worship, almost from the first. This is an almost incredible piece of heroic nerve to change the day of worship, in that milieu too, from the sabbath to the first day of the week. From the first, the early Christians felt a compulsion to meet together on, and celebrate, the day when they *knew* Jesus had conquered death and risen. There seems to be no other explanation.

3   The existence of the New Testament itself. Every writing is the

work of a man who believed in the resurrection. It is hard to see that they would even have bothered to put pen to paper had Jesus' life come to such a sudden and untimely end on the cross.

The fact of the resurrection is however not the only consideration. It is the *experience* of men and women down the centuries that provides the most telling testimony. Christians in every generation have come to know the *living* Christ: they have based their faith and hope on Jesus risen. Paul made this experience his topmost priority: 'I count everything as loss because of the surpassing worth of knowing Christ Jesus my Lord . . . that I may gain Christ and be found in him . . . that I may know him and the power of his resurrection, and may share his sufferings . . . (Phil. 3. 8–10). John refers to the same experience in terms of 'eternal life'. Christians down the ages have this experience, both of knowing him present and of being alive with his life. It is an experience that cannot be hid: it is to be seen in the radiant eyes and faces of those who know that their Redeemer lives, as well as in their attitude and approach to the whole of life. 'By their fruits ye shall know them.'

The significance of Easter for the world lies in the future new creation of all things. The resurrection means that this new creation has already begun, for it is an event of cosmic significance. In the resurrection a new power entered the world comparable only with the explosive force of the first creation. As such it heralded a new era for the universe, and certainly a watershed for the whole human race. The first man—for which Adam is a convenient shorthand—was made a living soul. The second Adam—now the first man of the new creation—was made a life-giving spirit. The resurrection meant that the world had died in the night and been reborn. It signified the storming of history. In fact it heralded the Kingdom, which has now dawned in the risen Christ who was crucified. If Jesus proclaimed 'The Kingdom of God is at hand', the resurrection proclaims the presence in power of him who was to come. The rule of death and elemental powers is at an end and the rule of God has begun. Since Easter, 'the Church understands the age in which it lives as the presence of the God who was to come . . . . the churches which acknowledge Jesus as Lord recognize in him the representative of the coming, all-redeeming Kingdom. They live in the power of his Spirit and no longer recognize any other masters.'[9] The power unleashed by the resurrection is

71

therefore purposely given for the inauguration of the Kingdom conditions, when all acknowledge God's rule. It is a power that will constantly express itself more gloriously through weakness. Just as it was the God-forsaken, humiliated body of the crucified Jesus 'whom God raised up', so it is the blind who will see, the lame who will walk, the lepers who will be cleansed, the deaf who will hear. It is a power at its strongest when human power is negated, a power that is seen in serving others not enslaving them, in loving others and not dominating them, in self-sacrifice rather than self-assertion (cf. Mark 10. 42–5). The Church of the risen Christ is the Church that lives out the Kingdom experience: it is made up of the poor who are blessed, the sick who are healed, the sinners who are forgiven and the prisoners who enter a new freedom. 'The Church is the fellowship of those who owe their new life and hope to the activity of the risen Christ.'[10] It is this 'activity of the risen Christ' within the members of his Body which is the power that heals. Only a healed Body is a healing Body; the Church is only true to its calling when it lives in the power of the resurrection, and uses that power for the healing of the nations until its risen Lord is Lord of all.

3 *The Christ who heals*

It used to be said that it was of no avail to preach the gospel or give Bibles to those with empty bellies. My reaction to this dictum which came from the mission field and was undoubtedly found to be an important truth, was that those poor unfortunates might well have understood a deal more than those with full bellies! For, as Jürgen Moltmann points out, the Bible's revolutionary themes—promise, exodus, resurrection, Spirit—come alive if read in the light of the experiences and hopes of the oppressed.[11] It is always the sick who need the physician. The *promise* is meaningful to an Abraham who has to leave his father's house, to an outlawed David, to a nation in exile: it is fulfilled in the crucified Jesus, 'for all the promises of God find their Yes in him' (2 Cor. 1.20). The *exodus* is the mighty work that forges a nation out of abandoned slaves. The *resurrection*, the mighty work of the New Testament, is God raising to life his forsaken and crucified son. The *Spirit* is given to a small remnant, to create out of nothing a whole new creation. His strength is always made perfect in weakness, and the source of that strength lies in the cross/resurrection event, to which the promises have always pointed, which the exodus foreshadowed and the Spirit confirms with signs following.

It was inevitable that after the cross/resurrection there should be a complete rethinking concerning the person and work of Jesus Christ. The person of Jesus and the presence of God's Kingdom became inseparably connected. We find Philip in Samaria preaching 'good news about the Kingdom of God and the name of Jesus Christ' (Acts 8.12). This is interesting because it shows that although 'Jesus and his resurrection' became the central part of the kerygma in the early Church, the proclamation of the Kingdom of God was in no way displaced.

> The post-resurrection christology, in which Jesus Christ is the centre of the kerygma, is rather the outcome of the realization that the Kingdom of God is present only in the person of Jesus Christ, so that one can only properly speak of the Kingdom of God by speaking of Jesus Christ . . . . the good news which Jesus preached of the dawning of God's Kingdom becomes, after Easter, the gospel of Jesus Christ and the proclamation of his Kingdom. [12]

This was in fact the logical outcome of Jesus' preaching and teaching about the Kingdom, for he made it inseparable from his own person. After the resurrection the disciples saw that the future rule of God had begun to be a reality in the words and works of Jesus. More than that: they realized that the rule of God would gradually became even more real and contemporary as they obeyed his command to proclaim that Kingdom by preaching and healing. They would be able to continue the work of Jesus for the Kingdom, now 'clothed with power from on high' (Luke 24.49). 'Truly, truly, I say to you, he who believes in me will also do the works that I do; and greater works than these will he do, because I go to the Father' (John 14.12). The ascended Christ now equips the Church with his gifts 'for the work of ministry, for the building up of the body of Christ' until the body and each of its members comes to full maturity in Christ (Eph.4. 1–13, cf. 1 Cor. 12). This gives glory to God and is the purpose of the Christ who heals.

Christians of every generation are called to follow and obey the Christ who heals. The reservoir of power consequent upon the cross/resurrection is freely available to continue this work which he saw as part of the work of his Father which he was sent to do. His teaching on the Kingdom will be for the Church the essential point of reference for the accomplishing of his work: it will also be the inspiration in the doing of it and the hope held out to those called to work 'for the Kingdom of our Lord and of his Christ' (Rev. 11.15). As the Christian faithfully goes about his work, he will find that Christ is present to heal and in that presence (*praesentia* = being in advance) the conditions of the Kingdom become a contemporary fact.

5

The Church moves outward

1 *The Pentecost experience*

We have seen how the Kingdom of God and the person of Jesus Christ came to have a close affinity in the consciousness of the early Christians. They had seen the conditions of the Kingdom being realized in the words and works of Jesus and now they came to regard 'the resurrection of Jesus as the divine confirmation of his mission'.[1] Those who had witnessed the post-resurrection appearances knew they were living at the dawn of a new age. This very real experience, which alone accounts for the new life of faith we see in the early Christians, became the door that opened into the history of the early Church.

There followed a parallel experience, equally real. Luke separates the two by a period of fifty days while the writer of the Fourth Gospel telescopes them into one event. Whatever the details may be, the essential fact is that as the resurrection witnesses were together in one place, they were filled with the Spirit which they described in terms of an explosion—wind of unnatural proportions and fire; this was the 'power from on high' they had been promised. It was both a group experience and very real personally, for it led to a release of their personalities and their latent gifts, together with a receiving of others, which they knew had to be used in Christ's mission to the world. They had been obedient and waited for the blessings of the crucified and risen Christ. Now the end of their waiting and the beginning of the new life had come.

This was the confirmation and focusing of their individual experiences of the risen Jesus. It did not matter where and how it happened though each locality would be evocative of some past experience with him, the soil of earlier faith: it might have been in Galilee where Jesus had sent his disciples after his resurrection to experience again the first visions of their calling; or by the sea of Gennesaret which would call to mind the teaching he had given them; or in the upper room with its enigmatic yet meaningful memories of the night before he died: all the experiences were so different and yet so vivid. What was of consequence was that they knew they had seen the Lord and were now having this experience confirmed by the outpouring of his power. Such an exploding force, consequent upon the resurrection, would change not only their lives but the direction of the world. They interpreted this explosive power as the Spirit of Christ and then came to identify it as the Holy Spirit who had brooded on the face of the waters at the first creation, had inspired the prophets, had overshadowed Mary and now, according to Jesus' promise, was exploding within them, indicative of a new creation. This 'power from on high' alone could fashion them into useful instruments for the preaching and healing work of the Kingdom. Only thus equipped could they become heralds of the new age. The power is always given to further God's purpose for his creation. The task of the Church is to be expectant and obedient so that it may be ready to be a channel of that power and so further the Kingdom of God.

2 *The obedience of the early Church: healings in Acts*

Little sister Mary Meliukov, one of St Seraphim's pupils who was to die at the age of nineteen after six years of monastic life, consecrated herself wholly to obedience. 'There is nothing greater than obedience' she would say to the sisters as they remarked on her radiant joy. The saints are glowing examples to us of this essential element in Christian discipleship (discipline!). The early Church was instant in its obedience to the commands given by its Lord both before and after his resurrection. The Holy Spirit brought all things to their minds, whatever he had told them, and guided them into truth. The Acts of the Apostles records these early essays in discipleship. It has been called the Gospel of the Holy Spirit, and so it is: it could also be called the book of obedience. It speaks of a new and eager desire to follow the commands of the risen Christ, because once confronted by the risen Christ there is only one possibility, a life of obedience. St Paul knew this only too well: 'Wherefore, O King Agrippa, I was not disobedient to the heavenly vision, but declared first to those at Damascus, then at Jerusalem and throughout all the country of Judea, and also to the Gentiles, that they should repent and turn to God and perform deeds worthy of repentance' (Acts 26. 19f). The experience has to be shared with others: like all God's gifts it can never be kept selfishly to ourselves.

That is the essence of the obedience which the risen Christ demands of each generation.

The early Christians' desire to obey led them to re-examine their first call and commissioning to proclaim the gospel of the Kingdom by preaching and healing. The overcoming of the sharpness of death by Jesus had now opened the Kingdom of heaven to all believers. The apostles therefore realized that they had been given this gift of new power to proclaim the risen Jesus and evoke faith in him. His mighty work had inaugurated the Kingdom. They must now proclaim that mighty work, using the same methods he had used and taught them, preaching and healing, word and deed always going together. In the mission and message of Jesus his healing work was no secondary consequence; it was the very means of the proclamation of the new age, of God's rule. The healing charisms given by the risen Christ to his Church would therefore be used to proclaim that the new age and God's rule had now begun. It was not long after the outpouring of the power that the disciples were given an opportunity to use it for the purpose for which it was given. Let us trace the history of their obedience.

The healing of the lame man at the temple gate called Beautiful together with Peter's word of explanation (Acts 3) and especially with his and John's defence before the rulers, and their sufferings at their hands the next day (Acts 4), form the perfect example of the early Church ready and obedient to proclaim the dawn of God's rule in deed and word by healing and preaching. The lame man asked for a small offering from the apostles and received riches beyond his comprehension: 'Look at us,' said Peter, 'I have no silver and gold, but I give you what I have; in the name of Jesus Christ of Nazareth, walk.' Peter then took him by the right hand and raised him up (*egeiren*, the same word used of the raising of Jesus in Peter's subsequent sermon and in his defence). For a Jew to walk is to live. The word is followed by the sacramental act, the taking by the hand and raising up. Peter both heals his lameness in the name of Jesus and enables his whole life to be lived in the power of Jesus Christ. As the crowd come running, there follows the other part of the proclamation, the preaching of the word. The whole incident, the healing and the preaching, is an opportunity (*kairos*) for God to be glorified.

Here at the very beginning of the Church's history, the Apostles obey the command of Jesus to heal the sick and preach the word, thereby proclaiming God's rule. Two whole chapters are devoted to this episode. The repetition and expanding of material, as we find later on with Saul's conversion or the Cornelius episode, is a sign from the author of Acts that he is recording a matter of supreme importance. The healing affords a literally heaven-sent opportunity for proclaiming the good news of Jesus Christ: 'By the name of Jesus Christ of Nazareth, whom you crucified, whom God raised (*egeiren*) from the dead, by him this man is standing before you well' (Acts 4.10). And again 'There is no other name under heaven given among men by which we must be saved'[2] (4.12). We note from this first episode in the life of the Church that there is already a shift of emphasis in the proclamation. The cross/resurrection has now opened the Kingdom, and Jesus and his works rather than his words become the keystone of the apostolic proclamation. He is now the 'good news'. Salvation lies in his name alone. But the point at issue here is that from the very first the members of the early Church were obedient to Christ in that they followed his method of proclaiming the good news in which healing and preaching were inseparable; while, because the good news was Jesus himself, the power of his Name ensured that their obedience was effective in furthering the Kingdom.

The juxtaposition of healing and preaching continues in Acts as the author proceeds to recount the history of the early Church. Among those cases specifically mentioned, after the lame man, comes *the healing of Saul's blindness* after his conversion (Acts 9. 17–19). The ministrant is an extremely unwilling and therefore exceptionally obedient Ananias. The incident demonstrates how his obedience embraced all the dominical commands:

Heal the sick	:	Laying his hands on him, he said,
Love one another	:	Brother Saul . . . .
Baptize all nations	:	He rose and was baptized.
Do this in remembrance of me	:	He took food and was strengthened.[3]

After this he was with the disciples for several days in Damascus. We can well imagine that some solid teaching followed the healing. How frequently God has to heal his greatest servants and bring them to an utterly new wholeness before he glorifies himself in them.

A Petrine episode follows the conversion of Saul at the end of chapter nine. At Lydda Peter finds a *paralysed Aeneas* (Acts 9. 32–5) bedridden for eight years and heals him in the name of Jesus with the direct statement, 'Aeneas, Jesus Christ heals (or has healed) you; rise and make your bed; (verse 34). The healing itself was the effective 'word' in this case for we read: 'And all the residents of Lydda and Sharon saw him, and they turned to the Lord' (verse 35). Meanwhile at nearby Joppa, *Tabitha had died* (Acts 9. 36–43). She had been a pillar of the Church. Her death prompted the disciples to send for Peter who was brought by them to the 'upper room' filled with mourners, admiring the relics of Tabitha's (or Dorcas')[4] skill as a needlewoman. 'Peter put them all outside' as his Master had once done, 'and knelt down and prayed.' Silent prayer is necessary in order to hear the Lord's word and be a means of communication between him and the sick person. Then Peter turned to the body and 'said "Tabitha, rise". . . . And he gave her his hand and lifted her up. Then calling the saints and widows he presented her alive. And it became known throughout all Joppa, and many believed in the Lord' (verses 40–2). Once again the sign itself became the proclamation. The work of healing evoked faith in Jesus' mighty work of death/resurrection and so led to belief in him as Saviour and Lord.

Two healings took place at Lystra during the first missionary tour, the first as a result of Paul's ministry to *a lame man who had never walked* (Acts 14. 8–10). Luke probably intended the similarities between this and Peter's healing of the lame man in chapter three, but there are differences, notably the fact that the preaching of the word came first, for the man 'was listening to Paul speaking'. As so often happens to a preacher, one person can stand out in a congregation as listening with exceptional intensity and expectancy expressive of a deep need. In this case Paul was moved to respond to his gaze. This in itself is an act of obedience to the promptings of the Holy Spirit, an opportunity (*kairos*) that we too often miss. Paul discerned that he had faith to be healed, and discernment is also a charism of the Spirit, preferable to our human judgements and used too little. Paul 'proclaimed' this healing for all to hear: 'Stand upright on your feet.' The healing was instantaneous, as a result of which they had a hard task in restraining the crowd from offering sacrifice to them. The situation became far more difficult with the arrival of the opposition party from Antioch and Iconium, who influenced the crowd to such an extent that *'they stoned Paul* and dragged him out of the city, supposing that he was dead' (14.19). Healing and suffering in the Church frequently go hand in hand. The Apostle is punished just as Peter and John were after the healing of the other lame man. As then, the Church gathered round, presumably for prayer. The effect of his colleagues' ministry was that 'he rose up and entered the city' (verse 20). Again Luke used a word, this time *anastas* from *anistemi*, which he had used of the resurrection in his Gospel. The healings in his name, the 'greater works' which Jesus foretold would be effected by the disciples, all bear a relationship to *the* mighty work of his death/resurrection and give glory to the God who accomplished it.

The next healing occurred in Philippi, the first Church in Europe (Acts 16.16ff). Luke was in Paul's party here with Silas, and it happened (once again) on the way 'to the place of prayer'. The person concerned was a slave girl possessed by *'a spirit of divination'* who made her owners a considerable profit by telling fortunes. Much to Paul's annoyance she followed his party, yelling, 'These men are servants of the Most High God, who proclaim to you the way of salvation.' Perfectly true but somewhat embarrassing from the lips of someone being used by 'the opposition' and it annoyed Paul. Finally he faced her and charged the spirit 'in the name of Jesus Christ to come out of her'. Suffering again followed for the Church: when the girl's masters saw she was healed, they took Paul and Silas to court. They were sentenced to be flogged and jailed. But out of this healing and the Apostles' suffering came the glorious opportunity to proclaim the victory of Jesus Christ, first to the prisoners 'who were listening to them' (verse 25) praying and singing hymns at midnight, and then to the jailer and his household when he brought them out of prison into his home after the earthquake. He washed their wounds and then he and his family were themselves washed in the cleansing waters of baptism. A meal of joyful thanksgiving followed. It was a spectacular beginning to the Church of God in Europe! The healing of the slave girl set the course of events, and the healing was perhaps not so sudden as the narrative suggests, but probably came out of the seed-bed of prayer. They were staying in the house of Lydia, the first convert there whom they had met and subsequently baptized at the place of prayer. As an eye-witness Luke is at pains to record this event prior to the healing. The Church's prayer is a necessary preliminary to any of its works in Christ's name.

On the following occasion, Luke was also with Paul and was therefore an eye-witness, this time to *a raising from the dead* (Acts 20. 7–12). The combination of a long address by Paul—our congregations would not thank us today if we preached until midnight!—and the hypnotic effect of the lamps which Luke specifically mentions proved to be too soporific for *Eutychus* and in his slumbers he fell out of the window on to the courtyard three stories below 'and was taken up dead'. Luke says this and means it, for he himself may well have verified it. The parallelism of the next verse to the raisings by Elijah and Elisha seems to show that Luke did have an actual raising in mind though my old teacher W. K. Lowther Clarke used to say that the only conclusion he could draw was that Luke wrote those chapters in a strongly Septuagintal style. Whichever may be the case, Paul fell upon him, embraced him and declared 'His life is in him.' 'And they took the lad away alive and were not a little comforted' (vv. 10 and 12). After the raising Paul again preached the word 'until daybreak'. The healing would have been another God-given opportunity to proclaim the risen Christ, the word following the deed.

The last *two healings, on the island of Malta,* both happened during the voyage to Rome (Acts 28. 1–10). The first was on Paul himself when a viper came out of the fire he was stoking 'and fastened on his hand', which means it bit him. The natives expected him to die, and watched him for some time, but he shook the viper into the fire and came to no harm. Once again this occurs during the course of a 'we'-section: Luke, the author and Paul's physician, was an eye-witness. Together they stayed with Publius, the chief man of the island, whose father had dysentery. Was this the notorious Maltese fever? Paul went in to him and prayed, laid his hands on him, and healed him. Other healings followed. The three days in Malta laid a foundation there for the Church in subsequent centuries. Only healings are recorded there, but there must have been an occasion for a goodly word. This was how Paul brought the good news of Jesus Christ to the island, having landed in the bay that now bears his name.

We have found in Acts ten specific healings: there are also ten other occasions in the book where we read of hundreds being healed, described in summary verses like those in the Gospels. The names of the ministrants below are in italics:

1 'Fear came upon every soul; and many wonders and signs were done through the *apostles*' (2.43). This follows the amazing number of conversions on the feast of Pentecost and the recording of the obedience of the early Christians who willingly accepted (the Greek word infers that nothing would make them budge from it) the fourfold rule of sharing the apostles' teaching and fellowship, the breaking of bread and the prayers (v.42).

2 'Many signs and wonders were done among the people by the hands of the *apostles*' (5.12). Again the fear (awe) of the people is mentioned (it followed the incident of Ananias and Sapphira) and that 'more than ever believers were added to the Lord'. The result was that:

3 'They even carried out the sick into the streets, and laid them on beds and pallets, that as *Peter* came by at least his shadow might fall on some of them. The people also gathered from the towns around Jerusalem, bringing the sick and those afflicted with unclean spirits, and they were all healed' (5.15f). There are similarities here with Jesus' own ministry (cf. Mark 6.56) and Paul's (19.12, *vide infra*). It is of interest that the verb for overshadow (*episkiazo*) occurs in four other places in the New Testament, always denoting the divine presence and power.

4 'And *Stephen*, full of grace and power, did great wonders and signs among the people' (6.8). The first three occasions have concerned the Apostles; this and the next two concern the deacons. Even if you lay on hands as a commissioning for serving at tables the Lord may well have greater ideas. The 'grace and power' that filled Stephen eventually led to the healing of Saul of Tarsus, truly a 'great wonder'.

5 'The multitudes with one accord gave heed to what was said by *Philip*, when they heard him and saw the signs which he did. For unclean spirits came out of many who were possessed, crying with a loud voice; and many who were paralysed or lame were healed. So there was much joy in that city' (8.6-8). The cure of paralysed and lame folk implies that the conditions of the Kingdom are beginning to prevail: the messianic age moves on from its dawn (Isa. 35. 3, 6). Such healings are notably frequent in Acts and it is the healings on this occasion that lead the crowd to listen to Philip's preaching of the word. The result was joy in that city.

6 'Simon himself believed, and after being baptized he continued with *Philip*. And seeing signs and great miracles performed, he was amazed' (8.13). Again the healing is inseparable from the preaching, the conversions and the baptisms. Yet, are not all these together the signs, the 'greater works' that Jesus foretold his followers would accomplish? Philip, we read, had been preaching 'good news about the Kingdom of God and the name of Jesus Christ'. Here is the place where the subject of the word is specifically noted to be both the Kingdom and Jesus. More often they are merged into one and the works of Jesus are the subject of the proclamation with the inference that they have inaugurated the Kingdom.[5] After the proclamation of the kerygma those who had divided the word would frequently appeal for their hearers to repent and be baptized. This happened here and signs did follow those who believed.

7 *Paul and Barnabas* 'remained (in Iconium) for a long time, speaking boldly for the Lord, who bore witness to the word of his grace, granting signs and wonders to be done by their hands' (14.3). The Iconium visit is filled out in the apocryphal *Acts of Paul and Thecla*; of the few factual pieces of writing this work contains, the description of Paul is the most interesting: 'A man of small stature, with his eyebrows meeting and a rather large nose, somewhat bald-headed, bandy-legged, strongly built, of gracious presence; for sometimes he looked like a man, and sometimes he had the face of an angel.' Such an outward appearance needed the grace and beauty of a healed personality, filled with the Spirit. Here again 'the signs' had followed the preaching and the resulting conversions. From Iconium they went on to Lystra and the pattern was repeated.

8 'All the assembly kept silence, and they listened to *Barnabas and Paul* as they related what signs and wonders God had done through them among the Gentiles' (15.12). Two points stand out: the first is that the reason why they rehearsed the signs and wonders before the Council of Jerusalem was to show that God's Kingdom was breaking in even in the Gentile world. The conversion of the Gentiles and how much of the Jewish law they should keep when they became Christians, was the main item on the agenda of the First Council. The second point is that they rehearsed the signs and wonders before the whole Church, that is, they gave their

testimony. Very rarely does this happen today, which may mean we have no testimony to give or that we are too timid to stand up and talk about the signs and wonders. The latter is more reprehensible than the former. To have been instruments of God's healing blessings to his people and then to keep silence would have been as unthinkable to a first-century Christian as missing the breaking of bread on the first day of the week or the prayer fellowship and instruction on a Thursday evening. It is still unthinkable in the African Church, where testimony plays a major part in Christian witness. Praise God for the incipient recovery of these signs of obedience in the Western Church today.

9 'And God did extraordinary miracles by the hands of *Paul*, so that handkerchiefs or aprons were carried away from his body to the sick, and diseases left them and the evil spirits came out of them' (19.11f). Like 5.15 (no.3), this seems to be a case of psychological suggestion or even mere superstition, but as Leslie Weatherhead remarked, it is more: it is 'an energy of love and power belonging to a higher spiritual order'. We may compare the customs of pilgrims to the catacombs during the first seven centuries who touched the saints' relics with their handkerchiefs and used them to bring healing to the sick; or in India, for instance, where the shadow of Gandhi was believed to have healing power. In this case the healing agents are Paul's handkerchiefs (the Greek word in this case is derived from the Latin *sudarium* = sweat rag) and aprons (again derived from the Latin *semicinctium* = the apron, used by Paul when exercising his trade as a tent-maker). On the sacramental principle, one possession could imply the presence of the total personality. Again, the preaching of the word accompanied the healings, for these occurred during Paul's two years in Ephesus where he hired Tyrannus' hall for his daily seminars.

10 'When this (the healing of Publius) had taken place, the rest of the people on the island who had diseases also came (to *Paul*) and were cured' (28.9); *iaomai* is used of Publius' healing; *therapeuo* of 'the rest'. There is no justification for translating the latter 'treated' as some have suggested. Had Paul treated the people without healing them not only would they have not been as generous when they set sail (v.10) but it would not have been a convincing word for the Lord Jesus. The Christian way is that

perseverance 'unto the end until it be thoroughly finished which yields the true glory'.

3 *Characteristics of the healing community*

There are many points that call for comment even after so brief a survey of the material in Acts. The most obvious is the invariable obedience of the first Christians to Jesus' commission to proclaim the good news by preaching *and healing*. They did not make a fuss about it; they merely got on with it. Confrontation with illness was not for them an occasion for depression or indecision; they did not consider it a stumbling block to the new life in Christ which they were proclaiming. Rather they accepted it as *ho kairos*, the opportunity given by God to proclaim his wonderful works and give him the glory. It was a confirmation of the word they were entrusted to preach. They knew they would be given the power and grace to heal if they responded with obedience to what their Master had taught them. They were therefore gladly obedient.

Obedience led to expectancy. It is obvious from the record of Acts that the early Christians invariably expected that the power to heal would be present. They knew that if they obeyed Jesus' commission he would be true to his promise to be with them and would 'confirm the word with signs following'. We shall find this same 'expectant trust', as Dr Leslie Weatherhead called it, in the letters of Paul and James. Until recent times, insufficient attention has been paid to this theme of obedience-leading-to-expectancy which was a hall-mark of life in the early Church. The Christian fellowship of those days became an embodiment of Christ's promise to be in the midst where two or three were gathered together.

The power of Christ was always experienced when they were together. This gave them a deep commitment to each other, in Pauline language to fellow members of the body, as well as to its Head. They soon realized that it was a corporate rather than an individual commitment they were making. Individuals functioned only as members of this 'fellowship of the Holy Spirit'. They were Christ's gifts to his body—'his gifts were that some should be apostles, some prophets . . .' etc—given for the purpose of building it up 'until we *all* attain . . . to the measure of the stature of the fullness of Christ' (Eph. 4.11ff). To put it at its most basic, no one is going to slope into heaven on 'their wild lone' like the cat in the *Just So Stories*. The power to heal and all the other gifts were given, as far as they were concerned, to build up the body, to help *all* towards that maturity in Christ so that *all* were being prepared for the life of the Kingdom of which Jesus had told them so much. They were all in it together. This was no strange thing to a Jew, as we have seen.

The commitment they felt to each other gave them a real joy in being together. Their realization of *being* the fellowship of the Holy Spirit and the experience of his gifts and power enabled them to radiate to others the strong sense of being loved by God ('In this is love, not that we loved God but that he loved us. . . .' 1 John 4.10). The knowledge and experience of this love led to this consummate joy. The joy led to a deep, inner peace, a new and healthy security of a healed personality (Gal. 5.22f). The result was that there was an attractiveness about the early Christian fellowship as there had been about Jesus.[6] The very act of being in the company was therapeutic, as it had been in Jesus' company. Just as the work of the Holy Spirit is to make Christ our contemporary, so the function of the fellowship of the Holy Spirit is to incarnate Christ and allow others as well as ourselves to experience him when we are 'together in one place'. The experience most needed in the Church today is of this kind of healing fellowship, which is no holy huddle but an outward-looking expression of corporateness with Christ in the midst. We have much to learn from the Jewish experience of the nation being married to Jahweh in order to be a light for the nations. The gifts and healing charisms of the risen Christ to his Body are for the healing of society and the world.

It was natural therefore that the healing work of the early Christian community should take place in an evangelistic context.[7] Just as Jesus had shown his love for others in ministering to people and healing their sicknesses, so the Apostles and their helpers had an intense desire to continue their Lord's healing ministry. We find it hard to realize that this desire to help others was a new phenomenon in those days. It would have made people stop in their tracks or at least turn their heads in an attitude of surprise. They would want to know more. What motivated these people's care and love for others? Men and women are again in our time wondering at the deep caring of devoted doctors and nurses, or groups of Christians, who incarnate this selfless caring today.

People are beginning to realize that it is a super-human phenomenon. It has a spiritual base: it is *inspired*, breathed into man by him who is the author and giver of life. This is what the Apostles' contemporaries also noticed. Their encounter with the healing ministry of the early Church was for them a disclosure moment, a confrontation with the good news of the risen Jesus. The healing work of the early Church was an instrument of evangelism which enriched the proclamation, creating new opportunities for the faith and mission of the Church. As we have often seen, and as the following passage from the *Apostolic Constitutions* serves to underline, deed and word go together:

> These gifts were first bestowed upon us, the apostles, when we were about to preach the gospel to every creature, and afterwards were necessarily provided to those who had come to faith through our agency, not for the advantage of those who perform them, but for the conviction of the unbelievers, that those whom the word did not persuade the power of signs might put to shame.

The healing ministry of the early Christians greatly influenced the spread of the gospel and occurred at certain key points in the mission; e.g. the healing of the lame man (Acts 3) gave emphasis to the events of Pentecost (Acts 2); Stephen's signs and wonders, together with his remarkable proclamation of Jesus as Messiah and his subsequent martyrdom, led to the great dispersion of the early Church beyond Jerusalem and into Gentile territory; the healing of Saul's sight led to the greatest missionary career in the Church's history; the exorcism of the Philippian slave girl led to urgent opportunities for evangelism in what became the first Christian Church in Europe. It is noticeable in Acts that every time there is a pushing out of the boundaries into wider spheres of missionary work, a healing heralds the event or subsequently gives it emphasis.

All these characteristics of the early Christian community—the obedience, the expectancy, the corporate experience, the attractive joy, and positive zeal—were used by Christ as effective instruments in his mission to the world. They were in fact proof positive of his power and presence among his early followers. The lesson which the Book of Acts has to teach the Church today is that when the power of the risen Christ is not only believed in but also allied to the preaching of the gospel, both Church and world will be renewed. For as Michael Green cogently says,

> There can be no doubt that in the early days of the Church the power of Christian evangelists was a factor to reckon with in addition to their love, the quality of their fellowship, the character of their lives, the courage of their deaths, and the joy and enthusiasm with which they bore testimony to their Lord.[8]

4 *Other New Testament passages*

The classic New Testament statement which has become the 'proper' for the healing sacrament in the Church's liturgy is to be found in James 5. 14–16:

> Is any among you sick? Let him call for the elders of the church, and let them pray over him, anointing him with oil in the name of the Lord; and the prayer of faith will save the sick man, and the Lord will raise him up; and if he has committed sins, he will be forgiven. Therefore confess your sins to one another, and pray for one another, that you may be healed. The prayer of a righteous man has great power in its effects.

By any reckoning this is a supremely important piece of didactic writing by James, originally to Jewish Christians the (then) world over, which has since the time of writing suffered from neglect and mistranslation. The word used for save here is *sozo*, which as we saw earlier carried the original meaning of saving a person from illness and death. In the Vulgate the Latin *salvo* was used. *Curo* or *sano* might have come nearer to the meaning of the Greek. As a result it was quite easy to permit this text to apply only to extreme unction, once the healing content of the passage was diminished. The Roman Catholic Church has now thankfully remedied this by specifically stating that Unction is a sacrament of healing. The full meaning of the Greek *sozo* has now been recognized. Also, we find again that *egeiro* is used for 'raise (him) up'; the power of the risen Lord is not far from the mind of the writer.

The sick person (or presumably his family if he is too unwell) is charged to call for the elders of the Church. How wonderful if this injunction was always carried out by members of our churches; what blessings would have accrued to such acts of obedience. The very act of calling the elders is significant for the sick person and brings an element of healing into the situation, for it is indicative of faith and is a positive response to what God is able to do. The elders are instructed to 'pray *over* him'. I remember the response of one patient and her beaming smile of gratitude and expectancy as she commented: 'Many have offered to pray with me or for me but not until now has anyone offered to pray *over* me.' There is a difference and James was obviously choosing his words well.

This is followed by the anointing with oil in the name of the Lord, who is Christ, the anointed of God. The writer then declares that the 'prayer of faith will save the sick man and the Lord will raise him up'. Both statements should be taken together for it is the Lord who heals, not our prayer; our prayer opens up the situation for the Lord to do his work. The prayer must be 'of faith', that is, expectant and trusting. It is able to have such a quality because of our knowledge of him to whom we pray. The God who raised Jesus is more than able to heal our infirmities.

The forgiveness of sins is also part of the ministry; it is in fact a 'bonus': 'if he has committed sins, he will be forgiven.' Sin may not have caused the sickness, but it is an obstacle to the full healing. And so the 'blood of Jesus cleanses us from all sin.' I shall be saying more about this passage below when we come to the actual ministry. In the meantime we can notice how James in verse 16 ends with a recipe for health. The early Church had made remarkable progress in the spiritual life for James to have written this in the first century. The New English Bible gives his epistle the title of 'Practical Religion', perhaps an encouragement to contemporary English-speaking Christians to put his teaching into practice.

This passage has given firm scriptural authority to the ministry of healing throughout the Church's existence. In the East, it has always been part of the Orthodox life and practice. In the West it has fallen into disuse for many centuries, but this century has witnessed a return by the mainstream Churches to this practice as we shall see shortly. James wrote his letter for the whole Church and it probably reflected the practice of the whole Church. It is exciting to live at a time when there is a universal return to the practice of the early Church in this regard.

If we turn to the rest of the New Testament we find that this ministry had not always been the normal practice for any accredited elder of the Church. St Paul lists 'healing' as one of the gifts of the Spirit in 1 Corinthians 12.9, while later on in the same chapter (v.28) he lists a number of functions which 'God has appointed in the church' including workers of miracles and healers. There seems to have been a process of consolidation and tidiness of administrative order at work in the early years of the Christian Church. In the first two decades the Spirit did indeed apportion 'to each one individually as he wills'. Paul's twelfth chapter of what is now our 1 Corinthians is an attempt to analyse and make some kind of order out of these spiritual gifts. He rightly saw that the Holy Spirit was a Spirit of order rather than disorder, as perhaps the Corinthians thought, but he also saw that these gifts were beyond human control in that they were direct infusions of grace for a particular purpose to further God's reign (= 'for the common good', v.7), whether it be wisdom and knowledge for the Apostles or administrators to rule the Church, or utterance of knowledge in the exercise of prophecy, or gifts of healing and working of miracles to be used by healers and helpers, or gifts of tongues and ability to interpret to deepen the awareness of the numinous in the worship. The order lay in their single purpose of furthering the Kingdom and in the fact that all were gifts of the *one* Spirit. By the time James wrote, although he realized that 'every perfect gift is from above, coming down from the Father of lights with whom there is no variation or shadow due to change' (James 1.17), there seems to have been a development in the administration by which the 'gifts of healing' are vested in the eldership of the Church. In other words, the gifts are still given as always to the Body and for the use of the Body, but for the sake of order are administered by its leadership. This would seem to be a natural development, but owing to the abdication of such leadership in many periods of the Church's history, the tendency has been for other members to exercise such a ministry, not always with edifying results. This has frequently brought the ministry of healing into disrepute, but the blame for this must be shouldered by 'the elders' for failing to exercise their leadership in this regard.

Apart from these two 'classical' texts concerning the healing ministry outside the Gospels and Acts, there are others:

1 'The signs of a true apostle were performed among you in all patience, with signs and wonders and mighty works' (2 Cor. 12.12). Here Paul is defending his apostleship and obviously views

the healing ministry as a sign of a true apostle. It is also good evidence that healing played a major part in Paul's proclamation of the gospel.

2 'Did you experience so many things in vain?—if it really is in vain. Does he who supplies the Spirit to you and works miracles among you do so by works of the law, or by hearing with faith?' (Gal. 3.4f). Here Paul appeals directly to the experience of the Galatians. The working of miracles is not under contention; only the way in which they are effected.

3 'In Christ Jesus, then, I have reason to be proud of my work for God. For I will not venture to speak of anything except what Christ has wrought through me to win obedience from the Gentiles, by word and deed, by the power of signs and wonders, by the power of the Holy Spirit, so that from Jerusalem and as far round as Illyricum I have fully preached the gospel of Christ' (Rom. 15.17–19). The good news of God's rule begun in Christ is proclaimed when signs and wonders accompany the preaching of the word. Here Paul tells how Christ has worked through him 'by word and deed, by the power of signs and wonders, by the power of the Holy Spirit', and therefore can justly claim, 'I have fully preached the gospel of Christ.' Our contemporary hunger for a religion of experience must soon teach us that both the word and deed—the signs that accompany the preaching of the word—are necessary if Christ is fully to be proclaimed.

There are also passages which refer to sickness, the most famous of which is that concerning Paul's thorn in the flesh: 'To keep me from being too elated by the abundance of revelations, a thorn was given me in the flesh, a messenger of Satan, to harass me, to keep me from being too elated. Three times I besought the Lord about this, that it should leave me; but he said to me, "My grace is sufficient for you, for my power is made perfect in weakness." I will all the more gladly boast of my weaknesses, that the power of Christ may rest upon me' (2 Cor. 12. 7–9).

This is an important piece of autobiography, as most probably is the passage concerning the 'out of the body' experience which immediately precedes it. The thorn in the flesh was not welcomed by Paul: it was to him 'a messenger of Satan'. He knew all disease was contrary to the divine will. But he saw its purpose—'to keep me from being too elated'. The experience rings true for many a Christian, especially for those in positions of leadership. As to the nature of the thorn, innumerable suggestions have been made. Most commentators have taken it to be some physical ailment, but it might well have been spiritual, some particular temptation, possibly sexual, as St Francis and many of the saints were to experience. 'My son, if you come forward to serve the Lord, prepare yourself for temptation' (Ecclus. 2.1). Whatever it may have been, Christians in every generation have been profoundly grateful for Paul's 'passion' because of the word given him by the Lord: 'My grace is sufficient for you, for my power is made perfect in weakness' (2 Cor. 12.9). I can testify that this word has been of inestimable help in my own ministry, both before preaching as well as before ministering Christ's healing. The emptying of self is an essential prelude to the receiving of that grace; perhaps we should therefore welcome such a thing as a thorn in the flesh to deflate us. For as Paul said, when we are weak, then are we strong with the strength of the risen Christ who can use that very weakness as an instrument of his glory and power.

Other passages in this category are:

1   1 Cor. 11.27ff, where Paul in giving guidelines for the celebration of the Eucharist, asserts that an unworthy or undiscerning reception of the sacrament can be the cause of weakness, illness, or even death.

2   Phil. 2.25ff, concerning Epaphroditus who 'was ill, near to death. But God had mercy on him.' Was it Paul's prayer over him with laying on of hands? We don't know. But Paul asks his readers to 'receive him in the Lord with all joy'. We are beginning to say our thanksgivings for healings in the Church today: for the greater glory of God those who recover should be received by the Body of Christ with all joy in the Lord.

3   2 Tim. 4.20, which refers to Trophimus being left behind ill at Miletus, though presumably he soon recovered.

4   1 Tim. 5.23, the thoroughly sane advice to Timothy, especially if he was doing some travelling, to 'no longer drink only water, but use a little wine for the sake of your stomach and your frequent ailments'. The fruits of God's creation are all his gifts for our health and healing to be taken with moderation—and thanksgiving.

George Bennett always used to say a 'grace' over medication before he took it, a good habit for all Christians to cultivate.

The New Testament also affirms there is a dimension to sickness other than the physical. References to 'weak and beggarly elemental spirits' (Gal. 4.9—where the word for weak is used elsewhere to describe cases of sickness, cf. Col.2.8) suggest that an inimical spiritual element may affect human beings. But the victory over such forces has been won on the cross where God 'disarmed the principalities and powers and made a public example of them, triumphing over them in (Christ)' (Col. 2.15, cf. Heb. 2.14f). The Christian must therefore expect to 'contend against . . . principalities . . . powers . . . the spiritual hosts of wickedness in the heavenly places' for which he will need 'the whole armour of God' and must 'pray at all times in the Spirit, with all prayer and supplication,' keeping 'alert with all perseverance, making supplication for all the saints' (Eph. 6. 12, 13, 18).

The Bible has many a recipe for our health. More importantly it tells us of the source of that power needed for our healing. Had we read it more diligently and taken it to heart as Dr McMillen has ably shown in his fascinating book, we should have had 'None of these diseases'.[9]

PART TWO

Healing in the Church

6

The Church moves onward

As we journey on from the Church of the New Testament we are left with a feeling of vitality and movement. The age of persecution has begun, but those who are facing the fiery trial radiate something of the charism of the risen Lord of the Church. There is still that explosive power within the community, the motive force of that 'service of reconciliation' which is seen in evangelization, now in preaching, now in healing, and always in the spirit of sacrifice and joy, pointing to him who is its source. Community centred and world orientated, it was a force to be reckoned with, for in the end it did turn the world upside down; it overtook the imperial power of Rome, the absolute power in the world at the time of Christ's birth, the power that sought to extinguish the Christian light in the first three centuries. Its victory however suffered the same disadvantage as that of Pyrrhus, King of Epirus, over the Romans at Asculum: it was gained at too great a cost.

During the first three hundred years of its history, the Church continued its proclamation of the risen Lord through its preaching and healing. The healing of physical illness, at any rate in the early period, was seen as evidence of the Spirit's work and presence among Christians and was a constant ingredient of the Christian life. Justin Martyr tells of Christian healings in the name of Jesus, while Tertullian identified people who had been healed. Irenaeus, writing more freely than others because Lyons was more distant from the centres of persecution, scored a point *adversus omnes haereses* by declaring that heretics did not have access to the power of God and so were unable to heal.

More importantly, he attested to a like range of healings as we found in the New Testament. He took the positive view that it is a natural activity of Christians to express the creative power of God through healing. Origen, writing fifty years later, witnessed to the power of Jesus still present to heal, but Cyprian, bishop of Carthage in North Africa and his contemporary, sounded the first note of alarm. Although he declared that healing still took place in the

Church he complained that it lacked strength in prayer, because the Church was growing more worldly and so giving power to the enemy.[1]

The Edict of Milan in 313 proved to be something of a watershed in the history of the healing Church. The threat of persecution over, and with Christianity now a *religio licita* and no longer proscribed, membership was more attractive and readily available so that the worldliness that Cyprian had discerned as incipient now flooded the Church. The result was a drop in the spiritual temperature, which led to a lack of awareness of Christ's healing power and a preoccupation with the great need to organize the Church, codify its law and systematize its theology. God raised up some of the greatest minds in history to serve him in this period, including Ambrose, Augustine, Jerome, and Gregory, known as the four Latin Doctors of the Church. The Eastern Church also had its intellects, Basil, Gregory of Nazianzus, Gregory of Nyssa (younger brother of Basil), John Chrysostom, all of whom accepted the Church's commission to heal, the first two having a good knowledge of medicine for their time. But after this golden age it was only individuals, men and women of the Spirit, who kept the flickering flame of the Church's commission and power to heal alight. Such were the desert Fathers, Martin of Tours, some of our own apostles of the north of England and Francis of Assisi. But a major shift in theological thinking had taken place: the more open and spiritual universe of Platonic thought had been superseded by the closed universe and rationalistic outlook of Aristotle, which had little place for direct contact between God and man or for healing. The belief in the miraculous, without the secure basis of a sound theology, became mixed up with superstition and the fanciful. Sickness and sin became indissolubly connected,[2] despite Jesus' own insistence that this was by no means the only view, and unction became a spiritual remedy[3] and merely part of the viaticum. The important factor was not to ensure healing in this life but a good existence in the next. Unction for healing therefore became unction for dying. It was seen to be substantiated by Jerome's translation of the word 'heal' as 'save'. This process has been reversed in the Latin Church only as recently as 1962 when the anointing with oil was reinstated as a sacrament of healing. In fact it was only in this present century that the Spirit of Movement was permitted to move the Church back to its pristine obedience to its

Lord's command to 'Heal the sick', away from an arid individualism to a new sense of the community and of the corporate implications of healing, and therefore forward in the service of reconciliation, a service it has begun to offer not only to itself (in the ecumenical movement), but to society and nations on a global scale. It is in the last quarter of this twentieth century that we have begun to witness the exploding world of healing.

1 *The renewal of the ministry in this century*

The very first time I heard George Bennett speak, he opened his address with the words: 'Many of us believe that with this century has begun the new age of the Holy Spirit.' It was a particularly striking thing to say in 1968 before the charismatic movement became news, and when the 'theological' message from across the Atlantic was that God was dead. At that time we were manifestly living in the 'Age of Uncertainty'.[4] Certainly this century has been an era of movements. The ecumenical movement is generally dated from the Edinburgh Conference of 1910 when William Temple acted as a steward. It was the National Mission of Repentance and Hope of 1916, which gave birth to the Life and Liberty Movement whose protagonist was the same William Temple with the vigorous Dick Sheppard at his elbow. Its avowed purpose was 'to win for the Church the liberty essential to fulness of life', and its leaders demanded a 'forward move' to this end. The move had begun towards that wholeness and health which William Temple saw as the one essential for the Church if it was to be used in furthering the Kingdom of God. This was accompanied by a desire to bring the Church's liturgy up to date and allow it to express the feelings and hopes of contemporary life. The Liturgical Movement was the outward expression of this aim which affected nearly every Communion and denomination. The Charismatic Movement was to come in 1968 and has probably in terms of the renewal of the Churches had more influence in so short a time than almost any other movement in history.

It was Bishop Stephen Neill who in his Bampton Lectures of 1964 referred to the Holy Spirit as

the principle of movement in the Church, through which it is constantly driven to look outside itself into the world by which it is surrounded, and to move forward into an unknown future, in which perils will have to be encountered, new questions will be asked, and new solutions will have to be found, with something more than mere reliance on the established past. . . . The Spirit is the spirit of adventure; it is through obedience to the movement of the Spirit that the Church makes its way into the perilous future and is able to survive.[5]

Certainly the principle of movement has been present within all the Churches in this century and slow as Christians often are to discern the signs of the times and the direction of this movement, few can doubt that it is of the Spirit. It must be so, for mighty works are frequently effected despite us!

The healing movement was in fact the first on the scene at the very beginning of this century. By its warning tremors and spring breezes it gave the first indications to the Church of the exploding force of the Spirit that would overtake it once again in our time. It was in 1904 that Dr Percy Dearmer, a famous Anglican scholar and liturgist, Conrad Noel, and others of a strong theological background, formed the Guild of Health to encourage co-operation with the medical profession in the practice of healing. The Guild continues to do valuable work, based on its headquarters at Edward Wilson House in London. The Aim of the Guild is 'To help people to experience within the fellowship of God's family the freedom and life promised by Jesus Christ'. Its objects are to implement this aim through prayer, sacrament, and counselling, through healing the polarizations between the caring professions and—something worthy of the Church's attention and of all the medical services—'To enable all members to study the interaction between physical, mental and emotional factors in well-being, and their relationship with the spiritual life in prayer and meditation.' Little wonder it has a very large number of affiliated healing prayer groups. On the 10th October 1905, James Moore Hickson founded 'The Society of Emmanuel' which changed its name to 'The Divine Healing Mission' (D.H.M.) in 1933. Hickson was a sensitive Anglican layman of tireless energy. With his co-founders he felt constrained to proclaim Christ as the Healing Saviour. He called on Archbishop Randall Davidson at Lambeth and told him all that God had laid on his heart for the revival of this ministry. The Archbishop commissioned and blessed him, charging him to go forward 'like the patrol of an army and come back and report'. He then dismissed him with the significant words: 'I will lead the main body forward.' From 1906–17 he held healing services, prayed and talked with groups up and down the country and established the Emmanuel League of Prayer. Always he and his colleagues— Bishop Mylne of Bombay and Prebendary Carlisle, healed of spinal trouble to do his great work of founding the Church Army, were among them—had two convictions laid upon them: the healing ministry was to be part of the preparation for the Lord's Second Coming; and that our Lord desires to use this ministry especially for the healing of his Body, the Church. On a visit to Iona in 1917 for a time of prayer and quiet reflection, Hickson was shown God's plan to take the message of the Healing Saviour to all the world. He began in the U.S.A. and Canada, then India, China, Japan, and the Philippines. He received the commission and blessing of the bishops in each diocese. People filled the cathedrals for the services and the bishops took part. In 1921 he set out again for Egypt, Palestine, Rome, and Paris; then to South Africa, Rhodesia, and on to Australia, Tasmania, and New Zealand. After this visit the Australian bishops wrote a remarkable document, testifying to the results of Hickson's visit which was richly blessed by God. His visit to Ireland in 1930 was still being talked about 47 years later at the healing festival I attended in Dublin in 1977. The work there has been continued and ably led successively by Noel Waring and Stanley Baird. The D.H.M., centred on Crowhurst, continues its witness to Christ the Healer today, for whom Hickson was a true apostle in this century. He as much as anyone has helped forward the revival of this ministry in the Churches.

Meanwhile in 1912 a girl of 23 was miraculously healed from death after five years of invalidism. Dorothy Kerin's health began to deteriorate rapidly after her father's death in 1902. By Christmas 1911 the two doctors attending her diagnosed tubercular peritonitis as her chief ailment. By 17th February 1912 the end was near: she had been deaf and blind for the past fortnight, and for the most part unconscious. The next day was Sunday and in the evening about 9.30 p.m. she seemed to breathe her last. Her breathing ceased and her heart stopped beating for eight minutes. She then seemed to be raised up in bed, sat up and opened her eyes. To her mother's and friends' astonishment she spoke: 'I'm well now; I want my dressing-gown. I want to walk', and repeated the request when the first time it went unheeded. She then got up and walked and asked for supper! Dorothy later revealed that she had seen 'a beautiful Light', out of which an angel of the Lord had called to her: 'Dorothy, your sufferings are over. Get up and walk.' Her healing led to detailed medical examination. She even stayed for six weeks with Dr Ash, a specialist in Portman Square, whose X-ray examination revealed that new lungs had replaced the old ones wasted away with consumption. Many doctors attested the cure. On June 30th the same year she gave a message to the Church and world which was given the whole of the first page in one of our national newspapers. She testified that her healing came from God alone and that she had been entrusted with a message to the whole world, 'a promise of healing to the sick, comfort to the sorrowing and faith to the faithless.'[6] The community and the church of Christ the Healer at Burrswood, near Tunbridge Wells, where the Church and the medical profession work side by side, and where regular services of healing are held, are fitting memorials to a great pioneer of the ministry in this century who lived for a further 51 years in total dedication to that message.

The Guild of St Raphael was founded in 1915 when the Guild of Health became interdenominational and, before the days of the ecumenical movement, some Anglicans were apprehensive about sacramental authority. Bishop Hough, suffragan bishop in the Southwark diocese, and Canon Roseveare, were the co-founders. Later on, its most prominent theologian was Dr T. F. Crafer, chiefly known as the author of *A Priest's Vade Mecum*, and it has had a long line of distinguished wardens including Bishop Edward Wynn, O.G.S., late of Ely. The Guild's quarterly paper was a small leaflet until in 1954 Prebendary Henry Cooper, initially with the help of Paul Shuffrey, editor of the *Church Quarterly Review*, raised its theological standard and at the time of writing is still editor of *Chrism*. He has given a lifetime's work to promoting the ministry of healing in the Church through the Guild and in 1958 played a major part in the Convocation debates on the Report to the Archbishops on the ministry of healing. The Guild's teaching and practice is 'that of the Lord Jesus Christ and His Apostles as revealed in the Gospel and handed down through all ages in Christ's Holy Catholic Church, i.e. by the Ministry of the Word, the Sacraments—especially the Anointing of the Sick—the Laying-on-of-hands, and the faith of the Church as expressed in corporate and personal prayer.' The Guild has always promoted close co-operation with the medical profession.

The Reverend Howard J. Cobb was raised from a bed on which he would have surely died. He was healed from sleepy sickness after receiving the laying on of hands from none other than James Moore Hickson, during which his church was filled with his parishioners in silent prayer. He saw it as a sign that he must give his life to the healing ministry. He became Rector of Crowhurst in East Sussex and in 1928 founded the Crowhurst home of healing now situated in the Old Rectory there.[7] From the first it had its connections with the D.H.M. Among the wardens of Crowhurst (and all have been great men and leaders of the ministry) was George Bennett who died on Ascension Day 1978. Trained as a medical student, the healing gospel of Christ had meant more than anything to George since he became a Christian. His experiences in the Coventry blitz and as a hospital chaplain, and later back at Coventry Cathedral where he began monthly healing services, strengthened his conviction. In 1958 he became chairman of the D.H.M. and Warden of Crowhurst later that year. His remarkable ministry there with his wife Margaret, is written up in the first of his books.[8] After eleven years he felt called to extend his ministry and, as President of the D.H.M. and supported by a Trust, he began conducting healing missions and clergy schools all over Britain, in Europe, and the United States. Many today owe their vision of the Christ who heals to his tireless work. Few can have exercised so great an influence on their fellow clergy and ministers and given such abiding leadership to a movement. Services of praise and thanksgiving for his ministry were held in York Minster and Holy Trinity, Brompton. At the latter he had frequently ministered at the regular services of healing, carrying on Godfrey Mowat's great ministry.

2 Initiatives from the Churches' leadership: the earlier Lambeth Conferences and the evolution of the Churches' Council for Health and Healing (CCHH)

These powerful initiatives given to the healing movement by individual leaders were matched by the leadership of the Churches. The subject of healing was carefully considered by a committee of the 1908 Lambeth Conference and again in 1920 when Resolution 63 requested the appointment of a committee 'to consider and report upon the use with prayer of the laying on of hands, of the Unction of the Sick, and other spiritual means of healing'. The committee's report was published in 1924[9] and included the following statement:

> Within the Church . . . systems of healing based on the redemptive work of our Lord . . . all spring from a belief in the fundamental principle that the power to exercise spiritual healing is taught by Christ to be the natural heritage of Christian people who are living in fellowship with God, and is part of the ministry of Christ through his body the Church.

The bishops assembled in the 1930 Conference commended the whole report. Morton Kelsey commented significantly: 'For the first time that I know of, a modern mainline church acknowledged in an official pronouncement that unction and laying on of hands can have a direct effect on the body.'[10] They also pressed for a growing co-operation between doctors and clergy, for the formation of regular intercessory prayer groups in parishes, but owing to their emphasis on preparation of the individual were 'not prepared to give any encouragement to public Missions of Healing'.[11]

Archbishop William Temple preached the opening sermon to the 1930 Conference on the theme 'God reigns', echoed by one of his successors at both York and Canterbury, Dr Donald Coggan, in his opening address to the 1978 Conference. (Does not the much neglected 'Kingdom' theology lie at the basis of this movement?) It was the initiative of these two Archbishops that led to the founding and re-founding of the Churches' Council for Health and Healing. The first meeting was held at Archbishop Temple's invitation in Lambeth Palace on 21st April 1944 in order to 'clarify the message and to educate Christian people by various means to provide knowledge of spiritual healing and fuller co-operation and understanding between doctors and clergy and all those engaged in health in the full sense'. It was to be one of his last initiatives for the Kingdom on this earth, for he died later that year. A series of such meetings over two years evolved a policy of forming a Council with the following purpose and function:[12]

1   To provide a common basis for the healing movements which stand on Christian foundations.

2   To draw into closer fellowship and co-operation the movements which share this common basis.

3   To co-operate with those guilds and other Christian agencies in the promotion of united prayer and witness appropriate to their common aim and basis.

4   To afford a recognised basis for the co-operation of doctors and clergy in the study and performance of their respective functions in the work of healing, and to promote this co-operation in thought and action throughout the country.

5   To explore the possibilities of establishing common centres of healing under adequate medical and clerical supervision.

6   To act as a centre for co-ordination and distributing experience and research, and to publish the findings of this exchange of thought.

7   To bring the work of healing into closer relation with the regular work of the churches.

Since that time many have worked hard to fulfil the Council's aims. Among them, the Reverend Geoffrey Harding brought a keenness and expertise to the directorship, a post he held for sixteen years. It was owing to his tireless work in visiting every Anglican diocese in England that in many was formed a local fellowship of health and healing. He left the Council in 1975 to create a centre for relaxation in one of London's Guild churches. In that same year Dr Coggan came to Lambeth and appointed Miss Janet Lacey, who had founded Christian Aid, as the new secretary. He also invited the leaders of the Churches to appoint new representatives. The new Council began its work at a time when the healing world was about to explode. Its foundations were laid well by its senior chairman Dr Kenneth Leese, who had been Vice-President of the Methodist Conference, and after two years it was able to appoint a General Secretary (Brian Frost) and a Travelling Secretary (the Reverend Peter Smith). The Council was then better able to devote all its energies to bringing together the many and varied strands of healing work and of health promotion and to form a focus of leadership for this influential movement.

Meanwhile, Dr Michael Ramsey, who assumed the chair of St

Augustine in 1961 as the 100th Archbishop of Canterbury, had also called together a body of priests and doctors to consider the whole field of health and healing. The result was the founding of the Institute of Religion and Medicine, which has its own organization, but works alongside the C.C.H.H. and has an ex officio place on that Council.

3 The 1958 Commission and subsequent Lambeth Conferences

In the decade after the second world war, the Archbishops of Canterbury and York set up a commission on the ministry of healing which reported its findings prior to the 1958 Lambeth Conference. The report is full of excellent material and deserves to be reprinted. The following is one of its 'purple' passages:

> The Church as the Body of Christ and as the community through which the Holy Spirit operates is charged with a Commission to heal the sick. Those who are called to minister to the sick have the duty of setting free all God's resources for health. They must contend with all that interferes with the process of healing. Since certain of these factors, such as anxiety or fear, are on the emotional or spiritual plane, many sick people are in need of an assistance which medical science by itself cannot supply. Many patients need above all else to be assured that in sickness as in health God's action, wholly personal, loving and creative, is working both in their innermost being and through those who are treating them. The pastoral and sacramental ministry of the Church brings this assurance to the patient and so helps to break down barriers deep in the personality which stand in the way of healing. Indeed it does more, by evoking the response of faith it allows the divine grace to act creatively and so determines the issue for health in ways beyond our present scientific methods of measurement.

The 1958 Lambeth Conference, like its predecessors in this century, discussed matters of health and healing, and resolved that every attempt at liturgical revision by any member church should contain a section on ministry to the sick. This should have brought down the curtain on a successful enterprise to gain full recognition for the ministry of healing throughout the Anglican Communion and it was not thought necessary to open the debate again when the Lambeth Fathers met in 1968. But after another decade in 1978 it was felt that some member churches were sitting lightly to the 1958 resolution. Again the subject was not on the agenda, but a private member's motion was put before the final plenary session, was passed, and so became a resolution of the 1978 Conference:

The Church's ministry of healing
The Conference praises God for the renewal of the ministry of healing within the Churches in recent times and reaffirms:
1 that the healing of the sick in his Name is as much part of the proclamation of the Kingdom as the preaching of the good news of Jesus Christ;
2 that to neglect this aspect of ministry is to diminish our part in Christ's total redemptive activity;
3 that the ministry to the sick should be an essential element in any revision of the liturgy (see the report of the Lambeth Conference of 1958, p.2.92).

The resolution certainly brought encouragement to all who had this ministry at heart and who longed for it to be at the centre of the Church's total ministry once again; while if it gained a solid place in the liturgical formularies of each church, this would mean that all future generations of ordinands would more than likely be instructed in this ministry, something which has too frequently been omitted from their training in the past.

4 *Global Initiatives for Healing*

The Anglican Church was of course by no means the only one in the field. Dr Leslie Weatherhead, greatly influenced by his experience as a chaplain in the first world war, in his writings and preaching had given a lead to his own Methodist Church in the field of health. His classic work, *Psychology, Religion and Healing*, most of which will stand the test of time, was published in 1951. It gained immediate influence outside as well as inside the Churches. He ended the book with these prophetic words:

Finally, let us never forget that there is a spiritual power to heal which has not been withheld. It has only been unappropriated. The slow development of our spiritual receptivity and insight hinders the recovery of thousands who could be healed by true spiritual healing. When the Church returns to her early devotion to Christ and creates united fellowships, even faintly like the small body of men who went out in the power of the Risen Christ and His Spirit to turn the world upside down, then a power more potent to heal than any atomic bomb to destroy will once more surge through sick souls and minds and bodies. It will be His own power and recognised as such. If disease is caused by the faulty reactions of a person—as is so often the case—then the supreme healing power will not be this or that treatment, let alone this or that drug, but *a Person healing*. Christians call that Person Christ. When He comes into His own, then the prayer will be answered which He Himself taught men to pray: 'Thy kingdom come; Thy will be done on earth, as it is in heaven.'[13]

Today the Methodist Church has an active Healing and Pastoral Ministry Committee as part of its Division of Social Responsibility, of which the Westminster Pastoral Foundation is a practical outcome.

The United Reformed Church has increasingly since the time of union turned its attention to health and healing concerns and has its own main committee concerned with these matters. This committee has produced an excellent study kit, 'Health and Healing' (1977) which, if amplified with more instruction on the sacramental means of healing, would be a best-seller in all the Churches. The Baptist Union also has its main committee on health and healing, presided over by Dr Stanley Thomas who was a surgeon in India for thirty years before becoming a minister.

Perhaps the most momentous step taken by the leadership of any Church in this particular field of ministry was taken by the Roman Catholic Church in the persons of its Bishops assembled for the Second Vatican Council. They pronounced that the Sacrament of Unction was no longer to be used solely 'in extremis', but as a sacrament of healing. (*Constitutions on the Sacred Liturgy* III 73ff).[14]

If the Anglican Church was not the only Church to experience a renewal of this ministry, neither of course was England the only country. Before the turn of the last century pilgrims were beginning to travel to the shrines of healing in large numbers—to Fatima in Portugal, to St Anne de Beaupré in Canada, and to Lourdes in

France where a medical bureau had been set up in 1882. Over one thousand non-medical cures there have been examined since 1918, fifty four of which had been accepted as miracles by 1957. Germany had witnessed a remarkable healing ministry in a village on the edge of the Black Forest under the Pastorship of Johann Blumhardt, a ministry that was commented on by the theologians, including Karl Barth who showed genuine interest; Bultmann however remained singularly unimpressed. There were also healings in Germany through the ministry of Theresa Neumann, whose spiritual gifts created the climate for healings to occur in her parish.

In America, the famous Baptist minister in Boston, A. J. Gordon, had written a book on the ministry of healing in 1882. He underlined the profound effect Christian healing had on peoples' lives in 'marked consecration' and 'spiritual anointing'. In the same city, Dr Elwood Worcester began in 1905 a ministry at his Emmanuel Church, whose congregation included physicians and psychiatrists, and who actively participated. Dr Loring W. Batten, who was on the staff of General Theological Seminary, as a result of this ministry began to minister himself. Later on Dr John Gayner Banks founded the Order of St Luke which flourishes today and not only in the States. The healing ministry of Agnes Sanford has come to be known through her books and the Schools of Pastoral Care. Other names include Kathryn Kuhlman, Tommy Tyson, and Oral Roberts who have all confronted those inside and outside the Churches with the reality of the healing gifts of Christ. Perhaps we in England are most grateful for a book that crossed the Atlantic in the shape of *Healing and Christianity in Ancient Thought and Modern Times* by Morton T. Kelsey, which will hopefully stand on the shelves of those engaged in this ministry and many others—and be frequently taken down and read—as the classic work on the subject in this century. [15]

Another American whose books have had a wide circulation this side of the Atlantic and whose ministry has been greatly blessed is Francis MacNutt, a Roman Catholic priest. [16] One of the first priests to be involved in Catholic charismatic renewal, he sees the lack of spiritual power in the Church and its ministers as the main blockage to the healing God wills. 'We need his *power* to transform us—we can't just teach and preach and then expect people to be changed.' And again: 'The basic problem is in us—we don't yet

109

have enough *life* and spiritual *power* to perform the healings that God truly wants us to perform . . . . I need to be more in union with Jesus, the source of that power, than I now am.'

In Scotland a Presbyterian minister, Dr J. Cameron Peddie, exercised a formative ministry and his book *The Forgotten Talent*, published by Fontana, is still a best seller. Possibly influenced by him, George Macleod made the healing ministry an integral part of the Iona Community and hundreds of pilgrims attend the regular services of healing on the island of Iona each year. Another famous Scotsman, the world-renowned scholar William Barclay, who had that great gift of communicating a wealth of learning in a simple and readable style, produced a fine book of *Prayers for Help and Healing* (Fontana 1968). His introductory essay on Christianity and Health has a message for all of us who have an interest in this ministry. Today the Reverend and Mrs George Fox and their colleagues in the Divine Healing Fellowship of Scotland continue this ministry, travelling widely from their home in Gargannock, Stirling, as also do Ian Cowie and his colleagues of the Christian Fellowship of Healing (Scotland). Both work closely together and with the C.C.H.H.

The ministry of Stanley Baird, an Anglican priest of the Church of Ireland, has already been mentioned. He was the Warden of the ministry of healing in Ireland responsible to the Anglican Synod. Originally set up in 1932, shortly after James Moore Hickson's visit, the ministry has gained increasing acceptance and a growing number of clergy become involved each year, in that they introduce a healing dimension into all their ministry. The ministry is centred on St Andrew's Church in Dublin. In 1974 a counselling and healing centre was set up with a part-time priest assistant warden in a former rectory in Belfast which has become a place of reconciliation in the city. Weekly services of healing are held in both Dublin (St Andrew's) and Belfast (the Cathedral). In Derry, the Bishop has allocated one of his churches (St Peter's) as a focal point for the ministry of healing and the priest in charge gives two days each week to the work. The whole work is undergirded by the Healing Prayer Union. An annual Festival of Healing is held in Dublin around the time of the Synod while the work of the Warden is extending now into other Churches including the Roman Catholic. In 1978 Stanley Baird preached at the first healing service (as such) to be held in York Minister, though he was quick to point out that we all hoped that every service was a service of healing. The Irish (ecumenical) Council of Healing has its headquarters in Belfast and Andrew McCombe its secretary came over with Stanley Baird to the C.C.H.H. Conference in 1978. The Presbyterian Church in Wales in the person of Dr Evans has promoted the ministry among its members while Norman Autton, for many years the Director of Training of the Hospital Chaplaincies Council at Church House, Westminster, has promoted the ministry within the Church in Wales and both are members of the C.C.H.H. Gradually there is a healthy network of communication being formed between the various bodies concerned with the ministry of healing in the churches of Great Britain and Ireland.

5 *Conclusion*

The healing dimension in the Church's ministry is receiving a renewed emphasis today, the like of which has never before been known in history. Certainly the Spirit has been saying something to the Churches through this century, as the bare statement of facts in this chapter has shown. The point of interest is that this word to the Churches has been heard right across the world, and right across the traditional divides between the Churches. Many will not discern this event of our times because their view of healing is too narrow. I hope however to be able to show in the final part of this book some of the many avenues in which Christ the Healer is at work. For the present, I return to the prophecy of James Moore Hickson.

'By their fruits ye shall know them' is a good yardstick in regard to prophets. I believe we are seeing some of these fruits of his prophecy as this century continues to unfold itself; and the pace is gathering momentum in this last quarter. God is preparing his Church for some great task he has assigned to it; and we must be found watching. There are still too many little things which prevent the watchmen and messengers from accomplishing their proper tasks. There are also larger 'thromboses', especially the lack of unity. How can we speak healthy words when the body itself is diseased? The task of the body is to prepare the way of the Lord himself (Hickson's other prophecy). Our vision is in need of healing for it becomes clouded when its gaze is removed from *him* and we make preparations for people and things other than *him*. The exploding world of healing is from him, a sign of his grace;

alone it will make us ready for him and heal our blindness. 'Lord, that I might receive my sight.' But first our plethora of paper must be recycled back into priedieux; our conferences become the Church at prayer; our endless talk become 'a time to keep silence'; our selfish regard and power-seeking become a new road of humility; our time of wealth become an opportunity for health.

7

The Church's Ministry

1 *The Holy Eucharist*

At the end of a chapter entitled 'The Eucharistic Theology of the New Testament', Alan Richardson declared that 'it is only in the eucharistic worship of the Church that the theology of the New Testament can be truly understood; this understanding arises at the point at which theology and worship meet and are no longer two separate activities, but one action of believing adoration.'[1] In any discussion of the Eucharist it must be borne in mind that participation in the ongoing, vital tradition of the Church's eucharistic worship is better than many words. It is here, in the very centre of the Church's life, that the salvation/healing which Christ came to bring is present in its 'timeless potency'. What are some of the main sign posts that point us to this truth?

First, the Eucharist is *the* healing sacrament for it is a making present of Christ and his grace. As the liturgical action unfolds we are enfolded in the love of Christ, who makes himself known to us in the breaking of bread. The manner of that making known is not that Christ is scattered over innumerable altars the world over and divided up among countless communicants. Rather, as St Paul and St Augustine among others have reminded us, unlike ordinary food received by the eater, the divine food of the Eucharist assimilates the eater to itself: 'The bread which we break, is it not a participation in the body of Christ? Because there is one bread, we who are many are one body, for we all partake of the one bread' (1 Cor. 10.16f). For in the Eucharist the Church is absorbed into the joy and presence of its Lord, or, as Alexander Schmemann puts it, 'the Eucharist is the journey of the Church into the dimension of the Kingdom' and again, 'the Eucharist of Christ and Christ the Eucharist is the "breakthrough" that brings us to the table in the Kingdom.'[2]

Because the Eucharist proclaims Christ as a present reality, who is 'the same yesterday and today and for ever' (Heb. 13.8) so it makes the past and the future a present reality. From the past it recalls into present reality the mighty event of the New Testament, the death/resurrection of Jesus: 'As often as you eat this bread and drink this cup, you proclaim the Lord's death until he comes' (1 Cor. 11.26). It is also the anticipation in this age of the final blessedness of the age to come; it is a foretaste of the Kingdom banquet. However, 'It is not a mere looking forward to something which shall be, any more than it is a mere looking back to events of long ago. It is the holding of past and future in the "now" of faith.'[3] It is the past and the future which contribute so deeply to the healing power of the sacrament in the here and now. The power of the new creation unleashed by the cross/resurrection event is present to a church that obediently recalls that event 'until his coming again'. It is a prophetic action that makes the healing work of Christ a present reality and so becomes an earnest (*arrabon*) of our coming to that perfect wholeness as the new community, which is the establishment of God's reign.

Every Eucharist therefore proclaims the present reality of the beginnings of the Kingdom, the dawn of God's time of salvation. The Church on earth is caught up into the worship of heaven, where the conditions of the Kingdom are already fulfilled. The Eucharist is the *sacrum convivium*, the holy and heavenly banquet, at which all the redeemed through the ages are present in the Head of the feast. St Augustine summarized it well: 'That whole redeemed community which is the congregation and society of the saints, is offered as a universal sacrifice to God by that High Priest who has also offered himself in suffering for us in the form of a servant, that we might be the body of so great a Head.'[4] This truth, so often forgotten, can be the source of great healing. Much of our depression and stress emanate from an unsatisfactory relationship with those gone before us. There is frequently much that is unresolved with our loved ones especially when they die. Why should all reconciliation and healing be left until the after-life? For our health it should be brought out into the openness of Christ and settled now; and the Eucharist is both the time and place for this healing to be received.

Unfortunately there has been much prejudice in many churches against praying for the dead. This prejudice itself needs healing! It has been the cause of much needless suffering and also of erroneous and harmful methods of trying to contact the departed. How can the love we have experienced with our dear ones be suddenly sundered in death? It is perfectly natural that we should

wish to continue to enjoy that love which was God's gift to each
other for all eternity. The healthy way to do this is in the setting of
the Christian Eucharist where 'with angels and archangels and with
all the company of heaven, we laud and magnify' God's holy
name.[5] Here our presence with one another in Christ can be experienced in the timeless present, 'the now of faith'. Here we can
say to Christ those things we would and perhaps should have said
to our dear ones; here we can receive forgiveness for what we did
say and do to our dear ones; here we can receive something of a
deeper *shalom*, an inner healing of the hurts that we received and
gave in the past, leading to a wholeness of personality which God
intends to fulfil in us in his Kingdom. It was a right instinct to
connect the so-called Comfortable Words with the sacrament:
'Come unto me all ye that are heavy laden and I will refresh you.'
The burdens with which we load ourselves by our sins both of
commission and omission are not meant to be carried around as
heavy, harmful, and useless luggage. They are meant to be brought
to the altar rail, which is the foot of the cross recalled vividly into
the timeless present, surrendered there *and left there*. The hurts
they have occasioned can then—and only then—receive the healing
touch of the living Christ. And we can then move forward again
towards that wholeness of being and be made ready to take the
place God has prepared for us in his coming reign.

Bishop Michael Ramsey catches this dimension when he summarizes succinctly something of the limitless and timeless benefits
of this central and vital act of Christian worship, Jesus' own
healing sacrament:

> Nowhere more vividly than in the sacrament of the Eucharist do
> Christians find through Christ an openness to the past and to the
> present, to heaven and to the world. The sacrifice of Christ on
> Calvary is present in the here and now in its timeless potency,
> and the homely bread and wine of a contemporary meal are
> made the effectual signs of Christ's self-giving. The Christian
> community on earth is one with the saints in heaven. Blending
> past and present, earth and heaven, the Eucharist is a prophecy
> and a prayer for our coming to the vision of God and for the
> coming of God's reign in the world.[6]

There are two more significant points about the Eucharist which
are relevant to our purpose. The first is that word and deed come

115

together in the Eucharist as they did in the life of Jesus and the early Church. The ministry of the word is a preparation for the action of the Eucharist—the offering, the breaking, the blessing, and the giving of the elements—and is also part of it. Neither can be separated from the other; nor could they have been in the life of Jesus. The Eucharist is a participation in the words and works of Jesus, until his coming again. It is interesting to note that in the Eastern Orthodox liturgy, no dichotomy is found between word and sacrament. The word is also considered to be a sacrament in that it transforms the person who hears it.

The other point is that the idea of the offering of the fruits of creation was always prominent in the Eucharist. In the ancient Church it was a sacrament of creation as well as redemption, just as every first day of the week was not only the day of resurrection but also the day of rogation and thanksgiving for the harvest. We have lost something of the primitive wholeness of life and worship to our detriment. True health demands that this dimension should be recovered. The sacrament of the Eucharist must again become the anticipatory celebration of a healed creation, a foretaste of the Kingdom of God.

> The eucharist is the sacrament of cosmic remembrance: it is indeed a restoration of love as the very life of the world . . . . Eucharist is the state of perfect man. Eucharist is the life of Paradise. Eucharist is the only full and real response of man to God's creation, redemption and gift of heaven. But this perfect man who stands before God is *Christ* . . . . he alone is the perfect Eucharistic Being. He is the Eucharist of the world. In and through this Eucharist the whole creation becomes what it always was to be and yet failed to be.[7]

2 *Anointing*

Jesus himself may well have used oil in healing the sick. It was a common, natural emollient and in the parable of the Good Samaritan, he told how oil was used with wine (a good, if primitive, disinfectant) for dressing the wounds of the traveller. Certainly the disciples used it for anointing the sick when Jesus sent them out to preach (Mark 6.13). It seems to have become common practice within the first century for we find some definite instruction in the

116

Epistle of James, in chapter 5. 13–16 (see pp. 88–89 for text and further comment.) James was a very precise person and a methodical writer. He would choose his words with care. If we are suffering on the one hand or cheerful on the other, the answer lies in our own hands. We can pray or sing praise, according to the occasion. But if we are sick—not suffering or bearing a sickness, but actually sick—then we need the Church's ministry. Christians who are sick need to make two 'phone calls, one to the doctor, the other to the priest/minister/elder. It used to be the bishop's job in the early Church to answer these calls—mercifully for them the telephone had not yet been invented—and his visit would be accompanied by the choir, because music was known to be therapeutic. Music is the food of health as well as love. Whether the music offered by some contemporary choirs would in every case be therapeutic is an open question!

The elders are commanded to pray over the sick person. I have always taken this to mean prayer with the laying on of hands, which is rightly part of the sacrament today. The injunction again is that more than one should minister in this way, for it is a ministry of the Church, not of an individual member. It is the 'elders' who are to be called, the representatives of the Church who minister in Christ's name. In practice this usually means the official, ordained ministry, especially for the actual anointing, though the same emergency measures could apply, as in baptism. For the laying on of hands, while accompanied by my ordained colleagues, I also think it right to have some representative(s) of the congregation, if possible someone who has been trained for this ministry, for at long last lay people *are* receiving training for such a ministry, though more trainers and trainees are needed.

Having prayed over him, the elders are to anoint him with oil. In the episcopal churches, the oil of the sick (*oleum infirmorum*) is usually blessed by the bishops during the Eucharist on Maundy Thursday. More and more is this practice being revived today with the beneficial result that the ministry of healing is increasingly and rightly taking its part within the normal, liturgical action of the Church. When the bishop performs this traditional function of his liturgy, he is providing one more point of focus for the unity of the Church and that is certainly part of the tradition. The service also gives an opportunity for the renewal of ordination vows, a time to seek again the grace of Christ to proclaim the Kingdom by preaching and healing. The oil used is normally olive oil, though any vegetable oil is now permitted. Like all medical remedies, it can however simply be blessed in the manner of saying grace over the food before meals, by the person who is going to use it. The actual anointing is effected by dipping the thumb in the oil and then making the sign of the cross on the person's forehead, as they were signed after their baptism. Sometimes the palms of the hands are also anointed. It is an act of consecration, used in the Old Testament to consecrate kings and priests, a practice still carried out today when the British sovereign is anointed during the coronation ceremony. It is the part of the present Queen's coronation which registered most vividly with many people, including I believe, with the Queen herself, for like all who receive anointing, there is the conviction that it is being ministered by the Anointed One himself, the Christ, the 'Chrismed' of God. In this sacrament we do indeed 'hail . . . the Lord's anointed'. The anointed person is thereby set apart for God's service and work, a person not only who is to proclaim the Kingdom, but in whom the conditions of the Kingdom can become a living reality. In fact it is the conditions of the Kingdom working out in the person which become the proclamation. The witness is given through *being* rather than *doing*.

Time and again in my ministry I have noted how the anointing sets off an explosive force in the person.[8] Sometimes it separates the person from his disease, giving him freedom from pain and a consequent ability to live a normal life even though his body may still be ravaged by the effects of the disease. At other times it leads to a complete healing, for a time at least if not more permanently. I well remember a call I received from a Christian friend, who was the surgeon in charge of this particular case, late one Sunday night. He generously rang to say that our verger was so seriously ill in hospital that I had better visit him that night rather than the following morning. Anne came with me and I took the oils. It was late and after 'lights out' when we arrived and so I asked for the curtains to be drawn round the bed. The nurse stayed with us as part of the praying Church. Many of our congregation were also engaged in urgent prayer for this dear man. I remember that it was with great difficulty that I performed the ministry; he was in an oxygen tent and had one or two drip feeds and other attachments. He was scarcely able to respond in any way as we began, but he did actually take part in the second Lord's Prayer and gripped our hands in recognition of what he had received before we left. His blood count was near to normal in the morning and he was back in church three weeks later. He died from the same disease two years later, but during those two years he gave a most valuable testimony not only to our congregation, but to the many hundreds of visitors who visited our church each summer. As someone remarked, his whole life was a song, a beautiful melody. Christ, the Anointed One, had allowed him to receive an injection of healing power which fashioned a new creation, something very beautiful for God.

There was a most interesting side-effect to this explosion of healing power, for indeed it was just this. Being a person of 'little faith' I had asked for the curtains to be drawn round his bed, partly to save myself embarrassment during the ministry—it is quite alarming how 'self' pops up in every situation, even when one's concern seems to be entirely for others—and partly not to distract the other men in the ward from their rightful occupation of trying to get off to sleep. When the nurse drew them back after the service, the men on the opposite side of the ward were sitting up in bed and beckoned me over. They silenced my attempts at apology and said that they did not know what had happened behind the curtains, but something had and they knew 'he'd be all right'. A week later the sister told me that a remarkable change had come over the men in the ward since that night; there was a new atmosphere of caring and concern for others; even most of the bad language had ceased. It taught me a very great lesson: the glory of God can never be hidden. The explosive force of healing and the consequent gift of health is for his glory and we have singularly underestimated this dimension as an instrument of proclaiming the good news of Jesus Christ. We must never be afraid of allowing his light to shine, for 'a city set on a hill cannot be hid' (Matt. 5.14, and let us take note of v.16).

'The prayer of faith' is also mentioned by James as an element in the healing. I hope I have emphasized sufficiently how essential a part in this ministry, and in every work of the Church, is the prayer of the faithful. This means particularly the prayer of the trusting, hopeful, expectant people of God. I believe the negative thoughts, as expressed in such phrases as 'if it be thy will', are harmful to such a ministry. The prayer of the people of God must be a positive aligning with the divine will which itself is always positive for good,

119

for God is good. The divine will may include suffering, but is nevertheless invariably orientated towards the good, as in the case of the divine Son himself 'who for the joy that was set before him endured the cross . . .' (Heb. 12.2). All prayer, as Jesus taught us in the prayer he gave us, must be directed towards the Kingdom, to the establishment of the Kingdom's conditions in the here and now preparatory to its fulfilment in the hereafter. Expectant prayer has a necessary emphasis in the adjective but it should be tautological. The prayer of faith has a healing potential as James here remarks because it is the trusting prayer of the expectant people of God, aligning themselves with the divine will, the kingly rule of God.

An obviously beneficial element of the anointing will be the forgiveness of sins, for you can not touch the fringe of Christ's garment and go away empty. I was taught that the confession of sin and receiving of absolution was a vital pre-requisite of receiving the sacrament. I still believe that sincere preparation where possible is good and helpful, but I have come to agree with the line George Bennett used to take: he believed that forgiveness was a 'bonus', part of the sacrament and a gift contained within it, as it is in baptism. Many recipients have witnessed to the amazing relief from the burden of sin which they experienced on receiving the anointing. For the rest, it is a help to our ongoing health if we have a 'soul friend' who can be our confidant and confessor, and who can continue to pray over us for our healing. 'The prayer of a righteous man has great power in its effects' (v.16).

I have included a rite for anointing in the Appendix. In any further revisions of the rite the connection with baptism needs stressing. As we were made regenerate, spiritually reborn, and joined to Christ in his death/resurrection at our baptism, so in the anointing we are being reconsecrated into that life which baptism began. This connection would be more obvious if oil was used again in baptism. Unction ought also to find its natural place within the Eucharist when the Body is gathered together. As Geoffrey Harding once wrote:[9] 'If baptism means renewal of life, anointing its restoration, and communion its continuing enjoyment, then anointing as it were looks backwards to baptism and forward to the Eucharist. It brings one aspect of the Eucharist into sharper focus—"Preserve thy body and soul unto everlasting life."'

I bring this section to a close by quoting a letter from a friend suffering from osteo-arthritis, and written after she had received the anointing:

> I can't begin to tell you how I felt after receiving the sacrament of Holy Unction. It was such a wonderful experience there are just no words. I'm quite sure now that I *shall* get better and free from pain, even if it takes time, and I feel now I have real strength to face whatever comes. Don't hesitate to let anyone know the benefit of those who have experienced it. I'm sure more would take advantage of it if they knew. One doesn't expect pain suddenly to go away, but it is the peace of mind which comes to one—all doubts and worries which had assumed such tremendous proportions have now just faded away, and the inward calm is something I just can't explain.

The more I ponder on my case histories, the more am I led to believe that the sacrament of anointing can itself be fairly described as a healing explosion.

3 *Laying on of hands*

This ministry has two roots: the one is theological, the other psychological. Theologically, it is an act of adoption. A rabbi adopted a pupil for the next course of study by laying on his hands. Jesus may well have acted in this way towards his disciples and so it became the outward sign of commissioning people to ministry. Barnabas and Saul, after the church of Antioch had fasted and prayed, received the laying on of hands to commission them for their first missionary tour. Presumably the adoptive element was expressive of the fact they were part of the church at Antioch and sent out as its emissaries. When used for healing, the laying on of hands adopts, draws the sufferer more closely, into the Body of Christ so that the health of Jesus Christ may be received by the sufferer through the body. It is a linking into the life and vitality, into the healing and health which find their source in Christ. Those who minister are used as the channel for this healing power, as the link in this chain of grace. There is another, partly antithetical, view which sees the ministrant drawing out from the suffer the healing properties inherent within him. I incline to the former view, knowing what blessings one receives oneself from the Christ who heals during a ministry.

Psychologically, the roots are deep indeed. Love is expressed by touch in so many ways. The mother's first instinct is to hug her child and so heal the trauma undergone in the birth. This physical contact in the pre-oral stage of a child's life is essential and should be prolonged if the spiritual damage resulting from the birth process is not to be lasting. Touch has greater *spiritual* significance than we realize. Every priest is aware of this as he celebrates the Eucharist. The laying on of hands, accompanied by the prayer of the Church, is a spiritual ministry of great power. All Christ's ministers are aware of this. I well remember the distinct feeling of being enfolded in, and embraced by, the eternal Body of Christ, the Church of the ages, when I received this ministry at my consecration as a bishop. I also felt a distinct commission as I was ordered, 'Heal the sick'. However, as regards this healing touch in general, more people than we suspect have been the recipients of a gift for relieving pain and discomfort in this way. Doctors and nurses frequently use a touch with their hand with obvious, therapeutic, results.

John Richards in a recent and most helpful monograph on the subject, traces the biblical ancestry of this act of the Church through both the Old and New Testaments and, quoting Acts 4. 29–30—'while thou stretchest out thy hand to heal'—concludes that the really important factor is that 'It is the *hand of the Lord* who heals, who blesses, who sends, who accepts, who equips and restores, and this cannot be over-emphasised.' This is why God is able to use this act of healing to enfold his children anew into his Son's health-giving body, despite the unworthiness of the ministrant. It is *his* hand which touches the sufferer. It therefore ought not to matter how the hands are laid on, but I used to notice the practice of George Bennett, who was trained to be a doctor before his ordination, and who placed one hand at the back of the neck and the other on the forehead or round the side of the temple. If there is a group ministering, one member may be led to place a hand on the affected part or area of pain.

As to the form of words, this may be varied according to the needs of each patient and it is better for the ministrant to be free to pray as he feels led or directed. If a more formal prayer is needed, that used at Burrswood is a fine one:

In the Name of God most High, and through his infinite Love

122

and Power, may release from all sickness be given thee. In the
Name of the Holy Spirit, may new life quicken thy mortal body,
and mayest thou be made whole, and kept entire, to the Glory of
our Lord and Saviour Jesus Christ.

Personally I have more frequently followed the pattern of the
prayer George Bennett used to say:

The healing mercies of our risen Lord Jesus Christ, present with
us now, fill your whole being, body, mind, soul and spirit, and
heal you. May he do away from you all that harms or hurts you
and give you his peace.   *But what if Not?*

In any teaching about this ministry, it is important to emphasize
that it is the touch of the Lord people are seeking. It is he who heals
and adopts the sufferer into the health-giving body of his Son. We
are his unworthy instruments. We can however rejoice that in this
ministry, particularly in regard to touch, the renewal movement in
the Church has brought a welcome informality and loss of embarrassment that has led to the unfreezing of some ecclesial
inhibitions. In this context we may hope for a more regular use of
this ministry.

Is it quite as simple as that? Why do some people appear to have the others gift of healing and others don't?

4 Absolution

Confession and forgiveness are central to the New Testament
teaching and the Christian experience. Jesus taught that it was
essential to forgive your neighbour if you yourself would desire
forgiveness, teaching vividly given in the parable of the unforgiving
debtor and articulated in what we now call the Lord's Prayer. The
parable of the Pharisee and the Publican demonstrated that
confession and not arrogance was the road to forgiveness. On the
cross, Jesus lived out the experience he had preached: 'Father,
forgive them; for they know not what they do' (Luke 23.34). The
grace of absolution has always been connected with the cross.
James indicated the ultimate benefit of confession and absolution
when he wrote (5.16): 'Confess your sins to one another, and pray
for one another, that you may be healed.'

The word that became the central symbol for this work and
teaching of Christ was reconciliation. Undoubtedly the main New

Testament emphasis is upon reconciliation as a corporate or community activity; we are all committed to this service or ministry: 'Brethren, if a man is overtaken in any trespass, you who are spiritual should restore him in a spirit of gentleness' (Gal. 6.1).

In the history of the Church the corporate element gradually became more individual and this ministry became closeted in the confessional. This process was reflected in the 1662 (Anglican) *Book of Common Prayer* where in the first exhortation in the Communion service, personal preparation is enjoined, first by self-examination, reconciliation with one's neighbours, a readiness to forgive, repentance and then, 'if there be any of you, who by this means cannot quiet his own conscience herein, but requireth further comfort or counsel, let him come to me, or to some other discreet and learned Minister of God's Word, and open his grief; that by the ministry of God's holy Word he may receive the benefit of absolution, together with ghostly counsel and advice, to the quieting of his conscience, and avoiding of all scruple and doubtfulness.' It has also been reflected over many centuries in the Roman rite of penance. The problem is not that the practice is unwholesome: far from it; very many have been led to wholeness and holiness through that sacrament. Many would be profited by its use today and much needless mental suffering would be avoided. Rather it is that because it has become centred on the individual, the ministry of reconciliation, once intended as a service to which all members of the body could contribute, has become a private matter between priest and penitent, with the emphasis on individual salvation rather than on corporate health. The result is that this ministry has been relegated to a siding, separate from the main line liturgy of the Church. Something has to be done to shunt it back on to the main line.

In the writings of the early Fathers, as Kenneth Leech points out in the appendix to his most helpful book on this subject,[10] confession and absolution were seen as the recovery of the Spirit. We can be thankful that this emphasis is being rediscovered today, partly as a result of the renewal movement especially among Roman Catholics. Confession is coming to be seen as a sacrament not only for the removal of sins but also for the healing power of the Holy Spirit. This element was expressed in early times through the laying on of hands during the administration of the sacrament. St Jerome wrote in the fourth century concerning the act of absolution: 'He imposes his hand on the subject and invokes the return of the Holy Spirit.' This was preparatory to the person being 'led by prayer into the midst of the people' and 'reconciled to the altar'. Absolution was obviously seen, not only as the receiving of forgiveness, but also as a giving/return of the Spirit in preparation for the restoration to fellowship in the body. The adoptive sign of the laying on of hands was therefore used.

This emphasis has now been restored in the reforms of the Roman Catholic Church promulgated in the new *Ordo Paenitentiae* of 2 December 1973, in which penance is seen as the renewal of baptismal grace and therefore as a reconciling act with God *and* the Church. 'Penance always implies reconciliation with one's fellowmen, who have suffered the effect of one's sin.' I believe these reforms have the greatest significance for all Christians. There are three different forms of the rite: only one is for individual penitents. The other two are for corporate use, one with individual, the other with corporate confession. Here are provisions for a public act in the 'main line' liturgy of the Church in which the penitent is seen as a concelebrant with the priest. There is an emphasis on the reading of the Word of God and opportunities for singing and silence. Throughout the *Ordo* there is an emphasis on the social aspect of grace and sin and the previous judicial language has been replaced by the symbols of wounding and healing. The language of reconciliation and emphasis on the power of the Spirit is uppermost in the new form of absolution.

All these are healthy reforms which hopefully will encourage more widespread—and ecumenical—use of this sacrament. I should like to see Christians other than Roman Catholics making use of such forms of service, if possible across the traditional and denominational divides. Such corporate expressions of penitence and seeking for forgiveness through the power of the Spirit could well give a thrust towards the unity Christians so deeply need and desire. The ecumenical celebration of the sacrament could contribute not only to the healing of individuals but also to the healing of the Church. The association of the sacrament with the healing ministry is in any case especially welcome since it sounds again a note heard, for instance, in Jesus' healing of the paralytic, where our Lord's forgiving of sin is associated with his healing work. Bultmann considered that this substantiated the claim of the Church to have received both these powers, for the Church 'demonstrates by her possession of healing powers that she has the right to forgive sins'. John Macquarrie concludes, after quoting this, that 'it is indeed in connection with healing, understood in the widest sense of reconciliation, that we must look upon this sacrament of penance'.[11] It may be only fair to him to say that he does not want the desirability of communal expression in the sacrament to obscure completely the fact that the Church has to minister to the individual in his specific guilt and weakness, though the individual receives the strongest healing by being bound more closely to the Body of Christ.

These reforms should restore this emphasis and recover the essential theological and pastoral dimensions of healing and reconciliation. Many, like Francis MacNutt, see this dimension as essential to the future of the sacrament: 'We need to add prayer for healing (to the sacrament) . . . . In my experience most situations of sin really need the help of healing prayer for the sinner to be truly set free.'[12] Certainly the priest's role as healer as well as counsellor receives emphasis in the new rite. It is not only however in the rite of penance that the Church ministers healing and reconciliation, and penance should be seen as but one part of its total service of reconciliation entrusted to it by 'him who reconciled all things to himself'. St Augustine declared that 'Forgiveness of sins may be found not only in the washing of holy baptism, but also in the daily recitation of the Lord's Prayer . . . in which you will discover as it were a daily baptism.'[13] Others have declared that the evangelical duties taught in Matthew 6 assist towards a daily cleansing from sin.

Kenneth Leech pleads also for a renewed connection between preaching and forgiveness, not only in order to teach about the confessional, but that the sermon should itself be seen 'as a vehicle of God's forgiveness', for 'preaching is an essential part of the cure of souls'. Many have indeed been convicted of sin and even healed during the time of preaching. Little wonder that a psychiatrist, Karl Minninger, has accused the Church of neglecting preaching in its concern for pastoral counselling. All these ministries must be fully used by the Church as God-given tools in the service of reconciliation with which she has now been entrusted. All are ways in which the word of deliverance can be ministered to man and the values of the Kingdom manifested in a creation the Creator wills to heal.

126

Martin Jones but
Lloy-Jones interesting
some interesting
point here.

5 *Exorcism*

Alec Vidler said in one of his 'Windsor Sermons': 'You have not really to bother whether the devil is best described as a person, or as a power, or as a supernatural agency—so long as you take him seriously. What you have to do is not to define him but to renounce him. And if you imagine he is leaving you alone at present, and that what I have been saying does not somehow apply to you, remember that will be the greatest feather in his cap. The devil is your opponent, not only your neighbour's.' When we minister in depth it will not be too long before we find that 'we are not contending against flesh and blood, but against the principalities, against the powers, against the world rulers of this present darkness, against the spiritual hosts of wickedness in the heavenly places' (Eph. 6.12). Small wonder that same writer advises us to 'take the whole armour of God, that you may be able to withstand in the evil day, and having done all, to stand' (v.13). What follows is not in any way an exhaustive guide to exorcism but merely a few guidelines for the parish priest, particularly with regard to the ever-increasing literature.

Work and study concerning this ministry were initiated in recent times by the late Bishop of Exeter (Robert Mortimer) who appointed a commission under the chairmanship of Dom Robert Petitpierre. Through his untiring work, Dom Robert has assisted many of us in our study and knowledge of this field of ministry. The report of his group is known as the *Exeter Report* and will remain part of the standard literature on this subject. The definitive work on this subject has been written by John Richards, entitled *But deliver us from evil.* [14] Beginning with that petition in the Lord's Prayer, where deliverance is seen as 'one, but only one, aspect of the Kingdom of God', he describes the healing Church and its ministry, 'the compassionate action of God working through his church', in its various forms. Rightly he emphasizes the corporate nature of the ministry. He then takes us through the history of the occult explosion and we accompany him on the occult journey. Having thus stated the problem of possession and defined his terms, he has a most helpful chapter on diagnosis, followed by two on exorcism, one of people and the other of places. Modestly he summarizes his work in a postscript:

127

> I have not provided a theology, but the raw stuff about which theology must be hammered out. That is the theologians' job, not mine. I have presented nothing that is not to be found in life . . . . A theological readjustment to accommodate the facts presented here would encourage the Church . . . . Four major aspects of the deliverance ministry are (i) its *pastoral relevance*—it meets peoples' needs; (ii) it is . . . *evangelistic* in that it prepares the way and points to Christ; (iii) it knows *no denominational barriers* . . .; and (iv) it *breaks down linguistic barriers*—by uniting together those of different traditions and terminologies.

He then concludes: 'The deliverance ministry, as well as contributing to the unity, effectiveness and relevance of the Church must, above all, drive the Church anew to the Exorciser—the Holy Spirit.'[15] So be it: a book for all ministers of the gospel.

While John Richards, who had been secretary of the Bishop of Exeter's Study Group on Exorcism for nine years and helped to bring out its valuable report, was writing his book, others were attempting to enable the Church to respond creatively to the 'occult explosion' at the beginning of the seventies. The Archbishop of York (Dr Coggan) had invited me to chair a group to advise him on this ministry in February 1973 and our first report was published at the end of 1974 just before he left for Canterbury. Intended as a guideline for ministry in the diocese of York it has apparently been of some use in many places, even abroad. In 'The Christian Ministry of Deliverance and Healing'[16] as we preferred to call it, after offering a catena of New Testament references for further study, we set out some basic guidelines for this ministry concerning the interview, diagnosis, preparatory prayer, consultation with the bishop and the medical profession (which we insisted was obligatory) and method and forms of service. We saw that discernment at this deeper level of ministry

> will derive from a constant awareness of the victory of our Lord Jesus Christ, an unwavering faith in the power of his death and resurrection to bring about a new creation and an attuning of ourselves to the eternal intercession of the Holy Spirit. A priest will soon be able to recognize whether the sickness is *obsessional* (Latin = sit down in the way of, besiege) when the sufferer is beset by exterior pressures leading to depression or jealousy (in

some instances); or *possessional*, i.e. when something has entered in, which is far more serious—and far more rare.

We also emphasized that what we offered were 'guidelines rather than tramlines; flexibility and spontaneity, centred in awareness of the presence of Christ and the bidding of the Holy Spirit, are the supremely important factors in this ministry of the Church.'

In the New Testament material we noted that exorcisms follow a closely similar pattern, though the details in some accounts are compressed: description of affliction; the presence or approach of Jesus arouses immediate violent antipathy; Jesus rebukes the demon, commands it to be silent and orders it to depart; violent reaction of sufferer; subsequent calm and deliverance and impact upon bystanders. It was the constancy of this pattern which inspired the basic structures of the liturgical forms which concluded the report. As a result of this work and subsequent events thrust upon us, such as the showing of the film 'The Exorcist' and a case that went tragically wrong in the north of England, most Anglican dioceses in this country have issued rules and guidelines concerning this ministry and bishops have appointed a properly trained panel to advise them. It is essential that this ministry should be firmly under the discipline of the Church.

The Church in Wales also issued *A Memorandum on Exorcism* prepared by the Reverend Norman Autton for the guidance of the clergy, sent to them privately, together with the name of the Diocesan Adviser. It covers much the same ground, following more closely the line of the Exeter Report. It is balanced and sane in its statements as the following will indicate:

> This Ministry is part of the total healing of the spirit-filled community and its pastoral care and prayer. It is a preparatory act, cleansing and clearing the way for wholeness. Deliverance should always be followed by the prayer of blessing, sacramental life in the church and committal to Christ in everyday life.[17]

The Methodist Church has also issued a Statement on Exorcism. Prepared by the Healing and Pastoral Committee of the Division of Social Responsibility, it was approved by the 1976 Methodist Conference. Like the others it insists on thorough investigation, consultation, pastoral care within the context of the life and worship of the church, a short (and unpublicized) ministry and after care.

According to my stated intention I have refrained from giving any direct instruction concerning this ministry. I have merely pointed to some of the available literature for study. I believe it to be a specialist ministry which needs both training and ongoing consultation between the caring professions. As far as my own experience is concerned, I have only been involved in one full scale exorcism in the whole of my ministry. This fact alone points to the rarity of the need for the full ministry. Frequently on the other hand one is consulted about infestation of places, often the result of not laying our dead to rest in the proper manner and omitting to pray for their peace. Frequently also one prays that people may be kept free from the snares of the evil one—especially over those who are about to receive baptism, over many who come for healing as well as over our dear ones in our homes, during the office of Compline, which also reminds us that our adversary goes about like 'a roaring lion, seeking whom he may devour' (1 Peter 5.8). Mercifully he who calls us to minister in this way has assured us of the victory over every adverse foe in the mighty act of his cross/resurrection.

6 *After-care*

The purpose of all deliverance and healing is the uniting of the one-time sufferer with Christ in his Body, the Church. Healing has both a personal and a corporate dimension. True wholeness is enjoyed by those who are integrated into the worshipping community. Everyone who receives Christian healing needs the love, the prayer, and the ongoing support of the Christian community. Some churches are still not alive to this responsibility; but thanks be to God, more and more are becoming aware of this task, and are pioneering new ways of caring for those who need ongoing ministry, including such imaginative and self-sacrificing experiments as extended families and Christian communes. Every congregation however should be trained to *be* the Church in this caring way.

Post-deliverance care will of course be of a special kind with a group (preferably) of Christians constantly surrounding the ex-sufferer with love and a gentle firmness that will enable him to break all the old bad habits and contacts and so be built up within the Body of Christ. This will include encouragement to a prayerful life in union with the Church, the regular reception of its sacraments and the reading of Holy Scripture. All the spiritual resources of the Church should be made available for the patient's convalescence, as well as the day to day caring of fellow members offering acceptance, fellowship, teaching and encouragement.[18]

Post-healing care also needs spiritual convalescence. In the past this has invariably devolved on the parish priest, who of course will still be responsible for seeing that the patient regularly receives the sacraments. But spiritual after-care is the responsibility of the whole Body and should always be seen as a corporate task. We are just beginning to unfreeze the talents that have lain dormant—they could do little else if they were frozen!—in the pew. My experience is that the people of God are hungry, not only for God's word and sacraments, a hunger that is on the increase, but also having been fed with spiritual meat, they are hungry and thirsting to be trained and equipped to be the Body of Christ in this way. Those of us who are in the ordained ministry ought to rejoice and it is our job to fill them. Now that we have removed that offending comma in Ephesians 4.12 (compare the AV and RSV) we have come to realize that the gifts of the ascended Christ to his Church are specialist skills in certain people, or better certain people called to particular functions (apostleship, prophecy, evangelism, pastoral care and teaching) *for the supreme purpose* of 'equipping God's people for the work of ministry, for building up the body of Christ' until there is a corporate sharing in the life of the Kingdom, when each has attained the measure of Christ's wholeness. You can't go it alone and be healed in isolation, neither can you remain aloof and decline to play your essential part in Christ's healing community. Every member needs to be equipped, built up, to be part of the healed and healing Body.

7 *On dying well*

At the heart of the Christian faith stands the death and resurrection of Jesus. For Christians, death should be a friend. Christ has been that way before us, overcome its sharpness and so opened up the Kingdom of God. St Paul is therefore able to say, 'For to me to live is Christ, and to die is gain' (Phil. 1.21). The early Christian attitude is finely portrayed by Ignatius of Antioch in the most moving of his letters—to the Romans in whose city he was to gain the martyr's crown:

> This favour only I beg of you: suffer me to be a libation poured out to God, while there is still an altar ready for me. Then you may form a loving choir around it and sing hymns of praise in Jesus Christ to the Father, for permitting Syria's bishop, summoned from the realms of the morning, to have reached the land of the setting sun. How good it is to be sinking down below the world's horizon towards God, to rise again later into the dawn of His presence! . . . . He who died for us is all that I seek; He who rose again for us is my whole desire . . . . Suffer me to attain to light, light pure and undefiled; for only when I am come thither shall I be truly a man. Leave me to imitate the Passion of my God. If any of you has God within himself, let that man understand my longings, and feel for me, because he will know the forces by which I am constrained. [19]

But this early Christian attitude to dying was soon lost and when the vision of Christ the Healer was dimmed, death became a matter of fear. From the time of Augustine, dying was looked on as a punishment, the result of the Fall. In the twentieth century, which has seen more than its share of violence and death, this trend has begun to be reversed. For although psychiatrists tell us that man is more tormented with the fear of death than ever before and undoubtedly he attempts to externalize it, theologians and modern martyrs among others have led Christians to have a more positive view.

For instance, one of the most healthy developments of modern times has been the spread of the hospice movement. Originally a hospice was a resting place on a pilgrimage to the Holy Land. Today the term is used for resting places designed for those nearing the end of their earthly life, 'a place of hospitality'. It is no mere coincidence that both the healing and hospice movements began in this century, roughly at the same time, the latter with the establishment of St Joseph's in London. It was not however until the 1950s that new impetus came with the establishment of the Marie Curie Foundation and the arrival at St Joseph's of Dr Cicely Saunders, who has been the inspiration and prime mover of the modern hospice movement. There are now some thirty hospices in this country, with many others in the planning stages and with the D.H.S.S. becoming increasingly involved.

The staff of the hospice are a team, for the most part a team of Christians who pray and share together, both among themselves and with the patients and their families. Their purpose is to transform this part of life from mere existing into real living. They give the patient the kind of unhurried attention he so greatly needs. Pain control is practised and distress relieved whenever and in whatever way it appears. Chronic pain can affect any of the four areas of growth that contribute towards a healthy personality.

> Chronic pain is usefully divided into physical pain, mental pain, social pain and spiritual pain. It is by teasing out the different components of a patient's pain and by treating them appropriately (without ever losing sight of the fact that this is pain contained in a person), that one can begin to help a person in his transition from living to dying. [20]

The team's purpose is to create a cheerful atmosphere which is genuine and welcoming, radiant with peace and love, and in which the fear may be eliminated so that every day may be lived. Each patient is treated as a person and all his needs and expressions of inner feeling are listened to unhurriedly.

> The real question is 'What do you let your patients tell you?' The true listener sees how the gift of insight is the work of the Holy Spirit and that we have to try to keep in step. Our work is to follow his leading, to be available and approachable and to learn that truth is so often in a relationship rather than in words. [21]

The team seeks to minister Christ through his sacraments of the cup of cold water and the washing of the disciples' feet, and learns how to relieve all distress, how to be silent, how to listen and how just to be there.

A most important part of the caring is for the families who are welcomed and integrated into the community. The team also listens to their needs, assisting their relationship with the patient from the very first and caring for them through to the end, particularly during the essential period of grief after their dear one has been laid to rest. They have to be helped to realize that the dying see through all unreality and that the masks which hid the truth and prevented full relationships are now removed. This can be a painful process. But this openness in the staff-patient-family relationships brings about the possibility of openness to God, and therefore the probability of a new relationship between the patient and his family and above all between them and their Creator and Redeemer. More may be achieved in terms of reconciliation, fulfilment, and faith in this part of a patient's life than in any other. We should be more than grateful to the hospice movement for teaching us not only how to die well but to live fully, without fear.

The elimination of the negative attitude to death and the gaining of a new vision of life from deeper knowledge of dying is also the purpose of a writer like Johann Christoph Hampe who in a remarkable book permits human experience to show how the moments before death are marked by an increased activity on the part of the consciousness. Of the elements which recur persistently in this period he places emphasis on three: the escape of the self (in which the dissociated self is able freely to observe what is happening to the body it has left behind), the life panorama (in which the dying experience their whole life passing in front of their spirits, but in a remarkable review and selection of what had been most important though they had never been conscious of this earlier), and the expansion of self (which is apparently dominated by the experience of light and colour, occasionally associated with music, accompanied by the 'feeling of weightless floating' and an 'intensification of the experience of reality' which alone explains 'the euphoric happiness' of which the reports continually speak).[22]

All the accounts from which Hampe marshals his evidence come from people who did not die at that time after all. 'They came back.' The final stage of dying can not be known. We need to learn more about consciousness which does not flicker out like a candle in the death process (an old medical view), but rather experiences an intensification of light, an experience that is frequently expressed on the serene faces of the dying, as though a new stage of superconsciousness has been attained. However we may judge the evidence Hampe provides, one fact stands out: death is not something to be feared.

For a Christian, dying is a matter of living. Life is the best preparation for death and a life lived with Christ is a journey with him from whom neither death nor life can separate us. It is his love, and the knowledge that 'having loved his own who were in the world, he loved them to the end' (John 13.1), which casts out the fear of dying. John Austin Baker puts it well in the following passage:

> There is only one way in which, with the world as it is, God can show himself good in respect of man's suffering; and that is by not asking of us anything that he is not prepared to endure himself. He must share the dirt and the sweat, the bafflement and the loneliness, the pain, the weakness, yes, and the death too. That would be a God one could respect, a God who put aside all his magic weapons, and did it all as one of us. A God who, when we cry out in our misery (as we all do), 'Why should this happen to me?' can answer truthfully, 'It happened to me too, not because I couldn't help it happening, but because I chose that it should, because it was right.' Then and then alone will our doubts be stilled, not because we understand, but because we can trust. [23]

Or as St Paul put it in his letter to the Romans (14.8): 'If we live, we live to the Lord, and if we die, we die to the Lord; so then, whether we live or whether we die, we are the Lord's.' From the peace experienced at many bedsides of the dying, I believe St Paul has got it right. Their whole demeanour has told of a coming together with 'the source and spring of all life'. For them, death has manifestly been the final healing.

8

Healing in the Local Church
A   Leadership

THE CONCEPT OF THE SHEPHERD
AND PASTORAL CARE

Differing traditions in the Church will have various names for their leadership—bishops, presbyters, priests, ministers, deacons, most of which derive from the New Testament. In his leadership, Jesus most obviously emphasized the serving element, both in his logia, 'I am among you as one who serves' and by what he was and what he did, he 'girded himself with a towel' (Luke 22.27; John 13.4). The image which he used to describe his role of leadership was that of the shepherd. If it is not readily understood in a technological age it is at least scriptural and is worthy of deep thought and study by those who are called to leadership in the Church today.

In his most helpful book *Soul Friend*, Kenneth Leech examines the image of the shepherd and draws attention to the fact that the Latin word *cura* which primarily means 'care' can also mean 'healing' and in Scripture the recurring symbol of shepherd holds together these two themes. 'In the New Testament there is a bringing together of the themes of the wounded healer, the slain lamb, the stricken shepherd, and the guide who nourishes the flock.'[1] In the Old Testament it was Ezekiel, sent to denounce the leaders of Israel, who called them shepherds, but shepherds who took care of themselves and never tended the sheep:

> The weak you have not strengthened, the sick you have not healed, the crippled you have not bound up, the strayed you have not brought back, the lost you have not sought . . . my sheep were scattered over all the face of the earth, with none to search or seek for them (Ezek. 34. 4, 6).

It was the Lord God who would come to show them what leadership of the people involved:

> Behold, I, I myself will search for my sheep, and will seek them out . . . . I will seek the lost, and I will bring back the strayed,

and I will bind up the crippled, and I will strengthen the weak, and the fat and the strong I will watch over; I will feed them in justice (34. 11,16).

This kind of leadership, so wonderfully revealed in the life of the Good Shepherd, a leadership that combines the caring and the healing elements, is the calibre of leadership that the Church needs and the 'flock' of God will expect. Of course, the concept of leadership has greatly changed in our time. No longer do the generals march at the front of the army nor bishops in front of the Church militant (if they ever did). We are beginning to learn in secular and religious life that Jesus' model of leadership will stand the test of time: for it is marked by a selfless devotion to the will of God, a willingness not only to serve others but to die for them, a love that knows intimately each individual in the flock, a humility that only desires the good and health of the other, a joy fulfilled in giving God the glory. This is the model set to all pastors of the flock by the Good Shepherd. 'Who is sufficient for these things? . . . Thanks be to God, who in Christ always leads us in triumph . . . as men of sincerity, as commissioned by God, in the sight of God we speak in Christ' (2 Cor. 2.14ff). For authority is ultimately not what is conferred by any human power upon a person, but what comes from the idea of unrestricted possibility or freedom of action enabling one to do what is permitted. The authority of creature over creation comes from the Creator alone (*ex-ousia*). We are almost back to the idea of spaciousness which lies at the root of being a whole person. Jesus spoke with authority, and not as the scribes, because he was always a man within himself, who had given himself enough space to allow freedom to move. The possibilities of his life and leadership were therefore unrestricted. He had a freedom, even on the cross, which men have sought in each generation. How can this freedom be enjoyed by the shepherds of today enabling them to have sufficient space to tend the flock?

Dietrich Bonhoeffer, whose life was marked by a spacious freedom even in prison, once said: 'Only by discipline does a man learn to be free.' The ascetics have always had the greatest freedom because they have by their discipline trained themselves to have that spaciousness in their lives. The pastor will need to exercise himself in Christian discipline or *askesis* (= training, making oneself fit through exercises, from which we get the word asceticism), if he is to care for and heal the flock. What are some of the marks of Christian leadership?

1 *A person of prayer*

I always like the story of the Indian tribe who had a special name for the visiting Christian minister. When translated it meant 'chief prayer man'. It is the description of the ideal Christian leader, whose chief occupation is prayer and who is therefore able to lead, to be chief of, the praying community. As an Anglican I have always been grateful for my training in the threefold diet of prayer which seems to be well balanced: the Eucharist, the office, and time for contemplative or silent prayer. Without the regular food of the Eucharist, a leader is in jeopardy of starvation even more than other Christians. It is his special privilege to obey the dominical command, 'Do this.' The healing power of Christ's own sacrament will be the spiritual food of him who has the commission to heal and care for the flock. He also needs the solid 'protein' of the daily office, which will help us to serve our contemporary scene the better by lifting us beyond it. The use of the psalter, our Lord's prayer book, provides a timeless nourishment for the spiritual life and the daily readings from Scripture are marrow to the bones. The leadership in the Church is directly responsible for ensuring that 'the voice of prayer is never silent'.

Bishop Michael Ramsey has always lived and taught the necessity of a life of prayer for any leader in the Church and therefore charged his priests to be men of prayer: 'We are called, near to Jesus and with Jesus and in Jesus, to be with God with the people on our heart.' Because of this belief he issued a warning to unfaithful shepherds: 'Amid the spiritual hunger of our times when many whose souls are starved by activism are seeking guidance in the contemplation of God, a terrible judgement rests upon the priest who is unable to give help or guidance because he has ceased to be a man of prayer himself.'[2] It is this life of prayer, meeting daily with God 'with the people on our heart', that finds its source in the Eucharist; Christian leadership demands a life of disciplined contemplation both in order to hand on the things thus contemplated (what have we otherwise to hand on?) and to be able to help others in their search for the spiritual realm.

Morton Kelsey out of his own experience sees that 'the total man must give himself to this encounter'. Frequently there are areas of life which have been forgotten or ignored. He therefore offers twelve guidelines for a spiritual odyssey which will ensure that all parts of our life are brought into the total relationship, so that we may be whole:

> Act as though you believe in the spiritual realm.
> Undertake the quest with serious purpose.
> Seek companionship and spiritual direction for the spiritual journey.
> Turn away from the busy-ness of the outer world in silence and introversion.
> Learn the value of genuine fasting.
> Learn to use the forgotten faculty of the imagination.
> Keep a journal.
> Record your own dreams.
> Be as honest with yourself as you can and get someone else to help you to be honest.
> Let your life manifest real love.
> Gird yourself with persistence and courage.
> Give generously of your material goods. [3]

Some would add a little to this, some would take a little; others would find it too introverted or lacking in a healthy earthiness, but much of it is useful and it is born of a living experience. In any case he makes his point that a return to a knowledge of the spiritual realm is one of the pressing needs of our time. Concerning those called to leadership in the Church, Evelyn Underhill once remarked: 'How shall they lead their fellow men out towards eternity unless it is a country in which they are themselves at home?'

A life of prayer also demands a discipline of the diary, a prayerful planning of one's life, even though emergencies come and every day is different, bringing new opportunities (a better word than problems). It is essential to vacate times in the diary just to be with our Lord—in prayer and worship, in reading, in passivity and silence, or in loving our neighbours. If there are no lines through the diary for these purposes how can we accomplish them? It is therefore beneficial to the spiritual quest if time with our Bible and books, time with our family, time for physical

139

exercise and relaxation and rest, especially a regular day off and holiday, are all entered in the diary thus bringing a necessary orderliness to life. In this way far more is accomplished, useless work and occupations jettisoned and less time frittered away.

All this is part of the equipment and *askesis* of the person of prayer, charged with leadership in the healing community, whose own life must first be healed and integrated if it is to be an example and give direction to the lives of others. In this the priest will also be greatly helped if in the early stages he has undergone a discipline of meditation, learning from the great methods of old such as the Sulpician or Ignatian, and so feeding himself on Scripture. But he must then progress, or come back, to the contemplative life,[4] a form of prayer marked by simplicity, stillness and silence, a looking, longing and listening (a good sequence). If prayer is 'the fundamental relationship of man to God, the state of attention to God, involving the whole personality', then its simplicity is its very directness. Here the Eastern Church has much to teach us, for instance in its use of the Jesus prayer, 'Lord Jesus Christ, Son of God, have mercy on me a sinner.'[5] It is used as an act of the memory, drawing Jesus into the memory and being drawn by him into his love, so that the memory is no longer a distraction to the necessary stillness but becomes ever more disciplined and healed.

This stillness is a vital part of pre-prayer. Fr Jim Wilson had a simple method of relaxing the body for prayer: sit in a good chair (with a convex back so that the spine is in a healthy position) upright with both feet flat on the floor, head up, hands on lap and eyes closed. Once in this position, feet and legs are relaxed, then arms and hands especially the hands, followed by the stomach muscles, the neck and face, and lastly the eyes. After several deep breaths, the process of mental stillness is begun by use of short phrases of prayer or just the name Jesus.

Silence or laying aside of thought, in which breathing plays an important part, is also a condition conducive to prayerfulness. 'Let the remembrance of Jesus be united to your breathing and then you will know the value of silence.'[6] It must also be remembered that Hebrew has the same word for Spirit and breath. Each breath (e.g. at the colon in the psalms) is an inhalation of the Spirit who is Lord and life giver. Such silence can help to reduce the overcrowding of the mind and so give the heart a receptive stillness and ability to listen to God.

Prayer however is not essentially something we do but is a gift from God, the action of God. One spiritual writer declared: 'Prayer is God who works all things in all men.' It is God's grace working in us and is therefore charismatic. To pray is to be set on fire with God, a fire that burns away the dross in human, sinful lives and kindles a flame for the Kingdom that is not easily quenched.

Prayer is no ejector seat from a flight dogged by problems; it is no push button to escape from life's realities. Prayer is a means by which Christ can heal our personality. He thereby imparts to us a wholeness which alone equips his servants to be his instruments of healing in the world, to be the leaven, a city set on a hill to give light to the world. Charles de Foucauld, a modern day *staretz* of desert spirituality, whose ideals are continued by Carlo Carretto and the Little Brothers of Jesus, lived in what he called the frigate, a long wooden erection shaped rather like the juggernauts that overtake law-abiding motorists on the motorways. At one end was the altar, a rough wooden box with the open Bible upon it. The other end was permanently open to the world so that anyone could come or go. This was to remind him that the purpose of his life of prayer was in the tradition of his Master—service of the world. At one end he met God. At the other he also met God—in his neighbour.

It is for this reason that any Christian leader who is called to heal (and which Christian is not?) must be a *pneumatikos*, a person of the Spirit, a person of prayer in order to fill that calling. Health and healing are God's gifts which it is our privilege to minister. How shall we fulfil our calling to heal unless through a life of prayer we know the Giver of the charism? In prayer alone shall we learn that 'He who calls you is faithful, and he will do it' (1 Thess. 5.24).

2 *A person of penitence*

At the end of Francis MacNutt's first book, *Healing*, he included 'a talk to priests' by the Reverend Tommy Tyson, a Methodist evangelist, in which the speaker urged his audience, priests of the Roman Catholic Church, to rediscover the power of the sacraments. In the course of the talk he pleaded with them not to do away with Confession.

The Holy Spirit [he declared] shows us who we are, separated

141

from God; then He shows us who we are in relationship to God. Then we simply make that exchange; that is what Confession is all about. We come to Confession because of a conviction of our sin. We are saying 'apart from God this is what I am'. When the priest hears our Confession he says: 'You are right: and the truth is you are a lot worse. But where sin did abound, grace does much more abound. And so, here is who you are before God. And here is how you go about appropriating that grace.' These ways of appropriating grace are simply a bridge to where people ought to be in Jesus. That is healing.[7]

It is a good notion of the sacraments—bridges 'to where people ought to be in Jesus', for the Latin word for priest, *pontifex*, means a bridge builder. He is the dispenser of the sacraments. But the word that must be learnt again in order to prepare people for this point of departure, for this crossing of the bridge, is *metanoia*. Usually translated repentance, it is an even richer word implying a drastic change, a change of heart, a change of mind and even a change of direction for one's whole life. The prime example of this was in the life of St Paul in which a dramatic change of direction took place on the Damascus Road, a true conversion (= turning round). The word even implies one more step because it presupposes a willingness to be changed and only the grace of God can effect such a total conversion as that. The sacraments are badges and tokens of this grace; they are the way in which we 'go about appropriating that grace'.

It is essential that the priest and leader of a healing community has a first hand experience of penance, this sacrament of *metanoia*, if he is to mediate such grace, such healing to others.

Be sure to criticize yourself in God's presence, [advises Bishop Michael Ramsey again to his priests] that is your self examination. And put yourself under the divine criticism: that is your Confession. Then God's forgiveness renews your freedom to be humble. If you use sacramental Confession, do not step out of using it. If you do not use sacramental Confession, ask yourself if it would not be a good thing that you should.[8]

This is a question that every minister of healing must face, for the greatest sickness in the world is the sin that separates man from God and the greatest means of health is *the* reconciliation once for all accomplished on Calvary. The Christian minister is therefore a person of the cross, one who bears about in his 'body the marks of Jesus' (Gal. 6.17), and who knows as a living experience in his own life the compassion of the Lord Jesus and is therefore able to show and minister it to others. It is this ministry which Christ has now committed to his Church, the ministry of himself, Jesus, Saviour, Healer.

> The good news is that when we encounter Jesus and yield to Him so that He becomes the centre of our being, He draws us towards perfection, showing us the way out of sin. Forgiveness, conversion and healing are facets of a single process through which God shows us His goodwill towards us.

The priest must have first hand experience of this inner healing, for as the writer continues: 'There is no disease which robs us of life in all its fullness more extensively and intensively than sin (this little word with I in the middle of it): there is no reconstruction or healing of the human personality more complete than that which Christ's forgiveness provides.'[9]

The leader of the healing community as a man of penitence will represent in his person the forgiving and healing Lord Jesus. He will chiefly witness to the truth of Jesus by what he is, a penitent. He will make his witness by his proclamation in preaching and teaching of the good news of *the* reconciliation, God's mighty act in the death/resurrection of Jesus, the source of man's ultimate healing and health.

3 *As prophet and pastor*

It is hard to separate these two functions of Christian leadership without detriment to one or the other. The pastoral role has briefly been discussed above in relation to Ezekiel's vision of the shepherding role of Jahweh. It was Ezekiel again who caught the vision of the prophetic role in his call to be a watchman for the Israelites: 'So you, son of man, I have made a watchman for the house of Israel; whenever you hear a word from my mouth, you shall give them warning from me' (Ezek. 33.7). The prophet's task is to 'wait still upon the Lord' until he have mercy upon him. The work of the prophet is the life of prayer and of waiting upon God in order that he may have the gift of wisdom to lead the flock and fulfil his pastoral function. It was because the shepherds of Israel had renounced their prophetic role that they were bad shepherds: they only listened to themselves and so were 'empty cisterns'. But the watchman of the Lord lives up to his name: his vigil is one of listening so that he may have something to say and the words will not be his but 'the very word of the Lord'. The true watchman will then be Spirit-filled, the *pneumatikos*, to whom is imparted the Word. As Bishop John Taylor has pointed out, 'It is this same combination of Spirit and Word that God imparts to men in that unique phenomenon we call prophecy, the nearest thing to creation that man can ever experience.'[10]

He will do much of his listening on his knees. He will also do much in his study. Time for reading is more essential as time goes on. If it is a definite entry in the diary it becomes part of the daily diet. A mind alert is a necessary part of the prophet's equipment. Cyril Garbett, one time Archbishop of York, once said he feared not so much a depleted Christianity as an ignorant one. At that time he took it for granted that the leadership was at its books. The prophet also listens to the voice of the world in all its secularity. A watchfulness of current events led the eighth-century prophets to a wide discernment of national and international movements. They watched them, let all activists take note, from afar and the distance seemed to increase the discernment of the right time to act or refrain from action, to speak or to keep silence. Incarnational religion takes the blame for a great deal of over-activism in the Church today. The incarnate Lord was however supremely in control of himself because of his nearness to the Father: his silence and his stillness were as articulate as his words and actions.

The Christian watchman and prophet is equipped to fulfil the role of the Christian pastor, the leader who watches over the flock given him by the Chief Shepherd. It was in the person of the Good Shepherd that the prophetic and pastoral found their fulfilment. It was Jesus of Nazareth who was both prophet to the old Israel and pastor to the new. At the very beginning of his ministry, in his own home town, the awareness of this fulfilment was articulated:

> The Spirit of the Lord is upon me,
> because he has anointed me
> to preach good news to the poor.
> He has sent me to proclaim release to the captives

and recovering of sight to the blind,
to set at liberty those who are oppressed,
to proclaim the acceptable year of the Lord
(Luke 4.18f; Isa. 61.1f).

He is the Lord's anointed, 'Great David's greater Son', sent to proclaim the good news as the prophet and watchman of the Kingdom, but also to feed and provide for the new Israel by the very signs that herald that Kingdom—the healing of the blind and the broken, which is the task of the shepherd. He is the Good Shepherd who knows his sheep and his sheep know him, because they enjoy the unique relationship with him begun by sharing his death and resurrection in baptism. He lays down his life for the sheep demonstrating that the one supreme norm of conduct in any situation is love, the fulfilling of the law. There are also other sheep of his whom he must also bring in, so that the flock may be one under one shepherd, for the kingdoms of this world must become the Kingdom of our God and of his Christ.

Like his Master, the Christian leader is called to unite in his ministry the prophetic and pastoral elements. 'Keeping the word at the Lord's mouth' he will be able to 'feed and provide for the Lord's family'. He will bring to the flock the good news of their release, of their recovery of sight, of their healing, of the Lord's favour. Without the prophetic ministry the pastoral will be ineffective. One of the great needs of the contemporary Church is a healed leadership and it is the prophetic side of our ministry, the waiting *still* upon our God, that will reveal the areas in ourselves that need inner healing, the Lord's deep-ray treatment. Those who have known such miracle in their own lives, the miracle of being 'ransomed, healed, restored, forgiven' themselves, are then fitted to become channels of healing. They become in fact ministers of Christ's healing to the flock he has entrusted to them. And as it becomes one (= whole, integrated) flock under the one Shepherd, so the healed Church becomes a Church of healing.

9

Healing in the Local Church
B   'In the process of the Spirit'

THE HEALING COMMUNITY

Dr Mowrer, a well known American psychiatrist, once explained to a group of church leaders why he was an atheist. It was, he said, because the Church had never learned the secret of community. He therefore felt it had failed him and others like him.[1] The charge is too near the truth for comfort. And yet from the very first, the Church has been 'called out' (the meaning of the Greek word *ecclesia*) to be a community. Historically this concept goes back as far as Abraham, called out of his father's house in order to father a great nation, like the sand and stars in number. The nation of Israel was called out of Egypt and freed to be the people of God, the community blessed by God for his own and variously called his servant, his son, his vine, his vineyard, his flock, his bride. This community was sealed by a covenant relationship with him, as were its members with one another. We have been at pains to point out that the Jew thought and lived *corporately*. For him, there was no life without the community. He was a member of God's people. Nothing could take away his solidarity with the tribe.

The nation of Israel prefigured the calling out of the new Israel, the Christian Church, in the release from their bondage in Egypt (redemption from sin), the crossing of the Red Sea waters (baptism) the journeyings in the wilderness (training for discipleship), the eating of manna (the Eucharist), and the entry into the Promised Land (the conditions of the Kingdom). The new community was also called to be God's people, the body of his Son, the fellowship of the Holy Spirit. And in the Acts of the Apostles we read of the exciting beginnings in the life of this new community.

It was, in Jürgen Moltmann's phrase, a 'community in the process of the Holy Spirit'. The risen Christ had come among them and breathed into them the new life of the Spirit. He had bestowed on them his resurrection gift of peace, the ideal new order of things, the eschatological conditions that obtain in the Kingdom, the very life of the new creation. The life-style and actions of the community therefore conformed to the principles of this peace, *shalom*. [2]

We read that 'they devoted themselves to the apostles' teaching and fellowship, to the breaking of bread and prayers' (Acts 2.42). Such a life-style kept them in the process of the Holy Spirit (the Greek word is very strong, more like 'persisted obstinately'). This is the life-style for the healing community today; we need solid teaching coupled with a tenacious desire to learn; we need deeper fellowship of a quality that is able to sustain the hurts of its members and pray and love them through their crises; we need such a hungering and thirsting after righteousness that can only be assuaged by the Bread of Life and the fruit of the True Vine; we need to pray with a persistence and devotion that will give the good Lord no rest until he makes the new Jerusalem a praise in the earth (Isa. 62.7). Above all we need to realize that all is from *him*, it is his gift—the teaching, the fellowship, the bread broken (and blood outpoured), yes even the prayer, for as a community in this process 'we do not know how to pray as we ought, but the Spirit himself intercedes for us with sighs too deep for words' (Romans 8.26). All is sheer grace, and of this the early community was profoundly conscious. Jeremias has pointed to this awareness of the boundlessness of God's grace as being 'the chief characteristic of the new people of God'. They were only conscious of their weakness; they praised God they were found worthy to suffer; they had every calumny levelled against them; they endured every type of physical suffering and privation; and yet they knew that very weakness to be the cradle of the Lord's strength, 'When I am weak, then I am strong' (2 Cor. 12.10). Truly it was 'amazing grace'. Little wonder they could not forbear from speaking to anyone who would listen of 'the mighty works of God' as they did at the very inception of this process of the Holy Spirit. For a Jew, the mighty work was the exodus; now for this new community it was the new exodus of Jesus' death/resurrection and all the signs and wonders of his life among them. The Kingdom experience had begun; the blind see, the deaf hear, the lepers are cleansed, the poor have the gospel preached to them . . . . Little wonder their lives were changed out of all recognition. Truly they were becoming a healed and healing community—in the process of the Holy Spirit. And we can only praise God as we begin to discern such signs in the Christian

community of our own time. We must not let down the likes of Dr
Mowrer again.

1 *The prayer group*

Cardinal Basil Hume and his fellow bishops of the archdiocese of
Westminster, wrote a pastoral letter to their people at the beginning
of 1978. Significantly it was entitled 'Prayer and Community'.
Equally significantly it was the pastoral paper *number one*, as
though its subject matter was considered to be of prime importance. In responding to their peoples' comments who in
previous dialogue had emphasized the need for personal conversion
to Christ, for communities of mature Christians and for prayer ('a
massive priority'), the bishops underlined

> two areas of Christian life that we are asking you to concentrate
> upon NOW
> > BECOMING A PRAYING CHURCH
> > AND MAKING THE CHURCH A FAMILY

They asked them to enter into two bonds: a bond of prayer and a
bond with people. One of their practical suggestions for im-
plementing these bonds was an encouragement to form, and
participate in, prayer groups, which 'a growing number of people
. . . find a very helpful way of *learning how to pray, of coming to
know our Lord* as a living person and of deepening the sense of the
Church being *a real family*' (my italics). I believe this was a genuine
use of *episcope*, for the role of the Church's leaders is to encourage
and enable God's gifts to his people to be used, that the Church
may truly become the Church. They are likely to be used the better
when people know how to pray together, thereby coming to know
our Lord in the context of the Christian family community.

In fact the seed bed of the Church's renewal in our time has been
the multiplicity of praying groups that have mushroomed through
this century with increasing rapidity. Right across the world from
Tanzania to Tennessee, clean across the denominational divides
from Catholicism to Quakerism, across the barriers of race and
colour, age and sex, Christians have been meeting in a world explosion of praying groups. This is another lesson the Church has
been learning from Jesus' example in our time. The circle of the
Twelve was not only 'a symbolic representation of the twelve tribes

of Israel and thus of the whole people of God'. It was also 'a section of the larger circle of disciples which Jesus summoned to discipleship from a still wider group of adherents'.[3] Within the concentric circles of the community there was the even smaller one of the three privileged disciples whom Jesus took with him to witness the raising of Jairus' daughter, the transfiguration, and his prayer of agony in Gethsemane. Commentators on these passages have suggested that he took them with him because he expected some trial of his spiritual stamina in which he would be glad of their companionship (G. B. Caird) or that the evangelist might have thought of them as the nucleus of the new Church (Lohmeyer). Both comments should be borne in mind when we consider the need of a prayer-full nucleus at the centre of a healing community. The Church has from the beginning been built upon the group foundation of apostles, prophets, etc., with Jesus Christ the corner stone of the whole building. The more groups there are, beavering away at prayer and other *essential* community activities in order to learn how to *be* the Church, the sounder the structure will be built. Suspicions about praying groups dividing the body should be allayed at once: groups who pray for healing nurture it and make it more healthy. They tend to 'build' rather than 'pluck down'.

I am frequently asked how such a praying group is formed. I can tell you how it is not formed, and that is by a pulpit announcement or an invitation pinned to a notice board! Rather, as Andrew went to call his brother Simon, and Philip went after Nathanael, it will 'happen' through a person to person call. How often Jesus speaks to us through our friends. George Bennett used to say that among the first to be sought out should be people who have known miracle in their own lives. The leadership should be prayerfully asking: 'Whom shall we call? Who will join us?' that they themselves may be led to those whom the Lord wills to call. Our own healing prayer fellowship was born out of those who had known the hand of God upon them, people to whom *he* had called us to minister, people in whom we had watched *him* at work in his healing power, people he then called together with us to be a nucleus of healing prayer in his body. Then we whom he uses to call others to such a ministry become the recipients of his healing grace too.

It is essential that these groups should be cells of the whole body, fully integrated into its life, and yet also feeding new life into the body. Integration will come through the whole group meeting with the whole body in the weekly Eucharist, as well as at other times for fellowship, teaching, and prayer (Acts 2.42). The group needs to be caught up into the worship of the communion of saints week by week in order to be enlivened with the divine life. The earthly body, in the form of each church, also has to become

> a living fellowship in Christ, offering deep and loving relationships, [for] the Church is the Body of Christ, and we are inescapably members of it; the Church is the family of God, and this is where we belong; the Church is the building of God, and each living stone is indispensable to the whole; the Church is the army of Jesus Christ, and each soldier must satisfy the one who enlisted him. [4]

The local church undoubtedly comes nearer to this ideal when members of the congregation are in the habit of praying together during the week. They thus become spiritually sensitive to each other and the needs of the whole Church and community and form deep friendships with one another. The whole atmosphere of the gatherings for worship then change. Members have the psalmist's joy in their heart—'I was glad when they said to me: "Let us go into the house of the Lord"' (Ps. 122). Their joy is first because they are going to worship the Lord and secondly because they are to meet people they love in him. There is nothing that communicates so quickly with the outsider than a congregation that is just so happy to be together. It is a most powerful instrument of evangelism which we have been too slow to apprehend. The joy of breaking bread together in the Lord's own sacrament feeds that joy and completes it and the grace of the sacrament continues the healing process in each member, so bringing an increase of health to the whole body. It is here too, at the central act of worship, that all the prayers of the week—the praise and the penitence, the thanksgiving and the intercession—are gathered into a glorious whole and offered before the throne of grace, in *the* sacrament of healing.

The methods of each group will vary considerably, according as they feel led and react to one another. Much will also depend on the preferences and talents of the group. Hopefully the Bible will feature significantly in the group's equipment. The reason why we are told we must get to know our New Testaments is because we need to know Jesus. There is no substitute to this for a Christian.

Each one needs a personal knowledge of his Saviour and the combination of the Lord's own sacrament with a regular meditating on the word of God in the Bible is the proven method of accomplishing this aim and fulfilling this need. Silence should also be part of the group diet, especially after the hearing of the word. Many are experiencing the blessings of silence in public worship too after a reading of the lesson or before the confession or after the Thanksgiving in the Eucharist. Silence in a group is a deep way of communicating both with the Lord and with each other and all silence has a therapeutic quality for every part of our personality. We keep silence in prayer in order to be attentive to God, for prayer is being with God, in his presence. Silence therefore leads to a realization of that presence; it is a time to wait on him, listen to him, look towards him. In contemplation this becomes the whole of prayer, not just an introduction to a time of prayer. Père Grou called it the prayer of the heart. Sometimes it is called the prayer of simplicity because of its childlike quality. Many are led to pray in this way focusing their attention on a crucifix or lighted candle (a mandala) with the repetition of some phrase (a mantra) like 'Jesus is the Light of the World', or the Jesus Prayer.[5] The important point is that these well-tried methods of prayer are not only for private use; the group can grow through the use of silence and through contemplative methods of prayer.

Many are also helped by these methods in the time of intercession. Frequently members are equipped with long lists of prayer requests. I know! for in addition to the regular cycle of the church's intercession, we receive from our healing prayer fellowship a monthly prayer leaflet with prayer requests for each day of the week and this is sent to 500 people and groups. Some find it helpful to take about four names each and offer them to the healing Christ during the time of silent meditation in which the whole group takes part. This gives an added depth to the whole operation. So also does a concentration on thanksgiving. It costs little to be grateful and yet how frequently this vitalizing ingredient of communication is lacking. The loss of real communication between people today can often be traced to a lack of gratitude. The psalmist knew that it was a joyful and pleasant thing to be thankful. Not for nothing does the chief act of Christian worship bear the title Eucharist for 'It is right to give him thanks and praise'. In the prayer of healing it is essential to give thanks for any blessings and for the setbacks, for both contribute to the wholeness God is preparing. The best advice was given by St Paul to his beloved brothers and sisters in Christ at Philippi: 'Have no anxiety about anything, but in everything by prayer and supplication with thanksgiving let your requests be made known to God' (Phil. 4.6).

An exercise for a praying group which can be both didactic as well as therapeutic is when at the beginning of the evening each member 'throws' into the middle the 'luggage' they have brought to the meeting. A good time should be allowed so that each one can spell out their problem or the care and concern they have for someone or some project. After all have had their say, then everything is prayed through, calmly and deliberately, perhaps without words when a particular problem seems too complex. Each member will pick up in this time of prayer something that has struck home to them about one of their fellows. But all will be surrendered to the Lord, and left at the foot of the cross. That is the place to leave our burdens; 'Come unto me, all ye that are heavy laden, and I will give you rest' is the word of comfort he says to each one of us. And there at the foot of the cross, as I can remember dear Bishop Joe Fison thundering to us undergraduates during a mission he was conducting at Trinity, Cambridge, 'there, is the place and the only place you will gain the blessing of the Holy Spirit.'[6] If a burden shared is a burden halved, a burden prayed through in this way is a burden taken away.

A group will ensure its spiritual health as a cell of the body if it also has an external point of reference. William Temple's over-quoted aphorism about the Church being the only organization which exists for the benefit of the outsider is perfectly true. This may be accepted by the group in the form of some activity like hospital visiting or conducting a service in old people's homes; or in money-raising for charities and overseas missions. Others may prefer to work with the young, running a young people's fellowship or children's week-day (Sunday) school. Others again will want to be those who undergird the whole parish and its manifold activity (and passivity) in sustained prayer, giving particular attention to the preaching and ministry engagements of the parish leadership. An external point of reference will prevent a hardening of the precatory arteries and ossification. There should also be an eye to new membership which may lead to a splitting of the group if it becomes too large. Some groups also feel called to have an open night for their hard-bitten or atheistic friends, at which food and drink may flow (in moderation!), but at which the main purpose is to speak a word for the Lord in the direct manner in which true friends can speak the truth in love. A praying fellowship which is thus oriented—spiritually, socially, and in the service of others, and in which all is done to the glory of God, cannot be far from being healed itself, and so is on the way to becoming an instrument of health for others.

Mention of my old college, to which I owe such a great deal, prompts me to close this section by offering the reader some words of my patient and excellent teacher:

> For all its essential communal context, God's love must first be apprehended in his love for me. Otherwise it is not apprehended as love, but only as benevolence or good will which fail to satisfy because they fall infinitely short of what love is. It is only to the degree in which I begin to apprehend God's love for me that I can begin to apprehend His love for all men. And that is the main spring of all Christian social action: Prayer begins as the opening of my heart and mind to God's love for me. And it never ceases to be that however wide, and indeed universal, the implications and demands of that love are discovered to be. . . . Our job is to put ourselves at God's disposal by the discipline of regularity, by faithfulness to our rule, and by the use of that common sense without which we can't do anything. But there our job ends. What happens when we pray is God's business, not ours. God will give us what He knows best. And what is best we see in the life of Jesus, in His joy and peace and stillness and confidence and trust. And also in His Passion, His bloody sweat, His death and resurrection.[7]

2 *The personal ministry*

Two phrases from the foregoing quotation are going to be helpful as we begin to consider personal ministry, the one about the apprehension of God's love for me being the key to my apprehension of his love for all men, the other about our job being to put ourselves at God's disposal. First of all there is a need to relate in a warm, loving way to those whom we seek to help. This can only happen if I have received healing myself and so have come to know the extent of God's love for me. For having been apprehended by his love nothing can separate me from it (Romans 8. 38f). Once I know God's love for me, I can know it for others and be used by the God of love to transmit his love to them. Those who know themselves to be loved can communicate that security to others by showing that love to them. Secondly therefore, we are utterly at God's disposal. Let him use us as seems to him best. The loving response to the supreme Lover is to put myself at his disposal, an attitude which George Bennett used to describe as kenotic, being utterly receptive because we have emptied ourselves for God's sake, eager to follow his every bidding. These are basic thoughts to anyone on the threshold of ministry to others.

I have called it a personal ministry rather than a private ministration because the minister will not be ministering alone. He ministers as a member of the Christian community. The foundation of his ministry will be the praying group, such as I have described in the previous section, who will undergird him in all his personal ministry. They need not know the name or circumstances of the patient, but it may be helpful to know the time of the interview, so that the praying can be concentrated at the particular moment. Again, he may not be alone with the patient: sometimes it is right for a trained team to counsel and minister together. If the ministry is to be under the seal of the confessional, that is of course quite a different matter: the ministry will be conducted according to the regular discipline of the Church in this regard. Just as the consultant however works in a team on his rounds, so sometimes it is better for the minister to be part of a team, especially when actual ministry is given, so that no cult shall spring up round the name of the minister. It is Christ who heals and we have the promise of his presence where two or three are gathered together in his name. The presence of others also trains people to see this as a ministry of the whole Church, and of no singular individual. Alone or in a group, the positive element of God's love and the utter willingness to be at his disposal should be present. These attitudes will communicate themselves and prove therapeutic.

The ministrant(s) should also convey to the patient his utter availability to them. Any form of busy-ness or impatient thumbing through the diary when the appointment is made is not conducive to the building up of that necessary trust and mutual confidence. The time at the patient's disposal should also be clearly stated, e.g.

'We shall have 45 minutes clear', and during that time no bells should be answered except by other people in the house and the telephone should be unplugged in the interviewing room. After all the time was booked by the patient and not by others. Being undisturbed is essential for the listening which will be the main task during the interview. I always tell those I train that they have been given two ears for the very purpose of Christian counselling: with one they will listen with all their worth to the patient, not only to what is said, but to what is left unsaid, and to what lies behind the various attitudes and postures adopted; with the other ear they will listen to God. George Bennett used to liken the situation to a triangle, with God at one apex and the ministrant and the patient at the other two. The purpose of the interview is then to eliminate the apex at which one is placed as ministrant so that the triangle disappears and all that is left is a straight line between God and the patient. I well remember being on the receiving end of this experience more than once in the confessional. I was so 'lost in wonder, love and praise' at God's forgiving power, the priest having done his work so well, that it was a long time before I noticed he was no longer there. That is what I call ministry. 'He must increase, but I must decrease' (John 3.30). It is when we are out of the way that the Lord can do his business with the loved one. It is through our weakness that he can reveal his strength. 'Our very power as ministers rests on our weakness and sinfulness. We can understand the bound state of others because we have been bound by our own sins and the sins of others. We can live in ourselves what the other is experiencing, because our experience is not that different.'[8] Frequently one cause of a blockage to the patient's healing is that the ministrant has failed to acknowledge his weakness and surrender the patient's problem to the Lord.

I had a salutary reminder of this when attempting to reconcile a married couple. The wife found it impossible to forgive past instances of the husband's infidelity. His genuine penitence failed to move her. It was only after the three of us involved in the ministry, the others being my wife and the minister concerned, had surrendered our utter inability to make any headway, that the break-through came and we were able to pray over them and then celebrate a renewal of the marriage vows. This is also the reason why I am utterly in favour of *Christian* counselling. First, the problems thrown up today are mostly far too complex for human

155

solution. New understanding of the problem and fresh light may be shed upon it, but too often the problem remains, *because of the concentration on the problem.* The Church on the other hand is not in business as a problem solver. Its job is to see that problems are surrendered to him who alone can make all things new. The Christian counsellor's purpose is to make himself redundant, so that the health-giving contact between creature and Creator is restored. This is what it means to be a minister of reconciliation. Secondly, a Christian minister is commissioned to restore and to build. When the structure is laid bare and the recipient of the ministry is an empty shell, helpless and hopeless, then the minister has something to give and something to say. By his commission he can speak with the authority of Christ and fill the void with all the fulness of God. His prayer over the person is an imparting of the presence of Christ, an assurance, as Bishop Michael Ramsey recently stressed in a talk on Christian prayer, that Jesus is near, the Holy Spirit is within and we are surrounded by a great cloud of witnesses, the praying Church. This is how the prodigal is welcomed again to his Father's house: he is brought again into the mainstream and joy of family life. He is not left to go it alone or with a nagging emptiness. He is filled with the fulness of God.

The interview will therefore invariably end in prayer. The person and the problem, hopefully separated in the time of counselling, will be brought to the foot of the cross and so to the place whence resurrection can take place. After a surrender of all that is blocking the road to healing which is made together before the throne of grace, the minister will pray over the person for his complete and inner healing and may well be led to lay on hands (with his companions if present) for that healing. He will feel an inner conviction of the rightness of this course of action if this is the will of the Lord for that person. The all-important attitude now and throughout the interview is a sensitivity marked by an awareness of God's presence in the total situation and an obedience to his promptings, not least in the actual words of the prayer and how it should be ministered. Both the awareness and the obedience will develop over the years from the surrender of ourselves in prayer to him who can do exceedingly abundantly, more than we can ever dare to contemplate or ask, and also from a real desire to put ourselves at his disposal. For the remainder, it is all his grace. We can only put ourselves in the way of it. He will do the rest. But even this assurance of faith and trust in that grace, especially if joined with a spirit of praise and affirmation, can itself be used by God for healing.

Please God the Church at large will become aware of his power present to heal, and obedient to his commission to use it. There are signs of a new awareness and obedience in many parts of the world. The Spirit is saying to the whole Church today, 'Wake up and believe in my power. Rise up and use it to heal my people.' After all it is he who has called them out of darkness into his marvellous light.

3 *The healing service*

Enough has been said already to emphasize the centrality of the Eucharist in the life and witness of the Church. It is *the* sacrament of healing because it is our Lord's own sacrament. The food he gives us in the sacrament is his own divine life in the forms of bread and wine which preserve our bodies and souls into everlasting (eternal) life. Nothing can add to, or subtract one iota from, the grace of the sacrament and its efficacy for the health of the total personality of the recipient if it is received with 'a lively faith'. Neither can any act of worship dislodge the Eucharist as the very acme of the Christian experience.

It therefore seems wholly natural for other sacraments to be celebrated in its context, for instance the sacraments of initiation, baptism and confirmation, to which the Eucharist forms the natural climax, and also the sacraments of vocation, ordination and matrimony, to which the Eucharist adds a seal and provides a fitting context for a concelebration with other members of the Body of Christ. It would also seem right, in view of this, that the sacraments of healing, the anointing and/or laying on of hands should similarly be administered in this context. It will ensure that this ministry is seen as part of the mainstream ministry of the Church, because it will be celebrated at the time when the Body of Christ is gathered together for its primary activity. It will also ensure that the patient is surrounded by the praying church, a vital part of this and every sacrament, while as in the case of the sacraments of vocation, the reception of our Lord's own sacrament will act as a seal and additional means of grace to what has already been given and received. For this reason, the communion should be seen to be the climax of the rite, as the new liturgies make increasingly plain. The ministry of the healing sacrament should take place earlier in the service.

In the new Rite of Penance of the Roman Catholic Church the priest receives the following instruction concerning the absolution: 'Following this prayer (for God's pardon), the priest extends his hands, or at least his right hand, over the head of the penitent and pronounces the formula of absolution . . .' (IV. A. 19 of the Introduction). It is good that the laying on of hands has been reintroduced into the healing ministry of absolution and it would therefore seem appropriate that when a healing ministration is offered at the Eucharist it should take place immediately after the absolution. In turn it will be followed very appropriately by the giving of the peace. The method of ministering the laying on of hands will be as set out above under that section in chapter seven. The ministrants minister to one another after the president has pronounced the absolution; then they offer a ministry to the congregation. In this context (of the Eucharist) especially, it should be seen to be a ministry of the whole Church and not of an individual, as too often it seems when each engages in a separate ministry to each. This does not prevent anyone from making a special (brief) request or mention of a name to their ministrant as they arrive at the altar rail. The ministry may close with a brief silence, the singing of the doxology, followed by the peace.

The healing service as an entity in itself and separate from the Eucharist has come into prominence in recent times. It has its critics, but the adverse criticism is far outweighed by the positive blessings of such a corporate ministry and the many 'signs following'. It also has the advantage of supplying a personal, shared, and spiritual experience in an age that is evolving from the institutional to the informal, from an emphasis on organized ritual to a more personal approach, from codified religious doctrines to an experience of faith, from academic to empirical knowledge (see p.179 re the paradigm shifts). For congregations which have been trained to be a healing community such services provide an experience which is of benefit both corporately and individually. In short they can lead those who share in the service to the disclosure moments which form a vital part of all religious experience and are steps to personal healing.

The service should be well prepared and advertised a sufficient time in advance in order to allow an adequate time of prayer. Those who are chosen to lead the ministry should have opportunities of coming together for prayerful preparation and should be quite clear as to their duties. Some members of the congregation may need help with their preparation: many will need after-care. The service should have an introduction of praise which will include a hymn of praise and prayer centred on the risen Christ ending with the Lord's Prayer. The service then has three main parts: the ministry of the word, the prayers, the ministration. The *ministry of the word* consists of a reading from the Bible followed by an address. Both will be proclamations of the healing gospel. Next comes the *time of prayer*, which may be shared prayer as many churches now enjoy during the time of intercession at the Eucharist, with, of course, a time for open prayer when it comes to mentioning the names of those who need and desire healing. Or it may take the form of a conducted meditation, beginning with relaxing prayer and followed by a 'sunbathing' in the beams of the divine Light, sometimes aided by the use of a Christian mantra or mandala. This can be a very helpful preparation for *the ministration*. A hymn (to the Holy Spirit) is useful at this point while the ministrants serve each other and then the people approach, quietly stewarded so that the right number come to each altar rail. It will have been suggested to them beforehand, that they may want to draw near for a ministry either for themselves and their own needs for we all need healing; or on behalf of someone else, who need not know (many blessings have come from this way); or they may want to offer themselves in an act of rededication to serve the healing Christ and ask to be shown the way. As at the Eucharist, it is good to have a time of silence after the ministration together with a thanksgiving, and end with the singing of the doxology. This may well be done with joined hands round the church since hopefully all feelings of embarrassment will long since have melted away as self-centred preoccupation has given way to God-centred attention and devotion. A hymn and a blessing/dismissal may conveniently close the service unless silence and informality is preferred.

Such services are spreading throughout many countries today, and in many places of worship from village churches and chapels to cathedrals. It is obvious that they bring a new sense of joy and purpose to the congregations who experience them, while those who minister the laying on of hands at these services are having their ministry renewed in many wonderful and surprising ways. The dry bones of a ministry which had given up prayer and was content with the formal duties springs to life again in new service to the risen Lord. It is also important that such services should be held in order to balance the personal ministry where the individual and his or her sufferings naturally receive most attention, though sometimes more than is good for their health. The healing service creates the corporate context for healing in the Christian community and the devotion of all is centred on the risen Christ. He is the centre of the community and the one who heals. The services also lead to an intensification of the life of prayer in the community: they throw up more needs and requests for prayer; they give a new purpose to the work of the prayer groups; they also lead to a new atmosphere in the worship and fellowship of the community which becomes marked by a radiant joy and expectant faith. This is the fertile soil which produces changed lives, for Christ.

George Bennett gave yet another reason for the holding of healing services:

> Perhaps it is the witness that such services give that is the most important thing about them just now. In these days when people are turning in all directions to find healing and peace, it is important that the Christian Church should be clearly seen to be preaching a gospel that has something very positive to say about sickness and disease. When the Christ is upheld in all his glory, He will draw all men unto Him. He is the divine magnet to whom men and women will turn if they are only able to *see* Him.[9]

PART THREE

Health and Society

10

Medicine, the Church, and Healing

1 *A health service*

The tragic polarization between medicine and the Church has a long history. It can be traced back at least to the twelfth century, when, in an effort to curb the power of the monasteries, the first Lateran Council (1123) forbad monks to administer unction or even visit the sick. When the monks began to study medicine this was also prohibited by the second Lateran Council (1139). The Council of Tours (1163) prohibited churchmen from practising surgery at all. The dissection of the human body was later declared to be sacrilegious and Innocent III, the formidable lawyer-Pope who sought to eliminate all deviations and heresy, pronounced through the fourth Lateran Council (1215) that bodily medicine might only be prescribed after the priest had ministered to the spiritual health of the patient. The position of the doctor became almost impossible. The process of polarization was completed by a decree in 1566 imposing on the physicians the obligation to enforce penance on the sick. Little wonder the gulf is taking so long to heal! Once again however it is this century which has seen the movements to put an end to the breach between medicine and the Church.

It was Dr Albert Schweitzer who once remarked that his only purpose with regard to disease was to annihilate it. In this he was remarkably at one with his Master's thinking. Jesus' one objective was the elimination of disease and the restoration of man to wholeness. This fact makes the attitude of the medieval church little short of a tragedy, for it was Jesus of Nazareth and Lord of the Church, more than any other religious leader, who showed the greatest concern for the physical and mental well-being of man:

> Sometimes it is forgotten that medicine owes its greatest debt not to Hippocrates, but to Jesus. It was the humble Galilean who more than any other figure in history bequeathed to the healing arts their essential meaning and spirit . . . . Physicians would do well to remind themselves that without His spirit, medicine degenerates into depersonalized methodology, and its ethical code becomes a mere legal system. Jesus brings to methods and

163

codes the corrective of love without which true healing is rarely actually possible. The spiritual 'Father of Medicine' was not Hippocrates of the island of Cos, but Jesus of the town of Nazareth.[1]

Many efforts have been made by many individuals, particularly in this century, to bridge the gap between medicine and the Church. A great step forward was made in 1947 when the British Medical Association approved a statement on medicine and the Church which declared that 'Medicine and the Church working together should encourage a dynamic philosophy of health which would enable every citizen to find a way of life based on moral principle and on a sound knowledge of the factors which promote health and well-being. Health is more than a physical problem and the patient's attitude both to his illness and other problems is an important factor in his recovery and adjustment to life. Negative forces such as fear, resentment, jealousy and carelessness play no small part in the level of both personal and national health. For these reasons we welcome opportunities in the future for discussion and co-operation between qualified medical practioners and all who have concern for the religious needs of their patients.' It will be recalled that this statement came just three years after William Temple's initiative in founding our Council of Healing. Both attempts at reconciliation proved to be in the nature of 'a bridge too far'; as my colleague, Dr Kenneth Leese, commented when quoting the B.M.A. statement in our C.C.H.H. booklet, 'This was in some ways so far in advance of secular medical thinking as to be almost totally ineffective in its impact on the post-war physician.' He then continued:

> This ineffectiveness has deepened the gloom of those within the profession who, as avowed Christians, have seen in society a developing secularism with its concomitant new emphasis upon materialism; the pressures for time-demanding cures rather than true healing; the trivia of minor complaints, the apparently disproportionate use of resources . . . and the real danger of a loss of respect for the dignity of human personality in the pursuit of scientific advance.[2]

This disillusionment, if such it be, may not only affect Christians in the profession as they view the rough road to a rapprochement with religion. Its cause may lie deeper still, in the divorce between medicine and healing. Jeremy Swain is but one writer who has diagnosed 'the true malaise of modern medicine' as 'a failure to understand its relationship with healing'. Scientific information has become the end rather than the means to the true end of human service to human people. One doctor writes:

> We are increasingly conscious of growing factual evidence that our patients go away from our consultations feeling emptily dissatisfied if all we offer them is pills and potions . . . . People have a 'gut reaction' these days that health is more than a physical problem and that their reaction to their illnesses and their relationship to their other problems is an important factor in their recovery and adjustment to life.

Of course, what has become known as the psychosomatic approach has played an important role in the revision of ideas as to how to treat illness. It gives recognition to the emotional, social, and family aspects which have influenced the course of a particular illness and seeks to help people to help themselves by gaining a greater insight into their own personality and situation. The resulting increase in maturity aids this recovery as total human beings. It must be said that given the time and alleviation from other pressures of their job, many general practitioners would like to work more along these lines than they are able to do at present and it is in this more open approach that there is real hope for the working together of the professions, especially among the younger generation.

It is in this very area that the concept of holistic medicine has done much to heal not only some of the disenchantment within the profession but also the gulf between medicine and the Church. It had long been evident that much disease had been psychosomatic in origin. The holistic approach demands that all aspects of living must be studied as a single reality. Sometimes individual aspects may be studied by abstraction, but the practitioner must remain aware that all other living processes are concomitant. In the main the approach is optimistic and therefore in accord with the theological approach of biblical authors such as the writer of Genesis. Inherent in man are constructive evolutionary forces goading him on to realize his given potentialities. This means that man by his very nature is striving for self-realization, and that his values evolve from such striving. The goal is therefore human growth at its most *whole*some and the way towards the realization of this goal is an ever-increasing awareness of ourselves and a true understanding of the essential 'me'. The purpose of holistic medicine is the liberation and cultivation of the forces which lead to self-realization.

It is but a small step forward from this peak of understanding to the summit, which has nowhere been better expressed than by the author of the Fourth Gospel and Paul in the New Testament. For John, the Word (who became flesh and dwelt among us) is the source of all life; he himself is the true life as the various 'I am' sayings indicate (John 6.35; 11.25; 14.6). This life of God is received by faith (6.40) and the recipient has already passed from death to life (5.24). Such life has the seeds of eternity within it (4.14) and is the means of man realizing his eternal destiny (the ultimate in self-awareness and self-realization?). Paul's view of life finds its origin in the resurrection of Christ, which has demonstrated the victory of life over death. Life for him is the life of Christ, who, through his resurrection, has become the author of a new life for mankind as the last Adam (Rom. 5. 17–21, 1 Cor. 15.20ff). The life of Christians is the life of Christ who lives in them. 'It is no longer I who live, but Christ who lives in me' (Gal. 2.20). Christians live the life of Christ (2 Cor. 4.10), and for them, once again, this is the ultimate in self-realization. It is not a vast gulf between the theology of the New Testament and growth—orientated psychoanalysis which, as Karen Horney claimed, 'has shown us that much that we have regarded as constitutional, merely represents a blockage of growth, a blockage which can be lifted.'[3]

It is towards this end of growth that humanistic psychology is orientated for it is 'a way of doing science which includes love, involvement and spontaneity, instead of systematically excluding them. The object of this science is . . . the liberation of people from the bonds of neurotic control, whether this comes from outside . . . or from inside.'[4] The Association for Humanistic Psychology was started in Britain in 1969, having begun its life seven years earlier on the other side of the Atlantic. Being concerned with 'human potential, it must include all that we have it in us to be, and therefore must include ecstasy, creativity, unitive consciousness and so on. . . . Humanistic psychology is asking for all of us to exchange the pain of alienation for the pain of awareness.' Because of its interest in Eastern philosophy and practice it has always been concerned with altered states of consciousness. It seems to me that much of this is common ground to both Christians and humanists. In fact we have Anglican priests who are researching in the field of altered states of consciousness with a view to teaching meditation as a form of therapy as well as entering the diagnostic areas of mental illness. It is to be hoped that the Church, particularly in the persons of its theologians, will apply itself to such studies and make an even more positive contribution by bringing a truly Christian dimension into these scientific researches. For Christians there can be only one liberation towards the full growth of self-realization and that is the freedom for which Christ has set us free (Gal. 5.1). The essential Christian truth is that the liberation of man does not lie within the field of his own capability. He can not come to his freedom by his own effort or by an act of his will. He can only take hold of the freedom Christ has already won for him by the mighty act of the new covenant. 'True freedom exists only where the Holy Spirit works in a man, becoming the principle of his life, and where man does not block his working . . . . it was given to operate above all in the communal life of the people of God.'[5] This needs saying loud and clear in the dialogue between the Church and those branches of medical science which are taking the holistic approach to healing.

2 *Pastoral Counselling*

The whole field of counselling is another 'bridge area' between medicine and the Church. As a process of helping other people it has become increasingly used in recent years, partly because of the growing sense of social responsibility especially among the younger generation, and partly because progress in the sciences of psychology and sociology has led to a deeper understanding of personal relationships and the reactions of people to their problems. The aim is to render the person more secure within himself or herself. Modern counselling has been defined as

> assisting an individual to develop insight and ability to adjust to successive events in his life through the appraisal of his capacities, aptitudes and interests; helping him to understand motivations, emotional reactions and compensatory behaviour;

and helping him to attain a degree of personal integration whereby he can most effectively use his potentialities and make the greatest contribution to the society in which he lives.[6]

Here can be seen a tendency towards this non-directive approach along the lines which Carl Rogers suggested in his *Counseling and Psychotherapy* (1942). Since then the emphasis has moved towards the relationship between the persons involved in the counselling exercise. An account of more recent methods is to be found in a book *Basic Types of Pastoral Counseling* by Howard J. Clinebell. It will be seen by the spelling of counselling that these books come from the States. In England, Dr Leslie Weatherhead pioneered the way of relating new developments in psychology to pastoral care. This work now finds its thrust in the Association for Pastoral Care and Counselling (APCC) which, among other groups, includes the Westminster Pastoral Foundation. Their work provides a necessary stimulation to the churches who have tended to lag behind in a field where the Christian contribution is vital.

In 1958 Dr Frank Lake, who had made an extensive study of the relationship between psychology and theology during his time as a medical missionary in Bengal, began his schools of clinical theology for small groups of clergy which took the form of periodical seminars over a period of two years. Four years later he had established a headquarters at Nottingham for the Association for Clinical Theology Training and Pastoral Care. The result of his researches was published in a massive work *Clinical Theology* (DLT 1966). His work has been of tremendous help to many clergy and ministers and through them to their parishioners. One doctor writes positively of Dr Lake's immensely compassionate prayerfulness, which she sees as an essential element in this pastoral method.

The modern pastoral counsellor is heir to the 'Shepherd of souls' without having replaced the legitimate role of the 'Soul Friend'. He will use more 'modern concepts with regard to personality and human relationships .... Healing replaces discipline ... sustaining has been substituted for comfort ... edification has given way to guiding. This healing, sustaining and guiding ... need as well a group within which the person can become a part and which will receive him as one of themselves. This implies a therapeutic community.' Interesting experiments are now being made in mental hospitals with the purpose of creating a therapeutic community through the process of changing roles, thus enabling all members of the hospital community to become more mature in their own. Among such hospitals is Claybury, on the eastern fringes of London, which has been written up in a series of essays from Claybury, *A Hospital looks at itself*, edited by Dr Elisabeth Schoenberg (Cassirer 1972). The Christian Church should also be in the process of becoming such a community and be able to sustain and guide those who are receiving pastoral counselling and care. For 'it is the spiritual aspect which is the distinguishing feature of counselling that is pastoral. . . . It works on the assumption that healing, or the process of reaching wholeness, is helped both by the methods of counselling, and by making it possible for the person to receive more fully the grace of God.'[7] The Church must be ready and equipped to make this vital contribution in a situation where the various disciplines involved in counselling are coming closer together.

3 *Hospital chaplaincy and inter-disciplinary relations*

As a statement of national policy, the Ministry of Health in the early days of the N.H.S. in Britain, laid down some significant guidelines; hospital authorities were advised that they 'should give special attention to provide for the spiritual needs of both patients and staff, and, in particular, should do everything possible to arrange the hours of duty of nurses and other staff (and of students at teaching hospitals) so as to enable them to attend the services etc. of their own denomination.' They were also advised that 'whenever the size of a hospital justifies it, a room should be set apart for use as a Chapel' and Boards of Governors were instructed to appoint chaplains, and 'these appointments should always be made in consultation with the appropriate Church authorities.'[8]

The chaplain has always played an indispensable part in any hospital. Through his ministry in the chapel and on the wards he provides a spiritual hub which can make all the difference to life in the hospital both for staff and patients. Indeed his ministry is to both and therefore the independence of the chaplain in the hospital setting should be maintained. He needs to be able to enjoy a good and close relationship with all members of the hospital staff, whether the person be a porter or a consultant. A chaplain is the pastor to all patients and staff of his denomination. His visits on the wards will be regular, both for counselling and encouragement, for prayer and the administration of the sacraments. He will have experience in the ministry of healing and in hearing confessions. He will be readily available to meet new staff (or patients) and to co-operate in student training and in induction courses, as well as in multi- or inter-disciplinary meetings. He will also relate to the families of patients, especially to those bereaved, and also to the local parish priests, as well as to colleagues of other denominations. In fact the work of the hospital chaplaincy as a whole will be run as far as possible on an ecumenical basis. He will also hopefully have a good relationship with the administrative staff, who not only are in a sense his employers on behalf of the D.H.S.S., but who will also run courses and conferences at his suggestion for medical and paramedical staff to meet chaplains and local clergy for mutual benefit in a learning situation.[9] The purpose of such gatherings will always have implications beyond the confines of the hospital community for, as Michael Wilson concluded in an article in *The Hospital*, 'The primary task of the hospital is to enable patients, their families, and staff, to learn from the experience of illness and death how to build a healthy society.'[10]

The C.C.H.H. has always attached great importance to that part of its policy which encourages co-operation between the Church and medicine, and particularly on the personal level between GPs and parish clergymen and ministers. In recent years the Council has sponsored a consultation on inter-professional referral at the Reading Postgraduate Medical Centre. It was acknowledged to be useful by those who attended, but it became obvious that the present generation does not find this an easy field of operation, partly as a result of the training which gives to both professions an exaggerated individualism and an expectancy of working within one's own discipline.[11] Hopefully the efforts of the R.C.G.P. and the Theological Colleges will inculcate wider implications of general practice and ministry in future generations. In the meantime it all rests on personal relationships and these are worth working at for the health of society as a whole.

It is possibly in this area that the hospital chaplain can do most to further happy relations between medicine and the Church, which in the end means a relationship on the personal level in each locality.

When we appointed a chaplain to the Selby coalfield, we wrote into his job specification the task of reconciling and interpreting to each other the coal industry and the local parishes and congregations. It is a difficult task but a vital one for the health of the community. Could not this be written into the contract of hospital chaplains, who, it seems to me, stand in a place of some advantage as regards both professions and have a real opportunity of bringing about harmonious and constructive relationships in the hub of the caring community? Many chaplains are parish priests (we linked our coalfield chaplain into a parish team ministry) and therefore begin with the advantage of being part of both the medical and ecclesial communities. Here are men who have the key to unlock the door to a harmonious working together. But possibly the task is at the moment needlessly hard; the first requirement is a re-orientation in the area of training.

4 *Co-operation for the future*

There are many hopeful signs in modern medicine that the emphasis is shifting from the sick patient to the healthy individual, from treating disease to attaining a positive level of health. Eric J. Cassell writes in a recent book, 'seeing their job exclusively as the curing of disease not only prevents physicians from effectively caring for the sick but also reduces their impact on the health of populations.' This is no paradox, he declares, but a description of the present position which, as a physician who is also involved in the field of public health and preventive medicine, he deeply regrets. He therefore pleads that a balancing force to technology in medicine must be restored. He foresees that this will only come 'by a return to a much wider view of the doctor's job, a view that restores healing to its place alongside curing as a trained and disciplined part of the physician's role'.[12] Such voices are welcome and the more there are, the more will they penetrate the innate, conservative thinking of both professions. What is needed in both professional colleges of training is the teaching that, according to the title of Cassell's prologue this is 'a time for healing'. His book is an attempt to separate doctors from their technology and their drugs and instead to view them as healers, for that is surely what they are.

Similar voices are being raised in the churches today where the same atrophying process has blunted the impact of the full time 'professionals'. The way of life in contemporary society has led to innumerable problems. The greatest need that society has therefore thrown up is for problem solvers. Clergymen and ministers are being dragged in as one of the many breeds who fulfil this need. But that is not the reason why the Church is in business. Its commission is to glorify God through the proclamation of the good news of Jesus Christ. Its aim is to do this through preaching, teaching, and healing. Its objectives entail the promotion of health and salvation not only for individuals, but for the whole community, society, the nation. In short, its purpose, like that of true medicine, should be preventive, healing rather than curing, salvation/healing centred rather than sin/disease orientated. It is said that Chinese mandarins used to pay their physicians only so long as they remained well; as soon as any one fell ill, payment ceased. We need to learn the wisdom of this approach, for the caring professions are in business to preserve health. Christians must again learn to *be* the leaven of the world, the new life bubbling up and infecting all around it with the new life of Christ. Structures and life-styles must be changed before the King of Glory can come in. Christians should be working *now* to create a social conscience about all that is best in health education and health prevention and promotion.

What are some of the things that are needful?

i The holistic approach needs to be emphasized in all disciplines and at all levels. High-level specialism has isolated various facets of health care which must be brought together again in order to serve the total health of individuals and the community. Medicine and the churches in particular should give a lead to the nation and influence its decision-makers in a drive towards total health. At the local level, self-help and family and community care should be encouraged. Nationally, those in government should be assisted in making holistic policies which are related to other social policies, and indeed to each other. (For instance, why is only a small budget given to the Health Education Council for a campaign against cigarette smoking, while vast sums are spent on the research and treatment of lung cancer? Is prevention no longer better than cure?)

ii   The widening of the concept of health care will lead to interdisciplinary dialogue and co-operation. It is essential that the seeds of this working together are sown early in the training of all personnel. Ideally, some of the training should be done together so that they get used to the idea of working in co-operation. The aim of total health demands this. All those in training should be taught how to work in teams and in group practice, something still lacking in clergy training. In contrast, after an evening's seminar with young doctors in their vocational training course I was asked why they could not have a priest as a member of their group practice. Demands from the younger generation such as this will hopefully not go unanswered. The subject matter of the training should also be given a more holistic approach. In the training of doctors, it is desirable that emphasis should be placed on preventive medicine, rehabilitation and geriatric care. This will bring doctors into closer contact with other caring agencies in a healing community. They will learn to advise management and trades unions in industry on physical culture, health education, the positive use of leisure, or factory and office breaks for callisthenics. Paramedical personnel must be trained to supervise rehabilitation services and advise the local community on how to cope with this end-stage of treatment, made all the more essential through the increase in numbers of old people owing to advances in medical science. Christians both clerical and lay should undergo practical training in health care along with their tuition in the faith. As we found in the life of Jesus, deed and word always go together. All in the health care business must learn again the art of healing. Treatment is not enough.

iii   The need for paramedical and caring personnel, especially in relation to the handicapped, will increase. 'Tomorrow's health services will be based on teamwork and the growth of the allied health professions.'[13] We are likely to witness an era of the emancipation of the handicapped, but they will need more personally assisted vocational training. Their contribution is that very need for it will bring more people together in order to promote the health of society, and Christians will have the opportunity of giving the lead. The dependence of the sick and handicapped is a source of enrichment to those around them who find themselves having to give. But those who are to give in this way, people who care deeply about the underprivileged and handicapped and chronically sick, will have to be found. Will there be enough people, especially Christians, in communities able to fulfil this need? Far more time and money must be spent on health education in schools to teach children not only to care for themselves but also for others. The Christian capital on which we have been living in the West will not last for ever. There must be a new inculcation of Christlike care and commitment not only for the health of the Church but also for the health of the Health Service and of the nation. Holistic health needs the motivation of the health-Giver.

iv   Part of this health education must be aimed at people of all ages concerning their own wellbeing. The health services have tended to make people lazy about their own health. People expect instant, chemical salvation—and some become angry when they don't receive it! Health is seen as a right, something which someone else is duty bound to dispense. Health education of a quality and quantity not seen before is needed to introduce family medicine and therapy, in which members of the same household are responsible for each other. Much of the increase in stress among the young results from bad parent-child relationships. A responsibility and caring for each other of a new quality would assist in curing that stress. Health education should have an immensely larger slice of the national budget.

v   For the health of the nation, someone—and soon—needs to question the values and goals in our country which are being fed to us by the media. The worst example is the unwritten assumption that good news is no news. A continual diet of bad news is bound adversely to affect the health of the consumer. Possibly a national survey might promote health in this regard as it did in Norway, where no one believed a social survey which found that most Norwegians thought their standard of living was too high. It therefore had to be done again—with the same result. In Britain we are so pressurized to have more and more that there might well be a similar and healthy reaction to being over-pressurized in this way as there was in Norway. It is also interesting to note that in Norway, out of a total population of four million, in four years 20,000 people joined a society called 'Future in our hands' whose object was to make the Norwegian society more participatory. This is also a coming trend in international health and will lead to a necessary re-examination of values and goals. In the meantime it is good that men and women are applying their thought to the inter-relationships between health, the mass media and the N.H.S. in our country, which pose important questions.[14]

vi   The problem posed against the health of each generation since the second world war has been that of nuclear energy. This will gain increasing importance during the next few decades. The W.C.C.-sponsored Ecumenical Hearing on Nuclear Energy (1975) has influenced Christian thinking without emerging with any clear-cut answers: 'Our group cannot put forward categorical recommendations. It would not feel justified in either entirely rejecting, nor in whole-heartedly recommending large-scale use of nuclear energy.' The main general agreement was that nuclear energy would 'be of no avail without a more equitable world economic order'. They sadly declared that a peace based on nuclear deterrence was 'at best precarious' and was 'not that kind of peace we are longing for, when we read in the gospel about peace on earth'.[15] What things (concerning this) belong to man's health? This debate concerns the health of all mankind.

vii   If health is considered as 'a process of dynamic interaction between people and their environments', what is behind the increase of aggression in contemporary life? We even use our motor cars as instruments of aggression. Conflict can be health-productive but how can aggression be contained so that it neither injures the aggressor nor anyone else?[16] Have we begun to think deeply enough about the health-giving (or destroying) properties of the environment? The voice of the medical profession and of the churches has not been heard on this 'interactive process'. Perhaps both have paid too much attention to the individual in their therapy and not enough to the corporate wound of the group which his disease may be articulating.

viii   A more thorough knowledge of environmental hazards is needed and interdisciplinary studies on medical ecology should be engaged in without delay. Otherwise the problems will become too formidable in number and totally insoluble. Noise pollution must be dealt with as well as air and water pollution. The internal combustion engine, especially with the high lead content of English (and only English) petrol, cannot be tolerated for many more years especially in inner cities and areas of housing. The researches of men like John N. Ott[17] of the Environmental Health and Light Research Institute in Florida on the effects of natural and artificial light on man and other living things should be more readily available and be given due publicity by an environmentally-conscious medical profession.

ix   One of the significant models for the future of local health care, influenced by the thought of Ivan Illich among others, is to be seen in a group of nine people in London who have teamed together in an experiment to run a communal care practice. Among them are people who have experience of women's health self-help groups, the medical and therapy worlds, acupuncture and counselling. It is financed in the same way as any general practice and has been going for some three years. An underlying philosophy of the practice is that patients are to be encouraged to take responsibility for their lives and that health and healing is a complex issue, sometimes involving the hospitals but sometimes involving a welter of other areas of life.

Since the new practice started its numbers have risen to 1,500 and patients are encouraged to feel part of it and to help each other as well as learn more about medical care. The day-to-day decisions are taken by the workers' group but on the third Wednesday of every month management collective meetings are open to everyone, when general issues about the practice are discussed: what is being done, how it could be done better. The nine people work part-time; two people are on call, one medical, one non-medical.

Underlying the experiment is an approach to health and healing as a whole person affair, involving the community, the environment, and not only the concern of specialists. The future certainly seems to be in the direction of this more democratic and human approach to medicine, but how many people in how many surgeries are really willing even to begin to look at health issues in this way? How mature as people do we really want to be? How responsible can an individual be in our kind of society? It is greatly to the credit of this group, that despite the pressures against experiment in this field and in British society generally, they have persevered and been willing to bring together various streams of thinking and acting which are at the moment held tightly apart. It shows that it is possible, even within the N.H.S., to adjust the models by which we are operating if we really have the will.

x   Finally, it is the spiritual element which will be the greatest contribution Christians can make to any dialogue with other caring professions. Sometimes in our dialogue with doctors, of which so much more is needed, we parsons try to be amateur psychiatrists. If we are thus qualified, all to the good, but let us first and foremost be men of God, 'chief prayer men', 'a band of men whose hearts God has touched', because we have experienced his power to heal. This goes for all Christians, especially those in the health professions; let us be totally unafraid to be seen as servants of Christ the Healer as we work among his people. So shall we assist our medical colleagues most beneficially and make with them the greater contribution to the nation's health.

am Ramsey.

11
Healing for Society

1 *The shifting scene*

Bishop John Taylor, writing recently to his diocese of Winchester, declared that he had sensed for a long time a profound change taking place in the consciousness of mankind. 'It is one of those mutations of the human personality which seem to happen at rare points in history—a shift of balance, of emphasis, of direction.' He perceived certain shifts in emphasis in contemporary life, among others those

> from submission to routine towards awareness of purpose, from passivity under authority towards collaboration and co-responsibility, from individual, self-regarding activity to corporate and social activity, from policies dictated from above to *ad hoc* decisions based on shared experience, from an over-riding preference for order to a belief in the creativity of conflict.

Others have similarly commented on this change and attempted some analysis. James Robertson marks out certain signposts to a self-fulfilling future in a thought-provoking work which pleads for what he calls an equilibrium economy.[1] This he calls the Sane, Humane and Ecological (SHE) Future. It is a plea to change direction in the belief that 'the key to the future is not continuing expansion but balance—balance within ourselves, balance between ourselves and other people, balance between people and nature.' It is the social and psychological, not the technical and economic, that is the way to future expansion. There needs to be a real drive towards 'learning to live supportively with one another on our small and crowded planet. This will involve decentralization, not further centralization.' It was E. F. Schumacher who told us we should have to rethink economics 'as if people mattered', the seldom-quoted subtitle of his oft-quoted book *Small is Beautiful.*[2]

Robertson sees this change of direction as a transformation, an essential part of which will be certain 'paradigm shifts', by which he means changes that take place from time to time 'in a basic belief or assumption underlying our perceptions and actions'. These he foresees as changing the emphasis away 'from the overdeveloped, structured, exterior aspects of life towards the under-developed, unstructured, interior aspects'. As examples he sees the transformation as entailing paradigm shifts

> from scientific and academic knowledge to intuitive understanding; from representative politics and bureaucratic government to community politics and direct democracy; from the institutional economy based on money and jobs to the gift and barter economy of households and local communities; from an arm's length relationship between professionals and their clients to a personally shared experience; from institutionalized social services to caring personal relationships; from organized religious activity and codified religious doctrines to personal spiritual experience.

I have quoted his ideas of the paradigm shifts at length for their general interest, but it is the last three which have a particular relevance to our purpose. In the case of the shift from professional relationships to shared experience he sees 'teaching and healing' as the key ideas. Of course it is far easier to have a professional relationship, to keep the person you are trying to help at arm's length, to prevent them from 'getting under your skin', in short, to keep the whole problem and the 'other' person externalized. The real question is whether a person can be assisted 'at arm's length', in a professional-client relationship. It helps the professional to reach for the prescription pad or say a formal prayer and get on with the next client, but how much it assists the client is anybody's guess. If those of us in the caring professions are really honest, we *know* that the people we have been able to help most have been those with whom we have identified as person to person and spent time with, listening patiently and diligently to what they are really saying and then possibly opening up with a personal experience of our own to demonstrate 'I have been there too'. In the field of Christian counselling it is the shared experience method that affords the deepest help. Shared prayer is then the natural outcome, as the whole situation is laid at the feet 'of him with whom *we* have to do'.

Given the hierarchical consciousness and system of conducting ourselves that we have inherited, certainly in the churches and I

179

suspect in all the caring professions, as one of the many legacies of the Roman Empire (the system has had the Church by the throat since the era of Constantine), it is indeed going to demand a deal of 'teaching and healing' before we can enjoy the shared experience syndrome, such as we find for instance in the primitive Christian community. There has to be much unlearning before the teaching and healing can enable this paradigm shift.[3]

It is my conviction that the renewal of the healing ministry is one of God's many gifts to his Church at this time that will enable this to happen. God is teaching us how to use, and be channels of, his power again. As well as being most exciting, it is proving most humbling, for every meeting before him is a shared experience: it is he who gives the power and both helper and helped are its recipients. The helper (a good biblical word, placed between healers and administrators in Paul's list of God's gifts to his Church at 1 Cor. 12.28), is just as much in the learning and healing situation as the helped in what can only, and truly, be termed a shared experience. It is when both helper and helped can open up to the Lord in prayer before and with each other that the 'Go-Between God' can bring his healing into the situation, so that both become 'the helped' by *the* Helper, *the* Advocate, who can then 'heal' them both into the wider therapeutic community, 'the fellowship of the Holy Spirit'.[4]

I have used the example of the milieu I know best, but this paradigm shift is obviously evolving in the political and economic fields where governing and governed are struggling to find a new concept of power-sharing. For the health of society it is apparent that men and women, who are rendered unhappy in work because of top-heavy superstructures, should become more involved in power-sharing through group participation and other means. They are sitting loose to the structures today because they see them as obstructing personal experience and this is an age which sets great store by the experiential. This is an area in which the Church can make a contribution to the future, showing by its own life of shared experience the way to a new paradigm of work for which men and women will no longer be dependent on an employing institution but will rather participate in defining, creating, and organizing their work themselves in a sharing experience. It is not beyond the ability of man to adapt to this new way of living; he has made longer leaps in the dark ages of the past. But it will require unlearning and re-learning, and healing for himself and the new evolving society.

The shift from 'institutionalized social services to caring personal relationships' will follow the same trend. The key ideas of 'welfare and care' have been well sown by the institution and for this we should be grateful. The N.H.S. was and is a great idea, but once ideas become institutionalized they become locked in an inertia of vested interests and power struggles. However, as Keynes said, 'The power of vested interests is vastly exaggerated, compared with the gradual encroachment of (new) ideas', and the new idea which is gripping many of the younger generation is 'how pleasant and joyful a thing it is to dwell together in unity' with the underprivileged and handicapped, the sick and the aged. The young are essentially a caring generation who will not be content to leave all the caring to the institution, but will forge caring personal relationships for themselves. This is one reason why they are seen to be rebelling against the institution: it has become too impersonal, too efficient if you like, too faceless. The welfare and care of the future will wear a more human face as the richness of personal relationships is tasted and enjoyed.

The evidence for this new 'feeling' among the young is easy to find. Many schools have initiated welfare schemes for the elderly. The young usually go far beyond the course of duty in these schemes and spend much of their spare time in forging these relationships. They belong to a generation that is becoming increasingly caring and concerned for the underprivileged, especially in the Third World. Throughout the world the new generation is politically and socially conscious. At home hospital visiting is becoming a leisure time activity. During a confirmation reunion and refresher week-end, a desire that was expressed most strongly was to do regular hospital visiting instead of one of their weeknight meetings for fellowship with each other. They had tasted the benefit of caring relationships outside their immediate Christian community which they experienced as an enrichment to the life of their community as well as to themselves. They are proving the dictum of Bishop Michael Ramsey, 'the Church which lives to itself will die by itself', to be profoundly true locally as well as nationally.

Robertson's final paradigm shift was that 'from organized religious activity and codified religious doctrines to personal spiritual experience', and he linked it with the key ideas of 'religious ministries and spiritual communion'. The disenchantment with dogmatic and over-institutionalized religion is manifest in the world today. The Beatles were among the first to turn the younger generation's eyes towards the East. Many have followed in their wake.[5] They were searching for a spiritual liberation which they were unable to find in Western Christianity. As David Edwards puts it in a comment on the post-Constantinian era, 'One disastrous aspect of the complex fact of Christendom was that Roman methods of law-definition and law-enforcement were applied to religion. It was as suitable as feeding a baby with a bayonet;' and again 'What made the orthodoxy enacted at those Councils (of the Church) spiritually disastrous was that it was gradually enforced by methods which would have aroused abhorrence in the first Christians.' The health-giving light of real 'religious ministry' and 'spiritual communion' was kept burnished by many holy men and women down the centuries, who were children of the Church, but as David Edwards again points out,

> when a twentieth-century layman looks at the record of Christianity (as Paul Johnson in his *History of Christianity* 1976 and Bamber Gascoigne in his *The Christians* 1977 have recently done) this dogmatism is what he is most likely to notice. And if he does identify Christianity with that spirit . . . he is likely to conclude that this religion is greatly inferior to other movements of thought. . . . It was inevitable that such a religion should fail to satisfy the deepest religious instincts and the highest moral aspirations.[6]

It is hardly surprising that many today, within and without the churches, have turned to the meditation techniques of the East, for example, Zen or Yoga, which do not depend on dogmas and which offer the aspirant peace of mind, renewal of spirit, and health of body. Some of the schools of meditation are in the big time, like Transcendental Meditation which can afford to provide the stateliest of stately homes for its adherents to practise their art.

Undoubtedly the Christian Church of the West is in need of spiritual enrichment in order to make the contribution to the health of society which it alone can make. Some of this will undoubtedly, and should be, found in the spiritual riches of the great Eastern religions, but ultimately the necessary spiritual resources must be found within its own tradition. This was the decision T. S. Eliot made, for although he remained fascinated by the inner peace of Buddhism (cf. his *Four Quartets*), he identified totally with Western Christianity. The Church in the West must bring again the riches of Christ to its progeny, the science-orientated, urbanized, industrialized, technologically-imprisoned, civilization of the western and northern hemisphere: the progeny, if it knows the things that belong to its health, must for its part face up to the challenge of Christianity, above all to its central figure, Christ the Healer. It could do worse than begin with the groping, humble, and yet magnificent response of Dag Hammarskjöld, Secretary General of the United Nations, who just before his untimely death made this entry in his spiritual diary:

> I don't know Who—or What—put the question, I don't know when it was put. I don't even remember answering. But at some moment I did answer *Yes* to Someone—or Something—and from that hour I was certain that existence is meaningful and that therefore my life, in self-surrender, had a goal.[7]

It is this 'goal', this response to the centre of all existence—call it Someone, or Something, or God—which Carl Jüng saw was vital (*sic*) to the life and health of human beings. Once that contact is lost, there is a situation of un-health. Once it is regained, health for society is more than a possibility. True healing requires an experience of the numinous.

2 *Resources available to Society*

How is the Church preparing to make the contributions to the health of society which it is vital for it to make? What is the present temperature of its spiritual resources? An external observer would have cause to be pessimistic. Centuries of dogmatism, and worse still the in-fighting to hold positions some of which were untenable, has left a Church in schism. Three quarters of a century of ecumenical movement has made great strides towards the healing of the situation, but a state of disunity prevails in the Church, which is bound to blunt the outward thrust of its evangelistic work (its *raison d'être*) and diminish its spirituality. Successive generations have added encrustations of institutional over-weighting and though a new breeze is eroding some of the outer layers, the structure still dominates, while some of the more important spiritual priorities are lost in its shadow.

The Church however is part of the world and its members are numbered among the human race (despite some of their critics!) and that very shift in consciousness we have been discussing is taking place in the Church also—and globally. To at least one observer from the inside a similar 'mutation' to that which happened after the Babylonian Exile to the Jewish nation, foreseen by Jeremiah (31.31ff) in his new covenant prophecy, and especially by Ezekiel (36.26ff) who 'sat' with them in the Exile, and the spiritually perceptive Deutero-Isaiah, whose great message also came to birth amid the same privations and suffering—a similar new consciousness to that which happened to the early Christians post-Easter and post-Pentecost, is happening to the Church today. This is no arrogant claim but a humble admission of fact. It is happening *to* us; we are not initiating it. The causes can be argued over, the manifestations examined, but it is still there. It seems that the global Church is undergoing a recharging of its spiritual batteries, presumably to equip it for bringing health and healing to society; and to the nations, for as William Temple reminded us (rather more poetically) we are only in business for the outsider. The Spirit is blowing its health-giving balm upon the rigid structures and has moved us on in ways which twenty years ago would not have been contemplated. Perhaps it was the prayer of that great and holy man of our century, good Pope John XXIII, which he prayed on the eve of Vatican II, 'O Holy Spirit, renew your wonders in this our day, as by a new Pentecost', which, as Cardinal Suenens declared 'opened a few windows in the upper room and let in the first breeze of springtime'.[8] Whatever may have been the cause, renewal is a fact of our time. As Robert E. Terwilliger puts it:

> God has been disturbing his Church again. He has made us think anxiously about him . . . . Now, for a season, has come an outpouring of new assurance to many Christians who have found a repossession of faith. Once again Jesus Christ and the Holy Spirit are vivid in the consciousness of Christians. It is possible to sense that in all of this we are in the grip of a divine action to which we must respond, alive and alert to its meaning. Christ is being made known to us by the Spirit; the Charismatic

Christ is being revealed in the mind and heart of the Church. This is theology in its deepest sense; this is the knowledge of God.[9]

What are some of the key factors of this renewal? Firstly, no Christian can deny that 'we are in the grip of a divine action'. This 'movement' has not come about because of human effort, a campaign or mission or programme for revival. It is happening— and I say this as a bishop who is called upon to minister in various parts of England—*before we get there*. We should not of course be surprised that God is on ahead; he always is as Moses learned at the burning bush.[10] The fact is that renewal is taking place in our time whether it be in a cathedral inspired to give a new lead to the life of the church at the centre of a diocese, in a college chapel whose worship has come alive because of disclosure moments given to individuals in praying groups, in a crowded city church known for its 'charismatic' renewal, or in any amount of small village churches where a new consciousness of the living Christ has gripped the congregation and is sending it about its business with renewed vigour. As Terwilliger commented, our obligation is to 'respond, alive and alert to its meaning'.

Secondly, it was noticeable at the 1978 Lambeth Conference, that the provinces of the Anglican Communion which had undergone the deepest renewal were those which were under political or social pressure, or were actually suffering persecution. For instance, a deep Christian love and joy and peace radiated from the leaders of a church, the political masters of whose country were attempting to divide the ethnic groups. The leaders of another church, under persecution, were filled with thankfulness and joy, as were the Apostles after their suffering (Acts 5.41). Renewal is both a sign to the Church that God has a great purpose for it to accomplish and the provision of the necessary spiritual fibre with which to accomplish it. It is also a warning that it must be ready. 'To whom much is given, of him will much be required' (Luke 12.48).

Thirdly, the renewal in the Church is an expression of God's will for his creation. He wills his Kingdom to come; he wills his creation to be healed. In short his will is health for man, that wholeness with which he sees us equipped in anticipation of his coming. The renewal movement in the Church has given Christians a new

185

consciousness of health and healing, expressed in a new caring for others as well as for their own physical and spiritual health. It is this action of God—for it is certainly far beyond our capabilities—which holds the greatest hope not only for the Church but for society and the world in our time.

There are of course facets of the Church's life which seem counterproductive to its health and apparently diminish the contribution it is able to make to the health of society. It is very hard for a Church in schism itself to bring a deep healing to society, whose reply 'Physician, heal thyself' can be readily anticipated. But what is the real divide in the Church today? I suggest it is not so much the traditional, denominational divide as instanced by the broad categories Catholic and Protestant, but rather a more personal division within each traditional grouping between those who seek to hand on the tradition unimpaired and those who desire to pioneer new ways, in ministry and liturgy for instance, in short between the conservative and the radical. The Church is undoubtedly suffering internal agony over such issues as women and the priesthood, and even over its liturgy, and these very issues tend to draw the lines of division across each denomination at this point rather than between them. May not this very division within the Church be a resource for the health of society, a way of showing the deep creativity latent in apparent conflict? Society is also in schism, deeply divided between those on the one hand who refuse to acknowledge evolutionary global trends as instanced in the 'mutations of the human personality' (John Taylor) or the 'paradigm shifts' (James Robertson), who are by nature afraid to make any leap into the dark unknown and who therefore cling, sometimes at any price, to the status quo: and between those on the other who, conscious or unconscious of mutation shifts or trends, wish to change the structures of society (or demolish them) and seek a different and better future than the past which they reject as meaningless, barren and wrong. Before anyone writes off the latter as wreckers and purveyors of dis-ease, it might be well to recall some words of Pope John XXIII in his opening address to the Second Vatican Council he had called:

> We are shocked to discover what is being said by some people who, though they may be fired by religious zeal, are without justice, or good judgment, or consideration in their way of

186

looking at matters. In the existing state of society they see nothing but ruin and calamity. They are in the habit of saying that our age is much worse than past centuries. They behave as though history, which teaches us about life, has nothing to teach them . . . . It seems to us necessary to express our complete disagreement with these prophets of doom, who give us news only of catastrophes, as though the world were nearing its end. . . . On the contrary, we should recognize that, at the present historical moment, Divine Providence is leading us towards a new order in human relationships, which, through the agency of men and, what is more, above and beyond their own expectations, are tending towards the fulfilment of higher and, as yet, mysterious and unforeseen designs. Everything, even those events which seem to conflict with her purposes, is ordered for the greater well-being of the church. [11]

If that was true in the early sixties it is even more true today, and not only of the Church, for God always works on a cosmic scale. His health is for all his people. The conflicts which are working themselves out creatively in the Church are reflections of the universal strivings of mankind. What is important is that the Church should be able so to believe in and use the power of the living God for its own health that it is able to contribute positively and creatively to the health of mankind. Here the healing movement has a great part to play for the eyes of the Church must be kept focused on the healing Christ at a time in history when he has so much to do and say. The movement has shown throughout this century the blessings of a positive response to the Christ who heals not only individuals but congregations and whole communities. More even than that, it has been used by Christ to gather in his 'other sheep', for it has met those outside the churches *at the point of their need*—where he met them. It has been like 'the patrol of an army': now, once again in Randall Davidson's words, 'the main body' must venture forth with its response. For the greatest blessing to the health of society today would be the total, corporate response by the Church catholic to the renewing power of Christ, present to heal. 'We are in the grip of a divine action to which we must respond, alive and alert to its meaning; Christ is being made known to us by the Spirit.' The power of the Lord does not change. We must; for the health of society, and for the glory of God; and in the changing we shall experience a transfiguration from glory to glory and so discover a new dimension of Christian unity—in Christ.

3 *Initiatives for health in Society and the Church*

One of the most interesting exercises recently undertaken by the C.C.H.H. has been the compilation of a directory of caring agencies in the field of health and healing.[12] The result showed that there are very many people involved in a large variety of bodies whose aim is to promote health in society. The agencies which are statutory or in some way connected with the N.H.S. begin a long list. They include the 228 Community Health Councils in England and Wales, 195 of which are affiliated to the central Association. The Therapeutic Community viewpoint has an Association, as do the Environmental Health Officers (6,000 members) and Nurse Administrators. Our concern for mental health is reflected in an All Party Parliamentary Health Group—'a voice in Parliament for mentally ill and mentally handicapped people'—while in 1975 a National Development Group for the Mentally Handicapped was set up. The B.M.A. has a membership of 64,000 doctors at home and overseas. Founded in 1832 it is now a registered trade union. There are also all the Royal Colleges. There is a slowly increasing number (at last) of agencies concerned with Health Education, including the Health Education Council itself. The Hospice movement has grown rapidly since its inception. Dr Cicely Saunders has been the inspiration to many in the profession who now care devotedly in an open and Christian way for the terminally ill.

There are many national organizations which may have charitable status or be more or less closely linked with other, even statutory, official bodies. Some of these are household names and have a fine record of devoted service: the Samaritans (1953) the National Marriage Guidance Counc.. (1938), the Tavistock Clinic (1920), or Age Concern England (1940). Many are devoted to serving the mentally or physically handicapped, like MIND formed out of three voluntary associations in 1946, the National Society for Mentally Handicapped Children formed soon afterwards, the Royal Association for Disability and Rehabilitation with more than

400 member organizations, or Sesame (1964). There are national associations of many workers in the field of health such as Social Workers, Counsellors, Jungian analysts, medical research workers, or osteopaths. Some societies have been founded to assist those with particular problems: SCODA (1971)—drugs; AA (1947: 1935 in the U.S.A.)—alcohol; ASH (1971)—smoking; Victims of Violence, which speaks for itself; or Gingerbread (1970), an association for one-parent families, with 400 groups in the U.K. Other groups care for depressives, autistic children, the widowed and their children, those about to retire, sufferers from migraine, or with the problem of rehabilitation (the Richmond Fellowship whose specialism is the provision of half-way houses). Others again are in the preventive area of health: Family Planning, the Royal Society for the Prevention of Accidents (whose ancestry goes back to 1916), the Noise Abatement Society (1959), and especially the Friends of the Earth, founded in the early seventies. There is some organization geared to care for most areas of our national life and health.

When it comes to the specifically Christian caring agencies, the list becomes even more formidable, as might have been expected. Most of the mainstream churches have a national health and healing group, though curiously enough the two exceptions are the Church of England and the Roman Catholic Church, though the former has several fellowships of health and healing at diocesan level, while the latter is open to the healing movement. The Church of Ireland has a well-organized ministry (1932) accountable to its General Synod and there is also an ecumenical Council (1965) centred in Belfast. In Scotland there are two ecumenical agencies, the Christian Fellowship of Healing (1957) and the Divine Healing Fellowship (1971). In England there are the ecumenical fellowships: the Guild of Health (1904), the Divine Healing Mission (1905), and the Anglican Guild of St Raphael (1915), as well as at least twenty homes of healing such as Burrswood, where the medical profession and the churches work together, Crowhurst, the headquarters of the Divine Healing Mission (both of them near the Kent/Sussex border), Green Pastures, etc. There are also Communities dedicated to the furtherance of health and healing such as the Glencree Reconciliation Centre and the Corrymeela Community (dedicated to work for reconciliation in Ireland), the Iona Community (founded by George MacLeod in 1938; weekly healing services are held in the Abbey Church on the island), or the Barnabas Fellowship (1971) in Dorset. There are innumerable centres for pastoral care and counselling, some members of the Association, others centred on local churches or Christian groups among which might be mentioned a Roman Catholic foundation, the Dympna Centre (1971), now ecumenical, specially for the assistance of Christian ministers, and also the St Columba centre in Cambridge, the St Barnabas Centre in Norwich, and others in York, Redditch, and many of the larger cities. The researches of Dr Frank Lake have created a discipline on its own in this sector of healing and led to the founding of the Clinical Theology Association. There are Christian agencies for young people away from home (Message Home 1976), rehabilitation (Coke Hole Trust 1962), alcoholics and drug addicts and various other forms of stress. There are also many agencies who are pioneering new ways or are more or less on their own and of which it would be good to see more in the field. Such are the Relaxation Society at St Mary Woolnoth founded in the mid-seventies by Geoffrey Harding who did a great work as secretary of C.C.H.H. for many years; the Newcastle and District Healing Centre (1965) whose aim is to give expert psychiatric and spiritual help; the Oxford Institute for Church and Society (1975) concerned with the relationship between Christian faith and society and specializing in the health field; and the Chaplain's Department, Royal Edinburgh Hospital, whose aim is the working out of an effective means of communication between the psychiatric services in hospital and in the community with the churches and related agencies. All these, it must be emphasized, are specific agents of caring *in addition to* the day-to-day work for health and healing carried out both by the churches' full time and part time workers, clerical and lay. Measured in business terms the churches are major multi-nationals in the sector of health and healing. This is the very reason for which they are in business.

There are more, some very large, organizations, too numerable to mention. Some are concerned with training or education, others with research, such as the Grubb Institute of Behavioural Studies (1969). Others again are involved in international co-operation, for example the Ciba Foundation (1947). The literature on the whole subject is vast, many of the above agencies producing their own magazine and/or other publications. There is indeed an exploding world of healing. Finally, among the vast number of organizations

I have not even begun to mention I want to end with just one whose aims seem particularly relevant to our purpose and highly commendable. It is appropriately named 'Health for the New Age'. It is international, a charitable trust and was formed in 1978. Its aim is:

To improve the quality of life in society by:

1 Re-introducing the human touch, compassion, and continuing relationships into the health care system.

2 Helping people to understand and accept responsibility for themselves and their health, and to develop and use their abilities by means of Positive Health Education.

3 Integrating conventional and unconventional therapies into a form of health care which deals with the whole person, within a caring community, based on a 'Community Positive Health Centre', where the first priority will be the promotion of positive health.

Such intentions 'are not far from the Kingdom of God', and society is well served by health agencies with such ideals. It should be but a small step from there to the health that is God's will for his creation and to being in the way of his healing power which alone can effect his purpose. But there are deep sicknesses and diseases from which contemporary man is suffering and much of our therapy is only a treatment of the symptoms. Only a deep ministry can touch the hurts that a war-torn century has inflicted on the inner being of man.

12

Healing for mankind and glory for God

1 *Transfiguration, healing and glory*

On the sixth day of August, in the year of our Lord nineteen hundred and forty-five, the Western powers dropped the atomic bomb on Hiroshima. The discussion on the moral justification and implications of such an act will continue while man possesses a moral sense; the decision must have been agonizing. What seems to have escaped the notice of most people at the time and certainly of those who took the decision was that the day chosen was the date traditionally set aside by the Church to commemorate the trans-figuration of our Lord. Perhaps this instance of insensitivity was because the West has never given the same recognition to the festival as the East. In the Eastern Orthodox Church it has a rank in the calendar equal with Christmas, Epiphany, Ascension and Pentecost; Easter alone has the primacy. Be that as it may, the event of that day in 1945 and the keeping of such a festival strikes a jarring note in the inner being of caring men. It is an event from which we all need healing.

The story of the transfiguration, recorded in all three synoptic Gospels, has fired the imagination of Christians down the ages and tested the ingenuity of scholarship. As Bishop Michael Ramsey once wrote:

> It stands as a gateway to the saving events of the Gospel, and is as a mirror in which the Christian mystery is seen in its unity. Here we perceive that the living and the dead are one in Christ, that the old covenant and the new are inseparable, that the Cross and the glory are of one, that the age to come is already here, that our human nature has a destiny of glory, that in Christ the final word is uttered and in Him alone the Father is well pleased. Here the diverse elements in the theology of the New Testament meet. [1]

The transfiguration has been used as a model for con-templation[2] as well as for revolution and politics.[3] I suggest that it is also a helpful model for healing. As Bishop Ramsey said, it is an

192

event that brings all things together—the living and the dead, the old and the new, suffering and glory, the age to come and the present, the human and the divine. I propose to use the transfiguration as a model for healing just as Fr Slade used it as a model for contemplation. He was inspired to do this by some words of William Temple in his *Readings in St John's Gospel*:

> As we read the story, though it all happened long ago, we apprehend present fact. It is not only the record of a historical episode that we read; it is the self-expression of that God in whom we live and move and have our being; so that whatever finds expression there is true now . . . . Our reading of the Gospel story can and should be an act of personal Communion with the living God.[4]

This is significantly true of the transfiguration and to have 'personal communion with the living God' is healing indeed. May 'whatever finds expression there (be) true now'. (The accounts may be read at Mark 9. 2–8, Matt. 17. 1–8, and Luke 9. 28–36 and should be 'digested' in their context.)

The context is in fact of supreme importance. The messianic secret has just 'exploded' at Caesarea Philippi but is followed by Jesus' prediction of his passion. Then comes the transfiguration. Immediately it is followed by conflict and healing (the epileptic boy) and all leads up to the 'exodus', the saving event of the death/resurrection. The transfiguration is like 'a watershed in the ministry of Jesus . . . a height from which the reader looks down on one side upon the Galilean ministry and on the other side upon the *Via Crucis*'.[5] As such it is a unique vantage point from which to view the life and work of the healing Christ. He is the central figure, the Christ of God, and alone gives authenticity to the use of the story as a healing model.

Like Caesar's Gaul, the story falls conveniently into three sections: the preparation, the transfiguration event and the results.

a The preparation

Uppermost in the consciousness of the disciples as they began the ascent of the mountain were two facts impressed upon them in the previous week: Jesus was the Messiah and the Messiah must suffer. This was the preparation of their mind, the first essential when we are to embark on a major happening in our life, whether it be marriage (the making of two lives as one) or the undergoing of an operation (which may possibly mean the removal of some part of the body for the good of the whole). Significant points of growth in our lives need some preparatory mental readjustment and a thinking through. Many people remain unhealthy because they have not made this initial mental preparation, especially in the case of marriage. All growth demands an initial growing in the mind.

The heart as centre of the emotions also needs preparation. Peter had spoken for them all in his confession of faith at Caesarea Philippi, and all now acknowledged Jesus as their leader. They had a commitment to him—personally. They learned what this commitment would mean—the denial of self and the taking up of the cross, 'for whoever would save his life will lose it; and whoever loses his life for my sake and the gospel's will save it. For what does it profit a man, to gain the whole world and forfeit his life?' (Mark 8.35f). These would be the demands on the disciples from which no one would be exempt. It would be a life of self-denial and unswerving perseverance. It would involve being taken away from the ordinary environment, the familiar landmarks of life, to a 'strange land', where the commitment would be tested. Again this is a necessary part of the preparation and much of the emotional disturbance which is part of modern life might well have been avoided by a simple preparation of the heart, some basic emotional adjustments to what life would inevitably mean if a commitment was given to a person, to a job, to a move far away from home, to a way of life.

Again, Jesus called them to share the experience by climbing a mountain. The body also needed preparation by some physical training. They had already had a preliminary physical preparation: they had left the security and comfort of home and joined the Master who had 'nowhere to lay his head'. This is not to say however that Jesus treated the body casually. On the contrary he invariably stressed the importance of it, both in relation to himself, for he was always a person within himself, whose every movement spoke of meaningful intention, whose very stillness was evocative of a unique power that was highly disciplined and supremely under control; and also in relation to others, for he spent a large part of his time (as we have already seen) in healing the sick and renewing the diseased faculties of men and women. The body is important as Peter, James, and John learned, for it was their only vehicle to take them up the mountain. This 'embryo destined for future development' also had to be adjusted for the tasks and growth that lay ahead. We are not much good with unhealthy bodies; our machines cannot take us everywhere. Physical fitness is important when seen as a means to an end—the experience of God. It is the only vehicle we have with which to share that experience. The stewardship of our body is an important step on the way to healing. Peter found in the transfiguration experience that his body was also spiritually important; overshadowed by the cloud, it picked up the sight and sound of the divine glory: 'We were eyewitnesses of his majesty. For when he received honour and glory from God the Father and the voice was borne to him by the Majestic Glory, "This is my beloved Son, with whom I am well pleased," we heard this voice borne from heaven, for we were with him on the holy mountain' (2 Peter 1.16–18). Brother Ass is not to be treated with disrespect. He is the vehicle for the mind and the heart.

Another lesson in the preparation is derived from the notion that man is part of a family. Jesus was surrounded by his earthly family, the company of disciples, from whom he had selected twelve. Now he was to select three. This was the effective size for sharing the experience. It is a warning against growing too large by becoming institutionalized or rigid about numbers or organization. The healed and healing family has to be small, adaptable, responsive to change, and without the rules and conventions which 'bind' together natural families. As the transfiguration experience showed, any attempt to make this family permanent, let alone to set up house, would be disastrous. (Jesus ignored Peter's suggestion about the tents.) The family is too large when our Lord ceases to be at the centre. The only healing then must be fragmentation. Jesus knew the effective size of a family. Apparently it can be shown that thirteen is the maximum number of balls of the same diameter which can be arranged so that each one touches both the other and the centre. To be healed, each member of the family must be able to share a rich corporate life in Christ. Families are made by a freedom to grow into the head, surrounded by fatherly love and with room for the free play of the spirit. They must also move as a unit. This nuclear family of the four, Jesus and the three disciples, went up the mountain together in preparation for the transfiguration experience. They did not ask to be left behind. Probably the other nine were disappointed at having to remain on the plain. But today, there are still too many members of the Christian family who positively wish to remain at the foot of the mountain, albeit absorbed in good works. This leads to the dissipation of the family energies, fruitlessly employed on peripheral concerns which distract from spiritual priorities. The divine presence is thus concealed: the world of men remains unhealed.

With regard to the preparation, one final point is of interest. It has often been said that the Bible speaks of a God who breathes. The common meaning of breath/wind/spirit to be found in the Hebrew word *ruach* lends emphasis to the importance of our human breath. It was seen by the Jews as the outward expression of the life-force inherent in all human behaviour because of the movement of air it involves. Climbers, like singers and those who play wind instruments, have to know how to use and control this 'life-force', both in the inhalation as well as in the suspension (or holding) and exhalation of the breath. Fr Slade talks of the cleansing work made possible by breathing in harmony with the rhythms of the Spirit. 'Inhaling the Spirit', he says, 'is a process of drawing the Spirit into the centres of the body . . . . As this is done we can think of ourselves as a potential mount of Transfiguration, waiting to be renewed and made glorious.' As he points out, climbing is a technique which enhances the ability to inhale, because the good climber's body is upright and he is compelled to use the abdominal muscles for drawing in the breath. In suspending our breathing we can direct the Spirit's energy to particular places in the centres of our body, or, in prayer, to special places and people. Exhaling is the direction of 'the out-breath to a point where (the Spirit's) healing and cleansing work is needed'.[6] This may be in ourselves, at some particular part of our body or life, or it may be in others where we then share in the healing movement of the Spirit as he hovers over the person or place which needs healing. It is this training in breathing, aided by such spiritual disciplines as the recitation of the psalter in the Office, which can bring healing into our life's activities and decision-making, for we learn to pause for breath before and after every decision we take and all we do. This gives an opportunity for the Spirit to speak and be the helper and guide in our life.

b The transfiguration event

The selected nucleus, after their mental, emotional, and physical preparation, arrived at a point at which they were permitted to penetrate the spiritual world. The initiative was with God: it always is, something we are slow to learn. Our role is to respond. Jesus is transfigured and they are given an insight into the resurrection life of glory. It is a moment of supreme awareness with the cosmic Christ at the centre and heart of all creation. As for Isaiah the son of Amoz, so for them the first impression was of their own inadequacy and humanity, of their own unworthiness and unfitness for such an experience. Peter 'did not know what to say, for they were exceedingly afraid' (Mark 9.6). They were after all very ordinary human beings, not very holy, not very brilliant, somewhat unimportant; they were types of everyman. The lesson God gives in the transfiguration event however, as in many of his dealings with man, is that his strength is made perfect in weakness. For St Paul the revelation came through a sickness (see page 91). To the chosen three it came in the contrast between the revelation of perfect wholeness, that of a healed person, seen in the glory of Christ, and their own weakness. This was the function of the cloud, to absorb all weakness in the divine strength, to take up the humanity into the divinity, to remove all that normally obstructs the human faculties so that a direct experience of glory and healing could be enjoyed. It is the experience of 'Jesus only'. This is the transforming into health: this is the transfiguration event.

The vision transformed all who took part in it. Our Lord was revealed in his glory to come, the disciples were healed as their weakness became charged with his strength, creation was clothed with the presence of God (the *shekinah*), and the infinite world was penetrated as Jesus held converse with Moses and Elijah. The vision was in fact one of true reconciliation and healing as the law of religion (Moses) met with the law of spiritual freedom and the whole prophetic tradition (Elijah) with Jesus in the midst, through whom God chose to reconcile all things. Peter's attempt to cling to this moment of reconciliation was ignored. The Spirit of movement blows as and where he wills and our role is to be ready, to respond and move on. 'Tell the people of Israel to go forward' (Exodus 14.15) was the order that preceded the mighty work of the old covenant. It is the message which if heeded will lead to a healthier

197

world today. God is always on ahead, beckoning us on. It is not for our health to look back as Lot's wife found out. The two laws as represented by Moses and Elijah will find the healing of their conflict in Jesus only. For the most part, and possibly for our health, as we have got to learn in the ecumenical movement, a creative tension is the order of things. The Church today is feeling the pressure of 'Elijah' on 'Moses' as the charismatic element seeks room for movement among the traditional. In the transfiguration event Jesus conversed with them both, or as Mark precisely says, both were talking to Jesus. We have to learn that the creative use of conflict is a wholesome and necessary part of healing. The point of tension in Jesus' ministry was frequently his dealings and relationship with the Pharisees. They stood for the law of religion while Jesus stood for spiritual freedom, though it was the genius of Jesus to fulfil both. On the mount of transfiguration the confrontation takes place once more, but with Jesus as the observer with whom both converse, whom both can serve. Luke adds a note on the subject of their conversation: it was the exodus, the way forward, which Jesus was to accomplish at Jerusalem—in a word, his death. This was to be the supreme healing. 'By his stripes we are healed.' This was the ultimate in transfiguring glory. The mighty event of the new covenant is the harbinger of healing for all creation.

The transfiguration event underlines the necessity of Jesus being in the midst. It also clearly demonstrates that not only weak human beings can be sharers in the glory and healing of the cosmic Christ. He is able to use any channel for his power and that healing and transfiguring power can also shine through a distorted universe, through a world in conflict, and still reveal the glory of God. The treasure can be had in frail earthen vessels: the glory can shine in the barren wastes of our wraths and sorrows.

The appearance of Moses and Elijah also makes luminously clear the unity of the material and spiritual world. God is a God of the living and all are present to him—on both sides of the grave. There is no middle wall of partition between the living and the dead. All are one in the transfiguring power of their Creator. In the death of Jesus the power of sin has been broken and the Christian delivered from the vicious circle of sin and death. This healing has made him a new creation in Christ: the old life has passed away, the new has come (2 Cor. 5.17). And the essence of this new life in Christ is that it is all of a piece, whole, eternal, shared by all the redeemed. This is a fact not grasped by very many Christians who feel cut off, parted from those they have loved in this life. They are not looking for the resurrection of the dead and the life of the world to come even though they profess it in worship. Here is a wound which for many needs healing. It is being exacerbated in our contemporary life by the wholesale abortions and crimes of violence. We are storing up for ourselves epidemics of dis-ease unless we are healed into a right relationship with our dead. Only the transfiguring radiance of the presence of Jesus can heal this wound of separation, which is not final or permanent, as St Paul knew for himself: 'If we live, we live to the Lord, and if we die, we die to the Lord; so then, whether we live or whether we die, we are the Lord's' (Rom. 14.8). That transfiguring radiance is experienced by Christians in the Eucharist, the sacrament of healing between us and our dead, in which we become one communion 'with angels and archangels and with all the company of heaven'. It is for this healing in the sacrament that Christians have continued to hunger and thirst down the ages and have gone away nourished with the Bread of Life and the Vine of Heaven. It is for countless millions the weekly transfiguration event at which the local body grows to include its departed members and all other Christians, and so finds Jesus in the midst.

c The results

The main consequence of the event was that the mountain had to be left behind. The Spirit moves us on; the tent pegs must be pulled up before the tents are allowed to become permanent dwellings. The place of vision must be quitted, but not forgotten. The event has been for a purpose: the preparation for service, that is, to play our part in the healing of those who suffer. 'The Transfiguration unlocks the messianic secret and uncovers a strategy of discipleship, e.g. of commitment, involvement and expectation, in a world whose time has come.'[7] We must ponder deeply its challenge, as did the three disciples, for Jesus led them down the mountain, according to Luke, in silence; they had much to absorb from the event. They would learn how the experience was the necessary condition for being used as a healer to bring health to an untransfigured world. Here was commitment, involvement, expectation indeed. In the gospel narratives the transfiguration event in the lives of the disciples is a preliminary to their sharing in Jesus' act of healing at the foot of the mountain. Here is a deliberate connection between the insight given and the service for which it was a preparation. It is all one. The moments of disclosure, so precious to our personal life in the Spirit, are healings given to us for the great purpose of healing which God has for his world. They are given to equip us to be servants of the Kingdom, to be witnesses to Jesus' ministry to fallen man. The mountain has to be left behind in order that the healing work of God can go on. As Calvin observed, 'The world is the theatre of the divine glory.'

At the close of the event the disciples had passed out of themselves into the cloud, that is, into a deep experience of Christ. This meant a death to the ego, to the individual self, and a rebirth into his body. The divine healing is a continual filling of the surrendered self with an increasing measure of the divine life. God is 'a tremendously rich reality' (Baron von Hügel). For us, as for the disciples, the result of the transfiguration must be a complete healing so that we, as members of his body, are able to communicate the divine power and the glory by bringing his healing to a disordered world, to make the conditions of the Kingdom a reality, in Paul Lehmann's phrase a 'kairotic action', 'designed for making room for the freedom that being human takes'.[8] What guidelines then, has this model for a world in need of healing?

2 *Health a human possibility*

One dis-ease that readily meets the eye in the world today is man's ill-preparedness and even unreadiness to accustom himself to the fast-emerging new order of things. The paradigm shifts that we thought of earlier are fairly far advanced. The march of technology (as instanced in the micro-electronics industry) is inexorable. The forces of totalitarian Marxism threaten to engulf many parts of the globe. The days of the sacral and hierarchical societies must surely be numbered, for a world society is emerging to absorb them in its rolling tide. The birth-pangs of the new age are being felt in much of the world, including the richer nations who are being forced to consider the poor, both by world opinion and their own radicals.

The major problems being thrown up by this world tide were reflected in a publication of preparatory readings for the 1979 W.C.C. Conference on the contribution of faith, science, and technology in the struggle for a just, participatory and sustainable society.[9] Part one is devoted to a theological and ethical evaluation of science and technology and their world-views, including the dilemma in the biological manipulation of human life. Part two tackles the problem of energy for the future, including what is perhaps the main global problem of today which requires resolution for our health—the problem of nuclear energy, and waste. Part three, concerned with food, resources, environment, and population, provides a useful survey of the whole ecological field ending with a consideration of 'the technological revolution and the oceans'. Part four turns to the problem of the distribution and control of scientific and technological power, and finally there is an examination of the economic issues in the struggle for a new society.

These are world problems but they impinge on each of our lives. The resolution or avoidance of these problems will directly affect our health and life-style. It is good that the W.C.C. is initiating dialogue concerned to alert mankind to these major responsibilities 'to make a deliberate transition to a sustainable global society in which science and technology will be mobilized to meet the basic physical and spiritual needs of people, to minimize human suffering and to create an environment which can sustain a decent quality of life for all peoples'. At least it shows a willingness to climb the mount of transfiguration. It even goes further, for it is an attempt to begin the training of man for this new world, mentally because it makes him aware of the problems, physically because it attends to the environment in which he will live, and emotionally because it initiates the long period of adjustment needed to accustom himself to global change. To take but one example cited in the symposium: the dominant problem raised by genetic engineering, apart from the fact that it raises questions which seem to be without historical precedent, is the conflict between individual and community rights. The teaching of Jesus, especially in relation to the Kingdom, emphasized the individual worth of each human being, in particular the weak, the poor, the sick, the outcast, and the despised. An individual has rights by being a child of God. Communities also have rights, for the Jewish nation to which Jesus belonged, or the Christian Church, are communities of mutual love and obligation. A population biologist concerned with eugenics would be more likely to opt for a programme to reduce the incidence of genetic abnormality for the benefit of the community, which would be likely to run counter to the will of the individual. Such a decision would fly in the face of the tradition of human rights held in Christian culture. The very same conflict obtains already in the treatment of mentally sick patients. Is the therapy designed in every case to help the individual or the community? Perhaps these alternatives are meant to stand as the Scylla and Charybdis, through which man has agonizingly to pass, and which will remain there for ever to catch him in his ceaseless voyage of discovery. But the alternative might be a valuable lesson learned from the converse of Moses and Elijah on the mount of transfiguration, where in that experience the conflict was held in creative tension until the whole was transfigured and suddenly there was no problem. That certainly could be called a 'kairotic' event and we may have to wait until such time as there is an obvious resolution, a new idea whose time has come. In the meantime the very conflict itself can provide healing.

World problems bring in a ceaseless tide of questions to be faced by individual countries. Put the other way round, the problems Britain is facing are a microcosm of the whole. Perhaps we have more than our share because the clearer the role a country possessed in the past, the greater is the amount of adjustment to be made in the present. The overview in society at a time when Britain played a dominant role in world affairs has now crumbled. The search for a role nationally leads to an uncertainty in the community. Groups of people emerge to pull the tiller this way, then that. The extremes always predominate in the tug of war and so today it is the National Front and the Socialist Workers who are making the most noise. The conflict will only be healthy if a large input of constructive ideas as to how to live in a pluralistic society and allow a healing power to be experienced in history, and even more a solid core of people of good will intent on contributing actively to the health of the newly emerging society, appears from somewhere to fill the dangerous gap in the centre.

The key question for this leaven which will fill the vacuum—let us call them 'society's healers'—bears on this very problem of identity. Who am I? What is my life for? In a recent article posing the question 'How healthy is Britain?' Brian Frost expressed the opinion that 'If Britain is unhealthy it is because it has stifled that question, or thought it did not matter', and urged that there should be a 'new articulation of our search for meaning'. I believe this is the primary question for our health as individuals, as a community, as a nation, as a global society. It is certainly the question we need to ask in Britain today.

We have already noticed the wealth of organizations devoted to caring for others in our contemporary society. We have almost become neurotic about it. But side by side with this outgoing thrust towards health is an ingrowing disease eating at our vitals. Its outward symptom seems to be a blind indifference to others, to our environment, and even to ourselves. There is a lack of respect for the lives of others shown for instance in the ever-increasing number of deaths and serious injuries on our roads. Part of this disease has even been given a name—motorway madness. The indifference shown to the welfare of others, especially to the sick and the deprived members of society, for instance by indiscriminate withdrawal of labour, has reached epidemic proportions. The human 'rights' of the individual have now acquired total predominance over the rights and claims of the community. The lack of care for others by those in positions of responsibility is instanced in a reluctance to take decisions especially on such matters as conditions of stress in urban and industrial areas, noise vibration, atmospheric pollution, e.g. from the lead content in petrol sold in this country. The indifference to our environment also has many manifestations, for instance in massive deforestation, indiscriminate dumping of waste leading among other things to water pollution (rivers, lakes, and even sea) and inordinate use of fossil fuels, particularly oil, in our century.

Even more remarkable is the indifferent way in which we treat ourselves. Over-consumption of food and drink, smoking and drug-taking (including the inordinate and culpable use of sedatives and tranquillizers) are but the more obvious of our masochistic tendencies. More serious are the number of suicides, which would be far larger but for the devoted work of the Samaritans, and the general malaise in failing to look after our personal health under the erroneous impression that it is the duty of the N.H.S. to keep us fit and not our own. Little wonder that doctors' surgeries and counselling clinics are frequently crowded. One might well be tempted to enquire which is the chicken and which is the egg? Is the disease-ridden indifference a neurotic response to the caring society expressive of the attitude, 'Someone will care for me anyway if I get ill or hurt'? Or is the caring society a response to the indifference shown towards the health of the community? Whichever way round, the balance seems to be weighted on the side of illness rather than wellness.

Is it possible to attempt a diagnosis? Probably not, and an attempt by one individual could well be dismissed as arrogance or folly. But somewhere, somehow, there must be Christian minds applied to the questions that confront us and it is good that so many Christians—and not only Christians—today are in fact giving themselves to ways and projects oriented towards the healing of society's ills. Hugh Montefiore in the sermon he preached at his installation as Bishop of Birmingham, stressed the need for

> new ideals, a new sense of self-esteem, which will unite us, energize us and unleash those excellencies of character and creativity latent within us all. . . . Such a society would affirm the unique value of each human person, so that there would be tolerance for others . . . where our main objective is not economic growth or growth in consumption, but rather personal growth, so that each of us may have a more human life. . . . Such worthy aims will not come from economics or from sociology, nor from science or from politics, but from the Spirit of God welling up in the hearts of men. [10]

I believe this is approaching the heart of the matter, for it is what comes out of a person that is decisive and will answer our two original questions: Who am I? and What is my life for? No amount of politics and economics can ensure this basic question is answered correctly. Such sciences come in at a later stage.

Jesus himself declared that it was not what went into a man that would destroy him, but what came out of him, from his inner being. He gave quite an impressive list of such diseases (cf. Mark 7. 14–23). It seems that there are too many of these diseases in the human heart at the moment for man to be well enough 'to affirm the unique value of each human person' or to enjoy that 'personal growth, so that each of us may have a more human life'. Man needs to undergo a cathartic process before the Spirit of God can 'well up in the hearts of men'.

Here our model of the transfiguration can help us again. The disciples, prepared as they were, went up to the mountain with their luggage of dis-ease within and fears without. The transfiguration experience absorbed all this in a process that was at once cathartic and invigorating and renewing. It led to such a vision of the Lord their healer (Jesus only), that creation, their own life, and the lives of others could never be viewed in the same way again. Creation and fellow human beings within it had to be served, not exploited. The Son of Man who came to serve, would equip them to do this in the same way this experience had equipped him—with the power and glory of God—to go forward to the second exodus. After this mighty act of the new covenant, it would be natural to spend one's life in the service and healing of others, suffering gladly if need be in union with the 'exodus' sufferings of the Master, whose power and glory would always be at hand. The mountain had to be left behind, but the experience remained as life was carried on in the service of others, and of oneself (in the form of self-affirmation rather than self-assertion) and of creation—on the plain and in the company of him who heals for all eternity.

I believe that the only word for this kind of experience is TRANSFIGURATION. In his article, Brian Frost expressed a similar opinion: 'We need therefore to live a new doctrine of trans-figuration, where flesh, spirit and mind are one new whole in a restored vision of a united creation.' This is the healing we need. It is the will of him who was once transfigured on that holy mountain that we should receive it. He will give it for the asking. Our lives would be a deal more simple if we would take him at his word. 'Ask, and it will be given you; seek, and you will find, knock, and it will be opened to you' (Matt. 7.7; cf. 7.11; 21.22; Luke 11.13; John 14.13f; 15.16; 16.23f).

There is one more fruit of the transfiguration, one more lesson to be learned from our healing model. How could the three disciples descend to the plain and be utterly involved in the healing and caring, the preaching and travelling, if all they had been assured of in the mountain experience was that their Master would suffer a cruel death? There seems to be only one answer: the vision they glimpsed gave them an unquenchable hope in the God of history 'who by the power at work within us is able to do far more abundantly than all that we ask or think' (Eph. 3.20). It is the power of the living God which applies the healing balm to the wounds within the human heart and it is the theological virtue of hope which concentrates our mind and whole being upon it. Hope, as the writer to the Hebrews tells us, is the 'anchor of the soul'

(6.19), for hope settles the inner being on God, purging it of the putrefaction which prevents that welling up of the Holy Spirit. It is the panacea for a person who has gone in on him- or her-self, for a community weighed down with its own difficulties, for a world with problems to face too large for its inhabitants to solve by their own unaided efforts. Hope produces fruitful and purposeful activity and is the source of the energy, courage, and endurance to carry it through to completion. It is the healer of selfishness, directing concern towards others and above all to God. It is the virtue needed by 'the healers' in the world today, for it will keep them aware of, and close to, the limitless reservoir of the divine power, available for the healing of creation, which is all *his*— Kingdom, power, and glory—who is able to do more than we can ever comprehend. Here is the fruit of the transfiguration, we have used as our healing model.

> The man who puts his life into the hands of Christ lines up his tiny forces with those of the God of history in working His purposes out. He becomes a fellow-worker with God in the defeating of evil and in the establishing of God's reign. The man who sees *that* begins to see the meaning of the universe and of his part in its onward march.
> O Lord, Who hast set before us the great hope that Thy Kingdom shall come on earth, and hast taught us to pray for its coming; Give us grace to discern the signs of its dawning, and to work for the perfect day when Thy will shall be done on earth as it is in heaven; through Jesus Christ our Lord. [11]

3 *Hope and the inner healing of man*

Dietrich Bonhoeffer and his friend George Bell, Bishop of Chichester, were probably among the first to discern the deep healing which would be needed by the Christian West following a second world war coming so soon after the first. Bonhoeffer laid some foundations of thought about this problem in his *Christian Ethics*. First he reasserted the reconciliation between the secular and religious world: God and the world have been reconciled in Jesus Christ enabling the Christian to live as a whole man in one world. Christians are prone to forget this basic work of healing accomplished by Jesus and so to compartmentalize their existence.

Bonhoeffer went on to say that Christ will be found among us, particularly in the Church when it confesses its sin, when it takes upon itself the sin of the world and confesses its responsibility for what has gone wrong in the Christian West. Ulrich Simon lent an urgency to this challenge in his book *The Theology of Auschwitz*, showing how forgiveness is a pressing problem to anyone, part of whose history includes the institution of concentration camps. Bell for his part gave his life to reconciliation between Christians and was one of the architects of the World Council of Churches. On a more personal level he involved himself in acts of reconciliation, personally welcoming Hitler's refugees. Later he and his wife entertained German prisoners of war and sent food parcels to Germany, something that, together with his stand against indiscriminate bombing, did little to enhance his popularity in a war-conscious Britain. [12]

It was thinking such as Bonhoeffer's among others (for instance Martin Luther King whose powerful sermons especially on 'loving your enemies' were so true to his Master), that led Dr Haddon Willmer of Leeds University to engage in a study which he calls 'the Politics of Forgiveness'. In a paper given at a seminar organized by the Glencree Centre of Reconciliation he began to identify some basic principles: 'What cannot be changed has to be forgiven', which led him to say that 'Forgiveness is a response to what cannot be changed but finds ways of changing the unchangeable . . . bringing to bear upon it a light that seemed to be unthinkable . . . the very power of a new life and a new hope.' It is when forgiveness is brought into this situation of hopelessness that the power of healing is released, enabling the whole situation to be transfigured. Sometimes the forgiveness is evoked by an act of repentance and when there is an admixture of both, the healing potential is increased. Sometimes however forgiveness must be given and received on its own or precede the repentance. The father anticipated the prodigal's repentance with an act of unconditional forgiveness and his action and bearing conveyed a deeper healing to the son than any words.

When this takes place in the political sphere there is a 'transfiguration of politics'. The power of healing is released into history, both into the past and into the present; it then lays the foundation of a new hope for the future. Festo Olang, the Anglican Archbishop in Kenya, related to some of his fellow members of

Lambeth XI how the greatest healing his country had received was when President Kenyatta first came to power and counselled his people to take no reprisals, to forgive and forget the oppression of the past, and so lay the foundation of a happy future. There followed one of the most stable periods in that country's history. It was an act that 'transfigured' the situation and brought healing to the people. This confirms another of Willmer's principles that the politics of forgiving is basic, for in it there is a certain kind of natural power which alone makes a community workable.

Individual members of the community therefore must also practise forgiveness continually if its life is to be marked by a condition of *shalom*. This will include the past as well as the present. Forgiveness is also a two-way event as the Lord's Prayer makes plain: it must be given and received. Only so can every member receive that inner healing so vital to his health as well as to the health of the community. The tragic occurrences of internecine strife in so many parts of the world at the present time, not least in our own country, are indicative of an unhealthy lack of forgiveness. The anger which so quickly flares up between fellow-workers and even between members of the same household results from a lack of being forgiven and cries out for a deep inner healing which no amount of sedatives and tranquillizers is able to effect. The initiative must lie with Christians who know better than anyone what it means to be forgiven:

> Ransomed, healed, restored, forgiven,
> Who like me his praise should sing?
>
> (H. F. Lyte)

'Men have a God given right to forgiveness and this is an obligation under which Christians should understand themselves to be standing', asserts Haddon Willmer. It would appear that the ball is in the Christian court and many Christians and others would acknowledge this fact and rejoice when a lead is given. A writer in Poland has called his latest (unpublished) work *PULP*, for that is what it has felt like to be a Pole throughout history. He shows how it has constantly been the Church which has cradled the hopes of the nation when politically speaking life seemed hopeless. Always the Church has been ministering to the inner wound of the nation's soul 'the infinite riches of Christ', and so effecting that healing from which the nation can once more take hope for the future.

This is the role the Church must find again in our time. Initiatives may be taken by its leaders, such as the penitential visit of Polish church leaders to Germany a few years ago, or the Call to the Nation by the Anglican Archbishops. Some churches may provide for such initiatives in their liturgies as the Roman Catholic Church has done in its services of penitence. It is encouraging to find these are well attended in Britain and hopefully they will lead to all the churches joining together in these expressions of penitence which have a profound power of healing both for personal and community issues. But more and more it must be the ordinary Christian clerical or lay at parish level who ministers forgiveness among his community at home, at work, at leisure. Once healed ourselves we have a particular responsibility to help our neighbour towards being healed inwardly by remembering, forgiving and receiving forgiveness.

It is as well to recall the part which remembering has in forgiveness and ultimate healing. We have, as Brian Frost wrote in a recent article 'How healthy is Britain?', 'to release the demons still trapped in history: wherever things have gone wrong, in a family, or a town or village or a country vis à vis other countries—and this is still a present fact in the consciousness of many—there is need for *healing of the memories*. . . . [13] That this needs to be done the pages of the daily papers placard before us' (my italics).

This is the very contribution the Church is able and equipped to make. Christians have always been good and persistent at remembering in a reconciling context in the Eucharist itself, the supreme sacrament of healing. As the result of a personal tragedy suffered through the situation in Northern Ireland, Dr George Lovell, a Methodist minister, movingly writes in an unpublished work:

> I see only one way to stop that chain of events: and that is for someone who has every right to take revenge refusing to do so. To say in effect, here inhumanity stops. I believe this is fundamentally what Jesus did. We and those who follow him, refuse to be a link in the processes of injustice at a particular point . . . . The central act of remembrance for the Christian Faith (is) the Eucharist where is death, sin, bloodiness to the Son of God, now institutionalised and celebrated in such a way that it cannot bring violence and hate but peace—*shalom*. Where

remembrance is right it seems that there is the possibility of forgiving, healing—of a renewed relationship with yourself, your neighbour, your universe, even with God.

This is the deep, inner healing which spells out the greatest hope for the human race. The Eucharist, as Dr Lovell said, is the central part of the Church's life in which such healing can take place and be sealed, for it is the great act of remembering, of forgiveness *and then* filling with all that is true, honourable, just, pure, lovely, gracious (Phil. 4.8). There are other healing sacraments (see chapter 7) which can also mediate this healing, together with counselling and deep prayer. I believe the Church will be increasingly called upon to minister at this depth as time goes on. My prayer is that she will not be cumbered about with too much serving of tables as the call for this ministry grows, for I perceive an unhealthy predilection to mimic the world through an excess of administration and busy-ness, which is inimical to the true vocation of Christians, and is frequently a timid excuse for avoiding the real responsibility of our calling. Too often the centre of the Church's life is communicated to those outside (and inside) as the structure of the Synod rules or the activities or even bishops! But good as these may be, they can not bring new life to God's people. Only the healing power that flows from the Lordship of Jesus Christ can do that. It is, I believe, essential that Christian leaders should become responsible for their own training in this ministry of deep healing. They must be ready and equipped to serve the Lord Jesus, the healing Christ, in this way. Once healed and trained themselves, they are ready to build up the Body of Christ for its role of furthering the Kingdom conditions in the community. Only the inner healing which the risen Christ can accomplish is able to bring new life and hope to ourselves, our church, our community, our nation, our world.

4 *The Kingdom, the Power and the Glory*

'The time is fulfilled, and the kingdom of God is at hand; repent, and believe in the Gospel' (Mark 1.15). The brief summary of Jesus' message still strikes a note of urgency today. The end has not come: that is of little significance. What is significant is that the Kingdom which is his coming reign casts its light and life, its joy and healing, its power and glory before it. It is this hope in God's future that will smite the disenchantment of our wraths and sorrows and transfigure man, society, creation. The Kingdom must be awaited by men and women who will watch and be alert, expect and prepare. The Kingdom evokes initiatives to prepare the conditions—serving, healing, loving, forgiving, so that the *polis* is the more ready to be transfigured into the Kingdom.

Meanwhile the Kingdom must be proclaimed by preaching *and* healing. It is this essential activity, the *raison d'être* of the apostolic Church, for which the promised power from on high is given. A disobedient Church will not experience this power and mankind will remain unhealed. This book is written in the conviction that an obedience shown in a renewed awareness of the healing dimension will give the Church an experience of that reservoir of power that will not only transfigure its own life, as the Body of Christ was once before transfigured on the holy mount, but will also bring that deep and inner healing to mankind and his environment, for which the whole creation groans and travails.

As the power of God continues to heal, the Kingdom will be no idle dream but his very real future, 'and we all with unveiled face, beholding the glory of the Lord, *are* being changed into his likeness from one degree of glory to another.'

For the Kingdom, the Power, and the Glory are *his*, now and for ever.   Amen.

211

APPENDIX

Appendix

From the
Book of Common Prayer according to the use of
The Episcopal Church (U.S.A.)

MINISTRATION TO THE SICK

In the case of illness, the Minister of the Congregation is to be notified.

At the Ministration, one or more parts of the following service are used, as appropriate; but when two or more are used together, they are used in the order indicated. The Lord's Prayer is always included.

Part One of this service may always be led by a deacon or lay person.

When the Laying on of Hands or Anointing takes place at a public celebration of the Eucharist, it is desirable that it precede the distribution of Holy Communion, and it is recommended that it take place immediately before the exchange of the Peace.

The Celebrant begins the service with the following or some other greeting

Peace be to this house (place), and to all who dwell in it.

PART I   MINISTRY OF THE WORD

One or more of the following or other passages of Scripture are read

General

2 Corinthians 1. 3–5 (God comforts us in affliction)
Psalm 91 (He will give his angels charge over you)
Luke 17. 11–19 (Your faith has made you well)

Penitence

Hebrews 12. 1–2 (Looking to Jesus, the perfecter of our faith)
Psalm 103 (He forgives all your sins)
Matthew 9. 2–8 (Your sins are forgiven)

When Anointing is to follow

James 5. 14–16 (Is any among you sick?)
Psalm 23 (You have anointed my head with oil)
Mark 6. 7, 12–13 (They anointed with oil many that were sick)

Appendix

When Communion is to follow

1 John 5. 13–15 (That you may know that you have eternal life)
Psalm 145. 14–22 (The eyes of all wait upon you, O Lord)
John 6. 47–51 (I am the bread of life)

After any Reading, the Celebrant may comment on it briefly.

Prayers may be offered according to the occasion.

The Priest may suggest the making of a special confession, if the sick person's conscience is troubled, and use the form for the Reconciliation of a Penitent.

Or else the following general confession may be said

Most merciful God,
we confess that we have sinned against you
in thought, word, and deed,
by what we have done,
and by what we have left undone.
We have not loved you with our whole heart;
we have not loved our neighbors as ourselves.
We are truly sorry and we humbly repent.
For the sake of your Son Jesus Christ,
have mercy on us and forgive us;
that we may delight in your will,
and walk in your ways,
to the glory of your Name. Amen.

The Priest alone says

Almighty God have mercy on you, forgive you all your sins
through our Lord Jesus Christ, strengthen you in all goodness,
and by the power of the Holy Spirit keep you in eternal life.
Amen.

A deacon or lay person using the preceding form substitutes 'us' for 'you' and 'our' for 'your'.

PART II   LAYING ON OF HANDS AND ANOINTING

If oil for the Anointing of the Sick is to be blessed, the Priest says

O Lord, holy Father, giver of health and salvation: Send your Holy Spirit to sanctify this oil; that, as your holy apostles anointed many that were sick and healed them, so may those who in faith and repentance receive this holy unction be made whole; through Jesus Christ our Lord, who lives and reigns with you and the Holy Spirit, one God, for ever and ever. *Amen.*

The following anthem is said

Savior of the world, by your cross and precious blood you have redeemed us;
Save us, and help us, we humbly beseech you, O Lord.

The Priest then lays hands upon the sick person, and says one of the following

N., I lay my hands upon you in the Name of the Father, and of the Son, and of the Holy Spirit, beseeching our Lord Jesus Christ to sustain you with his presence, to drive away all sickness of body and spirit, and to give you that victory of life and peace which will enable you to serve him both now and evermore. *Amen.*

or this

N., I lay my hands upon you in the Name of our Lord and Savior Jesus Christ, beseeching him to uphold you and fill you with his grace, that you may know the healing power of his love. *Amen.*

If the person is to be anointed, the Priest dips a thumb in the holy oil, and makes the sign of the cross on the sick person's forehead, saying

N., I anoint you with oil in the Name of the Father, and of the Son, and of the Holy Spirit. *Amen*

The Priest may add

As you are outwardly anointed with this holy oil, so may our heavenly Father grant you the inward anointing of the Holy Spirit. Of his great mercy, may he forgive you your sins, release you from suffering, and restore you to wholeness and strength. May he deliver you from all evil, preserve you in all goodness, and bring you to everlasting life; through Jesus Christ our Lord. *Amen.*

In cases of necessity, a deacon or lay person may perform the anointing, using oil blessed by a bishop or priest.

If Communion is not to follow, the Lord's Prayer is now said.

The Priest concludes

The Almighty Lord, who is a strong tower to all who put their trust in him, to whom all things in heaven, on earth, and under the earth bow and obey: Be now and evermore your defense, and make you know and feel that the only Name under heaven given for health and salvation is the Name of our Lord Jesus Christ. *Amen.*

[The Blessing.]

NOTES
SELECT BIBLIOGRAPHY
INDEXES

Notes

CHAPTER 1
Healing and Wholeness

1 Tom Storier, Professor of Science and Society at Bradford University, quoted in an article in *The Times* of 2 October 1978 by Kenneth Owen, the newspaper's technology correspondent, to which I am indebted for the above information.

2 Morton Kelsey, *Healing and Christianity* (SCM 1973), p. 305 to whom every student of this subject is indebted for this work.

3 Michael Wilson, *Health is for People* (DLT 1975), pp. 117ff.

4 Michael Wilson, *The Church is healing* (SCM 1967), pp. 17f. ✔

5 Donald Coggan, *Convictions* (Hodder and Stoughton 1975), p. 272.

6 Jürgen Moltmann, *Theology and Joy* (SCM 1973), p. 55.

7 Quoted in the *New International Dictionary of New Testament Theology* (Paternoster 1976), vol. ii, p. 778.

8 Stephen Neill, *Bible Words and Christian Meanings* (SPCK 1970), p. 33.

9 Basil Hume, O.S.B., *Searching for God* (Hodder and Stoughton 1977), p. 171.

10 A. M. Ramsey, *Sacred and Secular* (Longmans 1965), p. 3.

11 R. A. Lambourne, *Community, Church and Healing* (DLT 1963), pp. 103f.

12 Ibid.

CHAPTER 2
Health and the Kingdom of God in the teaching of Jesus

1 A. M. Hunter, *Jesus, Lord and Saviour* (SCM 1976), p. 47.

2 Cf. J. Jeremias, *New Testament Theology*, vol. i (SCM 1971), p. 98 in Study edn.

3 E. Haenchen, quoted by J. Jeremias, cf. article on 'King' in *The New International Dictionary of New Testament Theology* (Paternoster 1976), vol. ii.

4 Cf. J. Jeremias, op. cit., pp. 103ff.

5 See R. H. Fuller, *Interpreting the Miracles* (SCM 1963), pp. 26f, where he argues for its authentic witness to Jesus' healing ministry.

6 See Norman Perrin, *Jesus and the Language of the Kingdom* (SCM 1976), p. 46.

7 A. M. Hunter, *The Parables Then and Now* (SCM 1971), p. 40.

8 It is not within the scope of this book to discuss which is the original form of the prayer—the Matthean or Lucan version. Most scholars opt for the Lucan on account of its brevity, though the Matthean has a linguistic advantage. They were of course most probably from two different Churches.

9 J. Jeremias, op. cit., p. 199. Norman Perrin in his *Jesus and the Language of the Kingdom* was right, I believe, to apply the term 'tensive symbol' to the Kingdom as used by the Jewish community: I just wonder if he was right to apply the description to Jesus' use of the Kingdom. It is a well argued book for students of Kingdom theology.

10 Op. cit., p. 184.

11 See the final chapter.

CHAPTER 3
Jesus proclaims the Kingdom through his healing ministry

1 R. H. Fuller, *Interpreting the Miracles* (SCM 1963), p. 10. I am greatly indebted to his work and conclusions in this chapter.

2 This is what Alan Richardson did. See his *An Introduction to the Theology of the New Testament* (SCM, Study edn, 1958), p. 96. I owe much to the work and mind of this one-time dear friend.

3 J. Jeremias, *New Testament Theology* (SCM, Study edn 1971) vol. i, p. 92. For a full treatment of the critical evidence the reader is referred to the work of this scholar.

4 Op. cit., p. 20.

5 The term leprosy in the Bible does not mean the disease commonly so called today (Hansen's bacillus) but covers a wide variety of skin diseases.

6 See Dr Donald Coggan's helpful chapter on the ministry of healing in his *Convictions* (Hodder and Stoughton 1975), pp. 274f.

7 R. H. Fuller, op. cit., p. 51.

8 See Genesis 1, Exodus 18.9, Jeremiah 32.42, and Hebrews 9.11 and 10.1.

9 I.e. declaring black is white and white is black by ascribing to Satan the power of the Holy Spirit.

10 It is interesting that Jesus' formula includes exorcistic words: Rebuke, and Be Muzzled (RSV Be still).

11 Hans Kung, *On being a Christian* (Collins 1976), p. 231.

12 T. W. Manson, *The Servant Messiah* (Cambridge 1953), pp. 69–71.

13 Op. cit., pp. 35f.

14 Austin Farrer, *St. Matthew and St. Mark* (Dacre Press 1954), pp. 36f.

15 Cf. Sanders and Mastin in *The Gospel acc. to St. John* (Black's N.T. Commentaries), 1975 edn, pp. 13f.

16 There are references to more signs than these, e.g. at 2.23 and 3.2; also at 12.37f, which may have been the conclusion to the book of signs.

17 Or Bethzatha = house of sheep. Bethesda = house of mercy is however in most MSS.

18 Cf. Luke 13.2 and 4, where Jesus illustrates the point with reference to the victims of Pilate and of the tower of Siloam.

19 Cf. Sanders and Mastin, op. cit., p. 277.

20 Op. cit., p. 106. See chapter 7 below.

21 The Christian life is based on the rhythm between what Cardinal Newman called the market place and the desert.

22 T. Ralph Morton, *The Twelve Together* (The Iona Community 1956), pp. 42, 46.

23 J. Jeremias. *N.T. Theology*, vol. i, p. 237.

24 The order for the Visitation of the Sick, *Book of Common Prayer* (1662).

25 In his recent book, *A Reason to Hope* (Collins 1978), p. 10.

26 Cf. John 7.39, 'As yet the Spirit had not been given, because Jesus was not yet glorified.'

27 Ralph Morton, op. cit., pp. 134 and 140.

CHAPTER 4

The unleashing of Healing Power

1 Cf. J. Jeremias, *N.T. Theology*, vol. i (SCM 1971, study edn), p. 288. See also the commentary on these passages by Claus Westerman in the SCM O.T. Library (1969), pp. 92ff.

2 A. M. Hunter, *Jesus—Lord and Saviour* (SCM 1976), p. 96.

3 Jürgen Moltmann, *The Crucified God* (SCM 1974), p. 219.

4 Quotations from Jürgen Moltmann, op. cit., p. 47.

5 Hans Kung, *On being a Christian* (Collins 1976), p. 341.

6 Gerald O'Collins, S.J., *The Calvary Christ* (SCM 1977); this and the quotations that follow are from pp. 74–7. He also sees atonement as a call to man 'to uphold the objective moral health of God's world' perhaps through accepted (though not self-inflicted) suffering.

7 Rom. 5. 8–11 and 2 Cor. 5. 18–20. See also Col. 1.20 and Eph. 2.16.

8   Jürgen Moltmann, *The Church in the Power of the Spirit* (SCM 1977), p. 64.
9   Jürgen Moltmann, op. cit., p. 99.
10 Jürgen Moltmann, op. cit., p. 105.
11 Op. cit., p. 17. If we in the West cannot have a first-hand experience of the lot of the oppressed, a reading of Ronald J. Sider's moving book *Rich Christians in an Age of Hunger* (Hodder–I.V.C.F. copyright U.S.A. 1977) might help!
12 *The New International Dictionary of N.T. Theology* (Paternoster 1976), vol. ii., p. 387.

CHAPTER 5

The Church moves outward

1   J. Jeremias, op. cit., p. 300.
2   The Greek word is *sozo* (see p. 32f.)
3   Presumably Ananias would 'break bread' with him. In any case it signalled the completion of the cure, the coming to wholeness.
4   Tabitha is the Aramaic, Dorcas the Greek, for gazelle.
5   See the end of the last chapter.
6   This is the force of *kalos* at John 10.11. 'I am the good (attractive) shepherd.'
7   Cf. Michael Green, *Evangelism in the Early Church* (Hodder 1970), pp. 191f, from which the quotation is taken.
8   Op. cit., p. 193.
9   S. I. McMillen, M.D., *None of these diseases*. Lakeland 1966.

CHAPTER 6

The Church moves onward

1   Cf. Morton Kelsey, *Healing and Christianity* (SCM 1973), pp. 149ff.
2   See the office for the Visitation of the Sick in the 1662 B.C.P., which is a result of this theological thinking.
3   Cf. Thomas Aquinas, *Summa Theologica* III Supp. 29.1 quoted in Morton Kelsey, op. cit., p. 209.
4   The title of Professor J. K. Galbraith's lectures, published in a book of that name.
5   Stephen Neill, *The Church and Christian Union* (Oxford 1968), p. 295f.
6   Dorothy Musgrave Arnold, *Dorothy Kerin, Called by Christ to Heal* (Hodder 1965), p. 14.

7   His book, *Christ Healing* (Oliphants 1970 edn) has become something of a classic among books on this ministry.

8   *Miracle at Crowhurst*. Arthur James, Evesham, 1970. His other two books were *The heart of healing* (1971) and *In his healing steps* (1976).

9   *The Ministry of Healing*. SPCK 1924.

10 Op. cit., p. 117.

11 Lambeth Conference *Report* 1930, p. 183.

12 It was first called the Council of Healing. Dr Edward Winckley, who has since founded many homes of healing in South Africa and the U.S.A., author of *The Greatest Healer* (Arthur James 1978), was a founder member.

13 Leslie D. Weatherhead, *Psychology, Religion and Healing* (Hodder 1951), p. 495.

14 The relevant passage from *The Documents of Vatican II (1966)* is quoted in Morton Kelsey, op. cit., p. 242.

15 *Healing and Christianity*. SCM 1973. Another book, *Encounter with God* (Hodder 1972), gives a solid historical and theological background to the realm of Christian experience while his latest *The Other Side of Silence* (SPCK 1977), provides a rationale and method of Christian meditation.

16 Francis MacNutt, O.P., *Healing* (Ave Maria Press 1974), and *The Power to Heal* (AMP 1977); the quotations are taken from the latter, pp. 13 and 143f.

CHAPTER 7

The Church's Ministry

1   Alan Richardson, *An Introduction to the Theology of the N.T.* (SCM 1958, study edn 1974), p. 387.

2   Alexander Schmemann, *The World as Sacrament* (DLT 1966), pp. 29, 46.

3   Alan Richardson, op. cit., p. 372. See also the article by E. L. Mascall in *A Dictionary of Christian Theology*, ed. Alan Richardson (SCM 1969), p. 119.

4   St Augustine, *City of God*, X.6.

5   I'm sure Dr Edward Winckley has a point when he declares: 'Neglect of this unseen "company" has opened the way to Spiritualism, as neglect of the Healing Ministry of our Lord has led to the advent of Christian Science', *The Greatest* (Valley Press 1977), p. 73.

6   A. M. Ramsey, *God, Christ and the World* (SCM 1969), p. 116.

7   Alexander Schmemann, op. cit., pp. 42, 44.

8 See George Bennett, *The Heart of Healing* (Arthur James 1971), p. 62. He likens it to an atom bomb, the effect of which is to 'separate the roots of the illness from the personality of the sufferer'.

9 *The Laying on of Hands and Anointing. Principles of Revision.* A C.C.H.H. pamphlet, published when he was secretary.

10 Kenneth Leech, *Soul Friend* (Sheldon Press 1977), pp. 194ff, to which I am indebted for some of the ideas in this section and some of the quotations that follow.

11 John Macquarrie, *Principles of Christian Theology* (SCM 1966, study edn 1975), pp. 428f.

12 Francis MacNutt, O.P., *Healing* (Ave Maria Press 1974), p. 288.

13 *The Adornment of the Spiritual Marriage*, 2.

14 John Richards, *But deliver us from evil*, subtitled 'An introduction to the demonic dimension in pastoral care'. DLT 1974.

15 John Richards, op. cit., p. 219.

16 Known as the *York Report* 1974 (2nd edn 1976), published by the Diocese of York, 4 Minister Yard, York, YO1 2JE, from whom copies are available at 40p. post paid.

17 *A Memorandum on Exorcism*—for the guidance of the clergy (in Wales) (1974), p. 5.

18 Cf. John Richards, op. cit., pp. 190f.

19 From *The Epistle to the Romans* in Early Christian Writings, tr. Maxwell Staniforth. Penguin 1968.

20 Dr T. S. West, O.B.E., in a paper given at the First International Conference on Patient Counselling, Amsterdam, April 1976.

21 Dr Cicely Saunders, O.B.E., F.R.C.P., D.D., 'I was sick and you visited me', article in *In the Service of Medicine* no. 42 (July 1965), p. 2.

22 Johann Christoph Hampe, *To die is gain* (DLT 1979), chap. 3.

23 *Travels in Oudamovia* (1976), pp. 25f.

CHAPTER 8
Healing in the Local Church
A   Leadership

1 Kenneth Leech, *Soul Friend* (Sheldon Press 1977), p. 37.

2 A. M. Ramsey, *The Christian Priest Today* (SPCK 1972), p. 14.

3 Morton Kelsey, *Encounter with God* (Hodder 1972), p. 209.

4 Kenneth Leech, op. cit., pp. 184ff.

5 Our prayer fellowship uses an alternative ending, 'fill me with your love.' In its short form it is simply 'Jesus'. Orthodox guides insist that those who use it should be frequent communicants and penitents.

6 Ladder of Divine Ascent 27. Posture and breathing are important elements in prayer; cf. the experiments at the Anchorhold written up by Fr Herbert Slade, S.S.J.E., in his *Exploration into Contemplative Prayer* (DLT 1975).

7 Op. cit., p. 320.

8 Op. cit., p. 80.

9 Dr Edward Winckley, op. cit.

10 John V. Taylor, *The Go-Between God* (SCM 1972), p. 58.

CHAPTER 9
Healing in the Local Church
B 'In the Process of the Spirit'

1 Quoted by David Watson, *I believe in the Church* (Hodder 1978), p. 71.

2 Jürgen Moltmann, *The Church in the Power of the Spirit* (SCM 1977), pp. 291ff.

3 *The New International Dictionary of N.T. Theology* (Paternoster 1975), vol. i, p. 489.

4 David Watson, *I believe in Evangelism* (Hodder 1976), p. 125.

5 See Christopher Bryant, *The River Within* (DLT 1978), esp. chap. 8.

6 Many of my generation were influenced by his book, *The Blessing of the Holy Spirit'* (1952).

7 Harry Williams, C.R., *Becoming what I am* (DLT 1977), pp. 12, 49.

8 Michael Scanlon, *Inner Healing* (Veritas Publications, Dublin, 1977), p. 30.

9 George Bennett, *The Heart of Healing* (Arthur James, Evesham, 1971), p. 93f.

CHAPTER 10
Medicine, the Church, and Healing

1 J. W. Provonsha, M.D., *The Healing Christ*, quoted in Morton Kelsey, op. cit., p. 52 and Appendix A.

2 *Health, Healing and the Churches* published by the Churches' Council for Health and Healing at our office.

3 Quoted by Harold Kelman, D.D., in an article on the Holistic Approach in the *American Handbook of Psychiatry*, ed. Silvano Arieti, 1959.

4 John Rowan, *Ordinary Ecstasy* (RKP 1976); the quotations are from pp. 3, 99, and 133.

5 The *New International Dictionary of the New Testament*, op. cit., vol. i, p. 719f.

6 M. Alan Alerck, 'What is Counselling?' in *Marriage Guidance* (January 1967), quoted by Kathleen Heasman in *An Introduction to Pastoral Counselling* (Constable 1969), p. 2.

7 Kathleen Heasman, op. cit., pp. 8–10, 214.

8 Quoted in *A Handbook on Hospital Chaplaincy* (CIO 1978), p. 6. This excellent booklet was published for the Hospital Chaplaincies Council of the General Synod (Chairman: Ronald Bowlby, Bishop of Newcastle) and put together by its secretary and director of training, the Revd Eric Reid, Church House, Dean's Yard, London SW1P 3NZ.

9 E.g. in York. In Manchester, excellent courses on 'Curing and Caring' have been organized by the Greater Manchester Council of Churches for representatives of all the caring professions.

10 Michael Wilson, 'The primary task of the hospital', in *The Hospital* (October 1970).

11 See article by Dr David Rowlands in *Crucible* (July–Sept 1977), pp. 137–42.

12 Eric J. Cassell, *The Healer's Art* (Penguin Books 1978), pp. 17, 21.

13 Philip Selby, *Health in 1980–1990, a predictive study based on an international inquiry* (S. Karger 1974), p. 81. I am indebted to the thought-provoking material in this book.

14 Cf. *Health, the Mass Media and the National Health Service*, published by the Unit for the Study of Health Policy, Department of Community Medicine, Guy's Hospital Medical School, in 1977.

15 Quoted in *Facing up to Nuclear Power* (St Andrew Press, W.C.C., 1976), ed. John Francis and Paul Abrecht, which poses well all the long-term implications.

16 Cf. an article by H. Miller in *The Lancet* (1966), 2. 647.

17 John N. Ott, *Health and Light*. Pocket Books, New York, 1976.

CHAPTER 11

Healing for Society

1 James Robertson, *The Sane Alternative* (1978), pp. 18, 78, 80.

2 Cf. Gunnar Myrdal in *Against the Stream, Critical Essays on Economics* (New York 1972), p. 208: 'The concept of the GNP, and the whole structure of the theoretical approaches built up with the GNP as a central axis will have to be dethroned.' (Quoted in the WCC 1979 Conference preparatory readings, p. 231). An equilibrium economy that would not allow economic capital to expand at the

expense of the ecological capital would of course challenge fundamentally present economic thinking and practice.

3 The writers of the above W.C.C. publication (see note 9 to the next chapter) are of the opinion that 'in view of the present complexity of modern technologically organized societies we need more autonomy, a greater variety of groups, and more participation by people in (the) ordering of their everyday life. The demand for participation is not some sort of pre-modern pre-industrial romanticism outmoded by the demands of centralized complex organizations. Rather, appropriate solutions to such everyday problems as organization of work and organization of social services demand participation' (pp. 232–3).

4 Cf. John Taylor, *The Go-Between God* (SCM 1972), esp. his chapter on 'Playing'.

5 Cf. Robert Van de Weyer, *Guru Jesus*. SPCK 1975.

6 David Edwards, *A Reason to Hope* (Collins 1978), pp. 191–4.

7 Dag Hammarskjöld, *Markings*, quoted by David Edwards at the beginning of his chapter 'A Response to Life' in the above work.

8 Cardinal Suenens, *A New Pentecost* (DLT 1975), p. x.

9 Robert E. Terwilliger, *The Charismatic Christ*, co-authors Michael Ramsey and A. M. Allchin (DLT 1974), pp. 70f.

10 Cf. Stuart Y. Blanch, *The Burning Bush—Signs of our time* (Lutterworth 1978), esp. pp. 104ff.

11 Quoted by Paul Johnson in *Pope John XXIII* (Hutchinson 1975), p. 193.

12 *Your very good Health*, ed. Brian Frost (1980), for C.C.C.H. at St Marylebone Parish Church, Marylebone Road, London, NW1 5LT.

CHAPTER 12
Healing for Mankind and glory for God

1 A. M. Ramsey, *The Glory of God and the Transfiguration of Christ* (Longmans 1949), p. 144.

2 See Herbert Slade, S.S.J.E., *Exploration into Contemplative Prayer*. DLT 1975.

3 See Paul Lehmann, *The Transfiguration of Politics*. SCM 1975.

4 Quoted by Herbert Slade S.S.J.E., op. cit., p. 28. Those who know this book will realize the inspiration it has given me in what follows. For us in York, William Temple's affirmation still rings true especially in the chapel at Bishopthorpe where he 'wrote' his *Readings*—on his knees.

5 A. M. Ramsey, op. cit., p. 101.

6 Herbert Slade, S.S.J.E., op. cit., p. 67f.

7 Paul Lehmann, op. cit., p. 82.

8 Ibid., p. 235.

9 *Faith, Science and the Future*, Church and Society, W.C.C., 1978.

10 Hugh Montefiore, *Taking our past into our future* (Collins, Fount paperbacks), pp. 20f.

11 Donald Coggan, *Convictions* (Hodder 1975), p. 205.

12 Cf. R. C. D. Jasper, *George Bell* (OUP 1967); also Kenneth Slack's excellent little book. For Bonhoeffer, see his *Letters and Papers from Prison*, and the biography by his friend, Eberhard Bethge. With regard to the question of Auschwitz, Dr S. Davidson, senior lecturer at Tel Aviv University, has made some significant studies of the effect of the Jewish holocaust on the survivors and their children. The survivors project unresolved problems about what happened to their dead onto their children, who then reflect the conflicts and struggles of their parents in all sorts of antipathies. For healing to come there must be a healing of the group.

13 For a good exposition of healing of the memories, see Reginald East, *Heal the Sick* (Hodder 1977), chap. 10. The most profound book so far published is, to my mind, *Praying for Inner Healing*, by Robert Faricy, S.J. SCM 1979.

Select Bibliography

Arnold, Dorothy Musgrave, *Dorothy Kerin, Called by Christ to heal*. Hodder 1965.

Barclay, William, *Prayers for Help and Healing*. Fontana 1968.

Bennett, George, *Miracle at Crowhurst*. Arthur James 1970.

— *The heart of Healing*. Arthur James 1971.

— *In His Healing Steps*. Arthur James 1976.

— (Posthumous) *Commissioned to Heal*. Arthur James 1979.

Billington, Roy, *Health, a surprising Joy*. CMS 1976.

Blanch, Stuart Y., *The Burning Bush—Signs of our time*. Lutterworth 1978.

Brown, David, *God's Tomorrow*. SCM 1977.

Bryant, Christopher, *The River Within*. DLT 1978.

Cassell, Eric J., *The Healer's Art*. Penguin Books 1978.

Cobb, E. Howard, *Christ Healing*. Oliphants 1970.

Coggan, Donald, *Convictions*. Hodder 1975.

Cox, Harvey, *The Secular City*. Macmillan, New York, 1966.

Dearmer, Percy, *Body and Soul*. Isaac Pitman 1909.

East, Reginald, *Heal the Sick*. Hodder 1977.

Ecclestone, Alan, *A Staircase for Silence*. DLT 1977.

Edwards, David, *A Reason to Hope*. Collins 1978.

Faricy, Robert, *Praying for Inner Healing*. SCM 1979.

Farrer, Austin, *St Matthew and St Mark*. Dacre Press 1954.

Frost, Evelyn, *Christian Healing*. Mowbray 1940.

Fuller, R. H., *Interpreting the Miracles*. SCM 1963.

Garlick, Phyllis, *Man's Search for Health*. Highway Press 1952.

Green, Michael, *Evangelism in the early Church*. Hodder 1970.

— *I believe in the Holy Spirit*. Hodder 1975.

Gunstone, John, *A People for His Praise*. Hodder 1978.

Hammarskjöld, Dag, *Markings*. Faber 1964.

Hampe, Johann Christoph, *To Die is Gain*. DLT 1979.

Harper, Michael, *Spiritual Warfare*. Hodder 1970.

— , ed., *Bishop's Move*. Hodder 1978.

Heasman, Kathleen, *An Introduction to Pastoral Counselling*. Constable 1969.

Hickson, James Moore, *Heal the Sick*. Methuen 1924.

Hume, Basil, o.s.b., *Searching for God*. Hodder 1977.

Hunter, A. M., *The Parables Then and Now*. SCM 1971.

— *Jesus Lord and Saviour*. SCM 1976.

Jasper, R. C. D., *George Bell*. OUP 1967.

Jeremias, J., *New Testament Theology*, vol. i. SCM 1971.

Jung, C. G., *Memories, Dreams, Reflections*. Collins, Fontana 1963.

Kelsey, Morton, *Encounter with God*. Hodder 1972.

— *Healing and Christianity*. SCM 1973.

— *The Other Side of Silence*. SPCK 1977.

Kerin, Dorothy, *Fulfilling*. Hodder 1963.

Kung, Hans, *On Being a Christian*. Collins 1977.

Lambeth Conference Reports especially 1978 Resolution 8. CIO.

Lambourne, R. A., *Community, Church and Healing*. DLT 1973.

Lawrence, Roy, *Christian Healing Rediscovered*. Coverdale 1976.

Leech, Kenneth, *Soul Friend*. Sheldon Press 1977.

Lehmann, Paul, *The Transfiguration of Politics*. SCM 1975.

McMillen, S. I., *None of these Diseases*. Lakeland 1966.

MacNutt, Francis, *Healing*. Ave Maria Press 1974.

— *The Power to Heal*. Ave Maria Press 1977.

Macquarrie, John, *Principles of Christian Theology*. SCM 1966.

Manson, T. W., *The Servant Messiah*. Cambridge 1953.

Martin, George, *Healing—Reflections of the Gospel*. Servant Books 1977.

Melinsky, M. A. H., *Healing Miracles*. Mowbray 1968.

Merrison, Alec (Chairman), *Report of the Royal Commission of the National Health Service*. HMSO 1979.

Moltmann, Jürgen, *Theology and Joy*. SCM 1973.

— *The Crucified God*. SCM 1974.

— *The Church in the Power of the Spirit*. SCM 1977.

Montefiore, Hugh, *Taking our Past into our Future*. Collins, Fount paperbacks 1978.

Morton, T. Ralph, *The Twelve Together*. The Iona Community 1956.

Neal, Emily Gardiner, *The Healing Power of Christ*. Hodder 1972.

Neill, Stephen, *The Church and Christian Union*. Oxford 1968.

New International Dictionary of New Testament Theology. 3 vols. Paternoster 1975–8.

O'Collins, Gerald, s.j., *The Calvary Christ*. SCM 1977.

Ott, John N., *Health and Light*, Pocket Books, New York, 1976.

Peddie, J. Cameron, *The Forgotten Talent*. Fontana 1966.

Perrin, Norman, *Jesus and the Language of the Kingdom*. SCM 1976.

Ramsey, A. M., Terwilliger, Robert E., Allchin, A. M., *The Charismatic Christ*. DLT 1974.

Ramsey, A. M., *The Glory of God and the Transfiguration of Christ*. Longmans 1949.

— *Sacred and Secular*. Longmans 1965.

— *God, Christ and the World*. SCM 1969.

— *The Christian Priest Today*. SPCK 1972.

Reed, William Standish, *Surgery of the Soul*. Spire Books 1973.

Richards, John, *But Deliver Us from Evil*. DLT 1974.

Richardson, Alan, *An Introduction to the Theology of the New Testament*. SCM 1958.

— , ed. *A Dictionary of Christian Theology*. SCM 1969.

Robertson, James, *The Sane Alternative*. James Robertson 1978.

Roszak, Theodore, *Unfinished Animal*. Faber Paperbacks 1976.

Rowan, John, *Ordinary Ecstasy*. RKP 1976.

Rowe, Trevor, *Wholeness*. Cell Books. Epworth Press 1976.

Sanford, Agnes, *Healing Gifts of the Spirit*. Arthur James 1966.

Scanlon, Michael, *Inner Healing*. Veritas Publications, Dublin, 1977.

Selby, Philip, *Health in 1980–1990*. A Predictive Study based on an International Enquiry. S. Karger 1974.

Sider, Ronald, *Rich Christians in an Age of Hunger*. Hodder 1977.

Slade, Herbert, s.s.j.e., *Exploration into Contemplative Prayer*. DLT 1975.

Stapleton, Ruth Carter, *The Gift of Inner Healing*. Hodder 1976.

— *The Experience of Inner Healing*. Ecclesia Books 1977.

Suenens, L. J., *A New Pentecost?* DLT 1975.

Taylor, John V., *The Go-Between God*. SCM 1972.

Tournier, Paul, *Escape from Loneliness*. SCM 1963.

— *Learning to Grow Old*. SCM 1971.

Van der Weyer, Robert, *Guru Jesus*. SPCK 1975.

Vanstone, W. H., *Love's Endeavour, Love's Expense*. DLT 1977.

Watson, David, *I Believe in Evangelism*. Hodder 1976.

— *I Believe in the Church*. Hodder 1978.

Weatherhead, Leslie D., *Psychology, Religion and Medicine*. Hodder 1951.

Webster, Douglas, *The Healing Christ—Four Bible Studies.* Highway Press 1963.

Williams, H. A., c.r., *Poverty, Chastity and Obedience.* Mitchell Beazley 1975.

— *Becoming what I am.* DLT 1977.

Wilson, Jim, *Go Preach the Kingdom, Heal the Sick.* James Clarke 1962.

✓ Wilson, Michael, *The Church is Healing.* SCM 1967.

— *Health is for People.* DLT 1975.

Winckley, Edward, *The Greatest Healer.* Arthur James 1978.

World Council of Churches, Faith Science and the Future. Church and Society 1978.

York Report on the Ministry of Deliverance and Healing. (Chairman—the Bishop of Selby) York Diocesan Office 1974.

Index of Scriptural References

Index of Names and Subjects

241

207 Politics of Forgiveness
— Willmer.

e. — Kenya
— Zimbabwe.
— Europe.   Hello
                   Remind who
— Healing of memories.   X space